SUPPORT YOUR LOCAL
CONFEDERATE

✸ THE LOCHLAINN SEABROOK COLLECTION ✸

AMERICAN CIVIL WAR
Abraham Lincoln Was a Liberal, Jefferson Davis Was a Conservative: The Missing Key to Understanding the
American Civil War
Confederacy 101: Amazing Facts You Never Knew About America's Oldest Political Tradition
Confederate Blood and Treasure: An Interview With Lochlainn Seabrook
Everything You Were Taught About African-Americans and the Civil War is Wrong, Ask a Southerner!
Everything You Were Taught About the Civil War is Wrong, Ask a Southerner!
Give This Book to a Yankee! A Southern Guide to the Civil War For Northerners
Heroes of the Southern Confederacy: The Illustrated Book of Confederate Officials, Soldiers, and Civilians
Lincoln's War: The Real Cause, the Real Winner, the Real Loser
The Great Yankee Coverup: What the North Doesn't Want You to Know About Lincoln's War!
The Ultimate Civil War Quiz Book: How Much Do You Really Know About America's Most Misunderstood
Conflict?
Women in Gray: A Tribute to the Ladies Who Supported the Southern Confederacy

CONFEDERATE MONUMENTS
Confederate Monuments: Why Every American Should Honor Confederate Soldiers and Their Memorials

CONFEDERATE FLAG
Confederate Flag Facts: What Every American Should Know About Dixie's Southern Cross
What the Confederate Flag Means to Me: Americans Speak Out in Defense of Southern Honor, Heritage, and
History

SECESSION
All We Ask Is To Be Let Alone: The Southern Secession Fact Book

SLAVERY
Everything You Were Taught About American Slavery is Wrong, Ask a Southerner!
Slavery 101: Amazing Facts You Never Knew About America's "Peculiar Institution"

CHILDREN
Honest Jeff and Dishonest Abe: A Southern Children's Guide to the Civil War
Saddle, Sword, and Gun: A Biography of Nathan Bedford Forrest For Teens

NATHAN BEDFORD FORREST
A Rebel Born: A Defense of Nathan Bedford Forrest - Confederate General, American Legend (winner of the
2011 Jefferson Davis Historical Gold Medal)
A Rebel Born: The Screenplay (film about N. B. Forrest)
Forrest! 99 Reasons to Love Nathan Bedford Forrest
Give 'Em Hell Boys! The Complete Military Correspondence of Nathan Bedford Forrest
I Rode With Forrest! Confederate Soldiers Who Served With the World's Greatest Cavalry Leader
Nathan Bedford Forrest and African-Americans: Yankee Myth, Confederate Fact
Nathan Bedford Forrest and the Battle of Fort Pillow: Yankee Myth, Confederate Fact
Nathan Bedford Forrest and the Ku Klux Klan: Yankee Myth, Confederate Fact
Nathan Bedford Forrest: Southern Hero, American Patriot - Honoring a Confederate Icon and the Old South
Saddle, Sword, and Gun: A Biography of Nathan Bedford Forrest For Teens
The God of War: Nathan Bedford Forrest As He Was Seen By His Contemporaries
The Quotable Nathan Bedford Forrest: Selections From the Writings and Speeches of the Confederacy's Most
Brilliant Cavalryman

QUOTABLE SERIES
The Alexander H. Stephens Reader: Excerpts From the Works of a Confederate Founding Father
The Quotable Alexander H. Stephens: Selections From the Writings and Speeches of the Confederacy's First Vice
President
The Quotable Jefferson Davis: Selections From the Writings and Speeches of the Confederacy's First President
The Quotable Nathan Bedford Forrest: Selections From the Writings and Speeches of the Confederacy's Most
Brilliant Cavalryman
The Quotable Robert E. Lee: Selections From the Writings and Speeches of the South's Most Beloved Civil War
General
The Quotable Stonewall Jackson: Selections From the Writings and Speeches of the South's Most Famous
General
The Unquotable Abraham Lincoln: The President's Quotes They Don't Want You To Know!

CIVIL WAR BATTLES
Encyclopedia of the Battle of Franklin - A Comprehensive Guide to the Conflict that Changed the Civil War
Nathan Bedford Forrest and the Battle of Fort Pillow: Yankee Myth, Confederate Fact
The Battle of Franklin: Recollections of Confederate and Union Soldiers
The Battle of Nashville: Recollections of Confederate and Union Soldiers
The Battle of Spring Hill: Recollections of Confederate and Union Soldiers

CONSTITUTIONAL HISTORY
America's Three Constitutions: Complete Texts of the Articles of Confederation, U.S. Constitution, and C.S. Constitution
The Articles of Confederation Explained: A Clause-by-Clause Study of America's First Constitution
The Constitution of the Confederate States of America Explained: A Clause-by-Clause Study of the South's Magna Carta

VICTORIAN CONFEDERATE LITERATURE
Rise Up and Call Them Blessed: Victorian Tributes to the Confederate Soldier, 1861-1901
Support Your Local Confederate: Wit and Humor in the Southern Confederacy
The God of War: Nathan Bedford Forrest As He Was Seen By His Contemporaries
The Old Rebel: Robert E. Lee As He Was Seen By His Contemporaries
Victorian Confederate Poetry: The Southern Cause in Verse, 1861-1901

ABRAHAM LINCOLN
Abraham Lincoln: The Southern View - Demythologizing America's Sixteenth President
Lincolnology: The Real Abraham Lincoln Revealed in His Own Words - A Study of Lincoln's Suppressed, Misinterpreted, and Forgotten Writings and Speeches
Lincoln's War: The Real Cause, the Real Winner, the Real Loser
The Great Impersonator! 99 Reasons to Dislike Abraham Lincoln
The Unholy Crusade: Lincoln's Legacy of Destruction in the American South
The Unquotable Abraham Lincoln: The President's Quotes They Don't Want You To Know!

NATURAL HISTORY
North America's Amazing Mammals: An Encyclopedia for the Whole Family
The Concise Book of Owls: A Guide to Nature's Most Mysterious Birds
The Concise Book of Tigers: A Guide to Nature's Most Remarkable Cats

PARANORMAL
Carnton Plantation Ghost Stories: True Tales of the Unexplained from Tennessee's Most Haunted Civil War House!
UFOs and Aliens: The Complete Guidebook

FAMILY HISTORIES
The Blakeneys: An Etymological, Ethnological, and Genealogical Study - Uncovering the Mysterious Origins of the Blakeney Family and Name
The Caudills: An Etymological, Ethnological, and Genealogical Study - Exploring the Name and National Origins of a European-American Family
The McGavocks of Carnton Plantation: A Southern History - Celebrating One of Dixie's Most Noble Confederate Families and Their Tennessee Home

MIND, BODY, SPIRIT
Autobiography of a Non-Yogi: A Scientist's Journey From Hinduism to Christianity (Dr. Amitava Dasgupta, with Lochlainn Seabrook)
Britannia Rules: Goddess-Worship in Ancient Anglo-Celtic Society - An Academic Look at the United Kingdom's Matricentric Spiritual Past
Christ Is All and In All: Rediscovering Your Divine Nature and the Kingdom Within
Christmas Before Christianity: How the Birthday of the "Sun" Became the Birthday of the "Son"
Jesus and the Gospel of Q: Christ's Pre-Christian Teachings As Recorded in the New Testament
Jesus and the Law of Attraction: The Bible-Based Guide to Creating Perfect Health, Wealth, and Happiness Following Christ's Simple Formula
Seabrook's Bible Dictionary of Traditional and Mystical Christian Doctrines
The Bible and the Law of Attraction: 99 Teachings of Jesus, the Apostles, and the Prophets
The Book of Kelle: An Introduction to Goddess-Worship and the Great Celtic Mother-Goddess Kelle, Original Blessed Lady of Ireland
The Goddess Dictionary of Words and Phrases: Introducing a New Core Vocabulary for the Women's Spirituality Movement
Vintage Southern Cookbook: Delicious Dishes From Dixie

WOMEN
Aphrodite's Trade: The Hidden History of Prostitution Unveiled
Princess Diana: Modern Day Moon-Goddess - A Psychoanalytical and Mythological Look at Diana Spencer's Life, Marriage, and Death (with Dr. Jane Goldberg)
Women in Gray: A Tribute to the Ladies Who Supported the Southern Confederacy

REPRINTS
A Short History of the Confederate States of America (author Jefferson Davis; editor Lochlainn Seabrook)
Prison Life of Jefferson Davis (author John J. Craven; editor Lochlainn Seabrook)
Life of Beethoven (author Ludwig Nohl; editor Lochlainn Seabrook)
The New Revelation (author Arthur Conan Doyle; editor Lochlainn Seabrook)

Lochlainn Seabrook does not author books for fame and fortune, but for the love of writing and sharing his knowledge.

SeaRavenPress.com

Warning: SEA RAVEN PRESS BOOKS WILL EXPAND YOUR ★ MIND!

SUPPORT YOUR LOCAL
CONFEDERATE

Wit & Humor in the Southern Confederacy

CONCEIVED, COLLECTED, EDITED, & ARRANGED, WITH AN INTRODUCTION BY
"THE VOICE OF THE TRADITIONAL SOUTH," COLONEL

LOCHLAINN SEABROOK
JEFFERSON DAVIS HISTORICAL GOLD MEDAL WINNER

**Diligently Researched and Generously
Illustrated for the Elucidation of the Reader**

2021

Sea Raven Press, Nashville, Tennessee, USA

SUPPORT YOUR LOCAL CONFEDERATE

Published by
Sea Raven Press, Cassidy Ravensdale, President
PO Box 1484, Spring Hill, Tennessee 37174-1484 USA
SeaRavenPress.com • searavenpress@gmail.com

SEA RAVEN PRESS
SOUTHERN BOOKS, REAL HISTORY!

1st SRP paperback edition, 1st printing, May 2021 • ISBN: 978-1-955351-02-7
1st SRP hardcover edition, 1st printing, May 2021 • ISBN: 978-1-955351-03-4

ISBN: 978-1-955351-02-7 (paperback)
Library of Congress Control Number: 2021938775

Support Your Local Confederate: Wit and Humor in the Southern Confederacy, by Lochlainn Seabrook. Includes an introduction, illustrations, bibliography, and endnotes.

Front and back cover design and art, book design, layout, and interior art by Lochlainn Seabrook
All images, image captions, graphic design, & graphic art copyright © Lochlainn Seabrook
All images selected, placed, manipulated, and/or created by Lochlainn Seabrook
Image cleaning, coloration, & tinting by Lochlainn Seabrook
Title page soldier image from Lochlainn Seabrook's book, 'Heroes of the Southern Confederacy'
Cover image and design by Lochlainn Seabrook copyright © 2021

The views on the American "Civil War" documented in this book are those of the publisher.

PRINTED & MANUFACTURED IN OCCUPIED TENNESSEE, FORMER CONFEDERATE STATES OF AMERICA

SEA RAVEN PRESS

Dedication

Epigraph

"The Southern soldiers were always cheerful. The greater their trials, the brighter shone this quality. When pushed to the utmost on forced march, when rations failed, through biting blasts or scorching heat, they maintained their good humor and took 'fortune's buffets and rewards with equal thanks,' breaking into songs, gibes, and chaffings . . . under very adverse circumstances."

CAPTAIN WALTER G. MCRAE
7ᵀᴴ NORTH CAROLINA INFANTRY, C.S.A., 1901

CONTENTS

CHAPTER TEN

CHAPTER ELEVEN

16 ∾ SUPPORT YOUR LOCAL CONFEDERATE

NOTES TO THE READER

"NOTHING IN THE PAST IS DEAD TO THE MAN WHO WOULD
LEARN HOW THE PRESENT CAME TO BE WHAT IT IS."

WILLIAM STUBBS, VICTORIAN ENGLISH HISTORIAN

THE TWO MAIN POLITICAL PARTIES IN 1860

☛ In any study of America's antebellum, bellum, and postbellum periods, it is vitally important to understand that in 1860 the two major political parties—the Democrats and the newly formed Republicans—were the opposite of what they are today. In other words, the Democrats of the mid 19th Century were Conservatives, akin to the Republican Party of today, while the Republicans of the mid 19th Century were Liberals, akin to the Democratic Party of today.[1]

Thus the Confederacy's Democratic president, Jefferson Davis, was a Conservative (with libertarian leanings); the Union's Republican president, Abraham Lincoln, was a Liberal (with socialistic leanings).[2]

This is why, in the mid 1800s, the conservative wing of the Democratic Party was known as "the States' Rights Party."[3]

Hence, the Democrats of the Civil War period referred to themselves as "conservatives," "confederates," "anti-centralists," or "constitutionalists" (the latter because they favored strict adherence to the original Constitution—which tacitly guaranteed states' rights—as created by the Founding Fathers), while the Civil War Republicans called themselves "liberals," "nationalists," "centralists," or "consolidationists" (the latter three because they wanted to nationalize the central government and consolidate political power in Washington, D.C.).[4] In 1889 President Davis, who referred to the 1860 Democrats as "the conservative power of the country,"[5] himself explained the political situation at the time this way:

The author's cousin, Confederate Vice President and Democrat Alexander H. Stephens: a Southern Conservative.

> . . . the names adopted by political parties in the United States have not always been strictly significant of their principles. In general terms it may be said that the old Federal party [Liberal] inclined to nationalism [then a term for big government], or consolidation [that is, consolidation of power in the Federal government], and that the Whig party [liberalistic], which succeeded it, although not identical

with it, was favorable, in the main, to a strong Central Government [liberalism and socialism]. On the other hand, its opponent, the Republican [Conservative], afterward known as the Democratic party [until the election of 1896, when the two parties reversed, becoming the parties we know today], was dominated by the idea of the sovereignty of the States and the federal or confederate character of the Union [Americanism or conservatism]. Although other elements have entered into its organization at different periods, this has been its vital, cardinal, and abiding principle.

Since this idea is new to most of my readers, let us further demystify it by viewing it from the perspective of the American Revolutionary War. If Davis and his conservative Southern constituents (the Democrats of 1861) had been alive in 1775, they would have sided with George Washington and the American colonists, who sought to secede from the tyrannical government of Great Britain; if Lincoln and his Liberal Northern constituents (the Republicans of 1861) had been alive at that time, they would have sided with King George III and the English monarchy, who sought to maintain the American colonies as possessions of the British Empire. It is due to this very comparison that we Southerners often refer to our secession from the U.S. as the Second Declaration of Independence and the "Civil War" as the Second American Revolutionary War.

Without a basic understanding of these facts, the American "Civil War" will forever remain incomprehensible. For a full discussion of this topic see my book, *Abraham Lincoln Was a Liberal, Jefferson Davis Was a Conservative: The Missing Key to Understanding the American Civil War.*

A WORD ON EARLY AMERICAN MATERIAL

☞ In order to preserve the authentic historicity of the antebellum, bellum, and postbellum periods, I have retained the original spellings, formatting, and punctuation of the early Americans I quote. These include such items as British-English spellings, long-running paragraphs, obsolete words, and various literary devices peculiar to the time. However, I have corrected misspelled names to prevent confusion, and also *where possible*, inaccurate dates and locations (the inevitable result of old faulty memories). Bracketed words contain my additions and clarifications.

MY ILLUSTRATIONS

☞ In *Support Your Local Confederate*, as with many of my other works, I use "Civil War" images taken from original sources. In this particular case, this means that all of the pictures in this book are somewhere between 150 and 90 years old; in other words, they are antique illustrations, with all of the defects and imperfections found in old art. In short, matching faded and often blurry Victorian images to my Confederate material is intentional.

PRESENTISM

☞ As a historian I view *presentism* (judging the past according to present day mores and customs) as the enemy of authentic history. And this is precisely why the Left employs it in its ongoing war against traditional American, conservative, and Christian values. By looking at history through the lens of modern day beliefs—and, just as heinous, fabricating obviously fake history based on emotion, opinion, and political ideology—they are able to distort, revise, and reshape the past into a false narrative that fits their ideological agenda: the liberalization *and* Northernization of America, the enlargement and further centralization of the national government, and total control of American political, economic, and social power, the same agenda that Lincoln championed.[7]

Judging our ancestors by our own standards is dishonest, unfair, unjust, misleading, and unethical.

This book rejects presentism and replaces it with what I call *historicalism*: judging our ancestors based on the values of their own time. To get the most from this work the reader is invited to reject presentism as well. In this way—along with casting aside preconceived notions and the fake history churned out by our left-wing education system—the truth in this work will be most readily ascertained and absorbed; truth that has been rigorously researched and forensically uncovered by myself using the scientific method. As Confederate Colonel Bennett H. Young noted in 1901:

> History is valuable only as it is true. Opinions concerning acts are not history; acts themselves alone are historic.[8]

CONTINUE YOUR SOUTHERN HISTORY EDUCATION

☞ Lincoln's War on the Constitution and the American people can never be fully understood without a thorough knowledge of the South's perspective. As this book is only meant to be a brief introductory guide to these topics, one cannot hope to learn the complete story here. For those who are interested in additional material from Dixie's viewpoint, please see my comprehensive histories listed on pages 2 and 3.

CONFEDERATE HUMOR FROM
LOCHLAINN SEABROOK

INTRODUCTION

Here in the South when we think about Lincoln's War, it is usually nothing pleasant. We ponder the incredible courage our Conservative Confederate ancestors exhibited in seceding from a tyrannical and corrupt Left-wing government, and of course their formidable bravery on the battlefield. We cogitate too on the many severities and privations they experienced, fighting for four long dreary years against an implacable enemy, all the while covered in mud and gore, with cold, heat, hunger, dread, sanguinary carnage, and death their ever present companions. There was indeed *nothing* comical about the War for Southern Independence.

Despite this, "even misfortune has its funny side," as Old South Southrons used to say,[9] and irrepressible Johnny Reb was sure to comment on it at some point—even during the heat of battle. After all, "this was a remarkable characteristic of the Confederate soldier. He could throw off trouble, or face dangers, as occasion demanded. . . It was impossible to break or even check his spirit."[10] Indeed, he was "ever ready for any sort of sport or fun that offered itself to him"[11]—notwithstanding Billy Yank's daily attempt to end his military career prematurely.

As evidence of the Victorian South's keen sense of humor and fun I offer the work you now hold in your hands. It is filled with some 400 hand-picked examples of witty, playful, and hilarious jokes, stories, and tales that are sure to tickle your funny bone, nearly all of it engendered by Confederate wags: naturally jocular soldiers who were regarded by their martial band of brothers as "the life of the army in the hardest trials."[12] On full display is the Southerner's well-known erudition, philosophical sagacity, shrewd use of language, and whimsical views of everyday experiences. In describing this unique individual, Confederate Captain James Dinkins wrote the following in 1932:

> Much has been written about the bravery and daring of the Confederate soldier, and yet history will never do full justice to his genius. He will stand confessed as the greatest soldier of the past, but even this will not do him the credit he deserves. There were other features in the character of the Confederate soldier fully as remarkable as his courage. In every company there were one or more men or boys who everlastingly had some surprise for you. They were the comedians who furnished life and fun for the rest of the crowd. These fellows invariably made good soldiers, and by their pranks and jokes made the other men forget their troubles and the danger too. They were meat and bread when we were hungry, and they gave us new life on the march when we were worn out. Proper notice has never been accorded these fellows, but every old soldier will recall when he reads this the name of the men of his company who furnished the fun and who always had some poor fellow on the rack.[13]

May you enjoy reading *Support Your Local Confederate* as much as I enjoyed writing it.

Lochlainn Seabrook, SCV
A Son of the South
Nashville, Tennessee, USA
May 2021
In Nobis Regnat Christus

17 MONTHS LATER THE LIBERAL NORTH ELECTED THIS DEMAGOGUE PRESIDENT

SEA RAVEN PRESS

THE WORLD'S #1 SOUTH-FRIENDLY BOOK PUBLISHER

Restoring Dixie's honor
Defending traditional Southern culture
Preserving authentic Confederate history
One book at a time!

Nashville, Tennessee
SeaRavenPress.com

"NO YANKEES WERE HARMED
IN THE MAKING OF THIS BOOK."

Lochlainn Seabrook

Support Your Local
CONFEDERATE

Wit and Humor in the Southern Confederacy

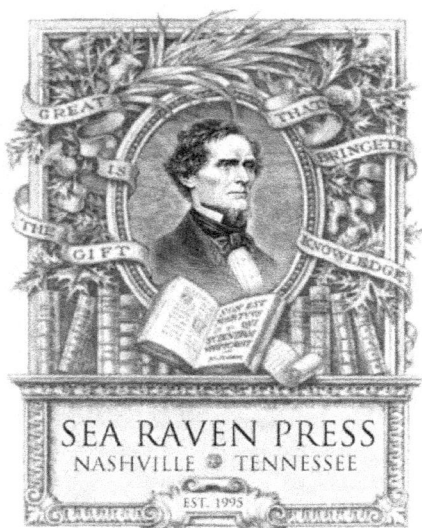

"Books invite all; they constrain none."
Hartley Burr Alexander (1873-1939)

CHAPTER ONE

REBELS GET THE LAST LAUGH ON A YANKEE GENERAL

☞ In the spring of 1862, when [U.S.] General Pope's big army, 100,000 strong, was encamped around Warrenton, Va., Mosby and his dare-devil [Confederate] rangers were engaged in a hazardous game of chess with the Yankees which abounded in remarkable moves on the part of the wary "guerrillas." All the men and boys as young as fifteen had gone to the war, leaving literally "the butcher, the baker, and the candlestick maker" to protect and to provide for the women and children of Warrenton. General Pope finally became angry and suspicious and issued orders for all suspects to be arrested, and the provost marshal formally convened his court.

THE "GRAY GHOST," CONFEDERATE RANGER JOHN S. MOSBY.

The first citizen of Fauquier to be arrested was a man by the name of Wolf, who resided in the upper part of the county. The next prisoner called to the bar responded to the name of John Fox, who was a shopkeeper in Warrenton. The judge remarked with a smile: "This is a coincidence to capture a fox and a wolf in the same trap." The guard then produced a quiet, inoffensive looking citizen, who called himself Rabbit, whereupon the judge frowned and demanded his right name. "I speak the truth," replied Rabbit; "that's my name. I'm a shoemaker by trade, and live in this town." The next was a comical looking little man, with a moonlike face and waggish gray eye. He chewed tobacco as if it was candy, and he had a voice like a cross-cut saw. When asked for his pedigree, he struck a pose and, in theatrical tones, spouted as follows for the benefit of the soldiers: "My name's Bob Coon. I'm the auctioneer of this 'ere town, and can prove it by reputable citizens." An uproar of laughter followed this sally, and the judge tried to look angry. "You fellows are assuming false names and ridiculing my authority. We will see who laughs last in this matter."

Coon established his identity, and as there was no longer any doubt as to his name, residence, and avocation, the court again became placid and dignified. "What's your name?" was asked the next man, a harmless

Hebrew, who gave his name as Bear, and his occupation as that of a merchant. The judge was nonplussed, but, appreciating the humor of the situation, remarked with a smile: "Have we gotten into a den of wild animals?" But the climax was reached when the last witness went on the stand. He was a local character and the popular Boniface of Warrenton. When he swore that his name was Louis Lion, and, moreover, that he was the proprietor of "The Lion House," there was such an outburst of hilarity that the judge lost his dignity, proclaimed that he was not in the army for the purpose of opening a menagerie, and adjourned the court *sine die*.

The sequel to the farce was the release of all the prisoners and a big laugh on General Pope throughout the rank and file of both armies.[14]

A BLACK SHEEP

☞ While scouting down on the Eastern Shore of Maryland, an aged woman, bearing the same name, was asked if she were a kinsman of General Palmer. She lived down on the Eastern Shore near where General Palmer's grandfather was born. "Did you all say he were a Gineral?" she asked. When she got an affirmative answer she was quite sure he was a kinsman. "But," went on the [Yankee] interrogator, "he was a general in the Union army."

"Well," she said, after a pause, her face lengthening, "there must be a black sheep in every fambly."[15]

A LONG WAY FROM HEADQUARTERS

☞ A Methodist circuit-rider met a Texan soldier and asked him what army he belonged to. "I belong to the __th Texas regiment, Van Dorn's Army," replied the soldier. "What army do you belong to?" "I belong to the Army of the Lord," was the solemn reply. "Well, then, my friend," said the soldier, dryly, "you've got a very long way from headquarters!"[16]

ROBERT TOOMBS' LUGGAGE

☞ It is a humorous incident in the stories told upon Robert Toombs, mention of whom is made in the diary of Alexander H. Stephens, herein printed, that when he had gone to the National Capital, from his home at Washington, Ga., to visit a gentleman of wealth, who met him at the station with his carriage, and in the good cheer of meeting forgot to inquire for his baggage until they had journeyed quite a distance. Then, startled at the oversight, he said: "What did you do with your baggage?" "I broke it," was Toombs' cool reply.[17]

WHO WON THE WAR?

☞ After fighting the same war for fifty-four years, somebody or other has to surrender, even if it happens to be the winning side. That's the reason Edward S. Upson, a white-haired man of seventy-seven years, is now held without bail in a Brooklyn jail on the charge of being a fugitive from justice from Trenton, N. J.

Once upon a time, when his hair was black and his limbs were lithe, Edward fought in the Civil War, on the Union side. Then he fell in love with a sweet young rebel down Virginia way, who married him. She's Mrs. Mary Williams Upson, and, as Edward told the judge, her only fault is she didn't surrender when Lee did. In spite of the fact that they lived together for fifty-four years, and regardless of the seven children out of fourteen they brought to manhood and womanhood, they still fought the war.

"She's a rank secessionist, judge," said Edward, "and she thinks the war's still on."

Even the knowledge that right, logic, and historical accuracy were on his side, couldn't win for Edward; so after the many years he decided to strike camp. He departed from Trenton for parts unknown. Arrested in Brooklyn, he is awaiting extradition papers to go back and face the charge of abandonment his wife has brought against him. "Now, listen, judge," argued Edward, "we won the war, didn't we?"

Did we?[18]

A YANKEE GIRL'S DEFINITION OF "CARPETBAGGER"
☛ A young lady from a Rose Creek, Minn., school gives this significant definition: "The carpetbaggers were people of the South who wore shirts made of carpets, so that the bullets would not go through."[19]

LOOKS CAN BE DECEIVING
☛ An incident that occurred the next day after the battle of Franklin [II], may illustrate how important good clothes may be in settling a preacher's identity. Pardon the use of the first person singular, and I'll tell it as it occurred:

I was chaplain of the 49th Tennessee, but as I was the only chaplain in the brigade, I did duty for the whole brigade.

Originally I enlisted as a private, and for a long time served as chaplain by detail, so I got to feel easier in the jacket, trousers and brogans of the private soldier than in a regulation uniform; and then, as I had no money to get a uniform, and as we had no chance to get anything from home, my plain apparel was a necessity.

From long exposure to the changes of climate and scene, my uniform became more picturesque than elegant. As we came into Tennessee the nights were often quite cold, and as I stood around the blazing camp-fires a sudden change of the wind would sometimes whip the blaze about my legs and scorch the lower extremities of my trousers. In the battle I had thrown off my jacket, and a shell exploding just over it had dropped a spark of fire in the middle of the back, which gradually spread until it burned a hole perfectly round and about four or five inches across.

Dressed "cap-a-pie," the following was my outfit: A hat made of brown jeans, quilted, and which when soaked took in half a gallon of water; a check cotton shirt, that would not meet about my neck, and had no button on the collar any how; my jacket, with the ventilator in the back; my trousers, fringed with scorched strings from the knee to the ankle; socks, with no feet but sound legs; shoes, in which sole and upper were only held together by strings.

My hair hung on my shoulders, and bleared eyes looked out from a long and scraggy beard that covered all my face.

In the battle our brigade lost dreadfully. The highest officer left, as I remember, was a lieutenant. We had large numbers of wounded. Our brigadier, General Quarles [C.S.A.], was desperately wounded. Every field officer and captain was killed, wounded or captured. We had a great many of our wounded in the buildings on the farm [Carnton Plantation, Franklin TN] of that noble gentleman, Col. John McGavock. After getting them placed as comfortably as I could, I started into the town to hunt up anything which might minister to their needs. The ladies of the old town were angels of mercy. They were abundant in their labors, preparing food, bandages and medicines for the soldiers. I looked in at a door and saw a dozen ladies hard at work on the very things I wanted. I never thought for a moment on my outlandish appearance, but addressed them in a manner that I thought was Chesterfieldian in its insinuating elegance.

The leader of the party and director of the work was an old lady, whose looks I shall always remember. She wore a cap with lace border, and a pair of silver bowed spectacles, the eyes of which were large and round. She was rather short and stout, and while her countenance beamed with business and benevolence, yet she had a quick, positive way, that seemed to settle things.

Bowing to the ladies, I addressed the leader:

"I have a great many wounded men to look after, and I should like to get anything that would relieve them, such as food, delicacies, clothing, bandages and lint."

The old lady looked at me rather doubtfully and then said, dryly, "Yes, I expect you would."

"Yes, madam," said I, "my men are in great need, and some of them very badly hurt; I want to get the things as soon as possible."

"Yes," said she, "you look like you needed them very bad yourself."

The ladies tittered at this pointed reference to my personal appearance, and I felt very uncomfortable, but I went on: "Madam, I assure you our boys need these comforts very much."

The reply, with almost a sneer, was; "No doubt of it: but how am I to know that the *boys* will ever get them if I give them to *you*?

I said, with some little feeling: "You don't think I would take from a wounded man, do you?"

Some of the ladies seemed to sympathize with me, but the old lady was inexorable. "Well, I don't know; I hear that a heap of you fellows are getting nice things for the wounded, and then eating them yourselves; I like to know who I'm sending by."

Drawing myself up with quite an air, I announced: "Madam, I'm the chaplain of Quarles' Brigade."

But the old lady was not even stunned. "Yes, yes, it is easy enough to *claim* to be most anything. Why some of you boys would *say* that you are Major Generals if you could make anything by it. You can't fool me."

The situation was getting desperate: the ladies were smiling audibly, and I was about to beat a retreat, when, happening to put my hand to my breast, I felt a paper, which was my commission. It was a formidable-looking document, with the great seal of the Confederate States on it, and signed "James Seddon, Secretary of War." At once I drew out the paper, saying, "Madam, I am sorry that you doubt my word; I shall not ask you for anything, but I can convince you that I am chaplain of Quarles' Brigade."

"NIGHT AMUSEMENTS" IN A CONFEDERATE CAMP.

As soon as her eyes fell on that seal, and she read the name and the office in the commission, her whole manner changed. She loaded me with all I could carry, and urged me to come back as often as I needed her help, and, following me to the door, she apologized to me in a confidential whisper, which could have been heard half a block away: "Now, parson, you really must excuse me; I didn't mean any offence, but I couldn't help it; for if I had been going to hunt a preacher, you are the last man I would ever have picked out."

The apology was satisfactory.[20]

THE POST OFFICE & THE LITTLE DEMOCRAT

☞ My seven year-old grandson persisted in playing about a small, nearby branch post office. He told me that the men "shooed" him out of the back office. I explained that only the employees were allowed in there, but that he could go in the front office, as that was for the public. He said, "But, Granny, I'm not a Public; I'm a Democrat [a Conservative then]."[21]

ECONOMICS & ENGAGEMENT

☞ "But darling, don't you want to marry a man who is economical?" "I suppose so; but it's awful being engaged to one."[22]

THE SPIDER WAGON

☛ One of the names given to the chaplain of the 49th Tennessee was more expressive than respectful. He was known throughout the brigade by every man in it. As he was always in good health, and quite strong in his limbs, he often carried some of the luggage of men who were weak or sick, and so often was loaded with a queer medley of frying pans, cartridge boxes, and sometimes a camp kettle. Now the North Carolina name for a skillet was a "spider," and the wagon carrying their cooking utensils was called a "spider wagon." A North Carolina regiment was camped near us, and this name amused us very much. One day as the chaplain came by under his load someone shouted: "Get out of the way there; here comes the 49[th's] spider wagon."[23]

A QUEER ORDER

☛ I remember the first battle order I ever heard. It was at Fort Donelson, in the fall of 1863. There were then only about half a dozen companies there, drilling and fortifying. The senior captain was Tom Beaumont, of Clarksville, with whom I messing.

In those days we had not given up all home habits; we wore white shirts and underclothes, had washing done, kept measurably clean, and every night went to bed in our tents, undressing and retiring "like folks."

One day it was rumored that the gunboats were in the river below us, and were coming up. About midnight, while all were sleeping soundly, the long roll began to beat in the company stationed on the river bank. At once there was a stir in the camp; officers were calling the men to fall in; there was hurrying to and fro. Captain Beaumont was always when on duty in faultless dress, and now he did not neglect his toilet. Quickly he put on his uniform, buckled on his sword, and stepped out of his tent to take command of his company.

But the men had not been as thoughtful as he. They sprang up and grasped their muskets, and formed line in front of their tents, but every man of them had forgotten to put on his trousers, and they stood there in the starlight, in their night-clothes, like "sheeted ghosts," trembling with cold and excitement. As the captain and I stepped out, and his eye glanced along the line, his sense of propriety got the better of his military ardor, and he shouted out his first command, "Confound your fool souls, go and put on your breeches!" In a moment the whole situation dawned on the men, and with shunts of laughter they prepared for battle by donning that needful article of apparel. But it was a false alarm, and they soon took off their breeches and went to sleep. Poor Tom Beaumont, brave and tender and true, as knightly a soul as ever drew sword—as colonel of the 50th Tennessee he fell on Chickamauga's bloody field.[24]

WHY AMERICA IS GREAT—1924

☛ The American Bankers' Association has given out some figures showing why America is great, in the following:

One hundred and ten million persons, occupying three million square miles of territory, and possessing wealth estimated at three hundred billion dollars.

Bank deposits aggregating approximately four billion dollars.

Outstanding insurance of more than Seventy billion dollars.

Five hundred million acres of improved lands valued at seventy-seven billion dollars.

Twenty-four million milch cows, forty million head of other cattle, forty million sheep, and sixty million swine.

More than three billion bushels of corn and one billion bushels of wheat produced a year.

More than sixty billion dollars' worth of manufactured products turned out in a year.

More than twenty-three billion gallons of crude oil produced in a year.

More than two hundred and fifty thousand miles of railroad.

More than two hundred and fifty thousand miles of commercial telegraph lines.

Eight hundred thousand miles of telephone lines.

Twenty thousand daily and weekly newspapers to disseminate information and to bind our people by ties of common knowledge for common purposes.[25]

THE TARDY HUSBAND

☛ They had one of their usual tiffs because hubby was home late for dinner. "You're always late," she said, indignantly. "You were late at the church the day we were married."

"Yes," he answered, bitterly, "but I wasn't late enough."[26]

CHARGING A GUNBOAT WITH THE BAYONET

☛ In the fall of 1864 I was at Fort Donelson, on the Cumberland River, where there were several companies of Confederate soldiers waiting to be organized into a regiment. At Fort Henry, on the Tennessee River, twelve or fifteen miles distant, the 10th Tennessee was stationed. At both places we were busy fortifying, especially against [Yankee] gunboats, of which we had heard dreadful accounts.

The 10th Tennessee was made up of Irishmen, as brave and witty a set as ever entered the service; with characteristic impetuosity, they were equally ready for a fight or a frolic, or to turn one into the other as occasion served. They were known as the "Bloudy Tinth."

I remember a story about this regiment that went the rounds at Fort Donelson, and I tell it as it was told to me:

One day while they were busy digging and fortifying, a report came to them from a breathless picket that a gunboat was just around the bend, coming up the river, and would blow them all into "smithereens" in a jiffy. At once there was immense excitement.

There was not much order nor discipline in those days, so the whole regiment at once dropped pick and shovel and rushed to the colonel's quarters to know what to do. They had muskets and bayonets, but not a round of ammunition. The commander was Col. A. Heiman, a fine old soldier, a German, quiet, cool and deliberate. He was busy writing, and as the crowd came clamorously about his tent he took in the situation. He knew that the river was too low for a gunboat to get in cannon shot of the fort, so he merely looked up from his papers, saying, "Oh, take 'em mit to payonet, poys; take 'em mit to payonet," and went on with his writing, while they went back to their quarters. In a couple of hours, having finished his work, and almost forgotten the incident, he strolled down to the bank of the river, and there was the "Tinth," drawn up in line, with set faces, shoes off and trousers rolled up, and bayonets fixed, ready to charge the gunboat as soon as she appeared. And they were sadly disappointed that she didn't come, for "they'd have got her sure, bedad, if she had shown her nose."[27]

FRENCH-SPEAKING FROGS
☞ At Port Hudson we were encamped next to the 30th Louisiana Regiment, made up of French-speaking men. On the 14th of March, 1863, [U.S. Admiral] Farragut and his [Yankee] fleet attempted to pass up the river, and the bombardment was terrific. The scene at night was sublime. We were all ordered to the trenches, in anticipation of an attack by land. While we were standing in line, in the darkness, close to the quarters of the 30th Louisiana, we noticed that the frogs in the numerous ponds seemed much excited, and were croaking incessantly in a kind of low, continuous chatter. One of the boys listened a moment, trying to make out what it meant. At length he announced the explanation: "Boys, these frogs have been camped so long by the 30th Louisiana that they have learned to talk French."[28]

THE MYSTERIOUS FRENCH LANGUAGE
☞ French was a mystery to most of our rural Tennessee boys. They never could get used to the strange sound and the rapid utterance. As some of them were lounging by the riverside at Port Hudson, they heard some French-speaking women, who were engaged in washing, talking to each other. One of our boys called to another: "Run here quick, Sam, and hear this woman talk; she can just give *one* flutter of her tongue and say more in a minute than you can in a week." Sam was noted for slowness of speech.[29]

THE CENSUS
☞ A census taker made his rounds in an isolated village. He gave one of his official papers to a woman that she might fill in the required answers. One of the questions, instead of reading, "Married or single," had it "Condition as to marriage." The woman filled in the answer thus: "Awful

hard up before. Wuss after."[30]

OUCH!
☛ Author. "Have you read my new book?"
   Friend. "Yes."
   Author. "What do you think of it?"
   Friend. "Well, to be candid with you, I think the covers are too far apart."[31]

MONEY VALUES
☛ In these days of financial stringency and monetary discussion, this may illustrate the depreciation of currency.

In January, 1864, we were in camps at Dalton, Ga. I had just been paid off, and a great deal of my money was in one dollar bills. The dollar bill of the Confederacy was a red hacked piece of paper about six or eight inches long and about three inches wide. Of course, when a soldier is paid he wants to buy something to eat; so, as I heard of a man who was selling ginger-cakes in a camp about a mile away, I went at once. I resolved to spend a whole dollar in gingerbread. My memory recalled with delight the generous square that I used to buy for five cents from the old cake woman when I was a boy. I found my man. He had constructed an oven on a hillside, and he baked bread in one cake about three feet square. I imagined that my dollar would about buy a whole square—would probably exhaust his stock. So, with an air of riches, I handed him my red-back and said, "Give me the worth of that." He wasn't disconcerted, but just took my dollar and laid it on his square of cake and cut out the exact size of my dollar and handed it to me. I never realized before that money is a *measure* of value.[32]

A MISSISSIPPI BRIGADE AT WORK.

SOME EATING REMINISCENCES
☛ When rations were scant and the boys were hungry, they talked a great deal about the good things to eat they used to have at home, and which they expected to get when they reached home after the war. They grew enthusiastic over imaginary dinners.

One Billy B. was, when at home, noted for his excellent table. He felt deeply our narrow bill of fare, and so drew largely on memory and hope to supply the deficit. He was a shouting Methodist, and expressed in lively style his emotions. He would begin to tell what he would do when he got back home. In a gentle voice he would speak of getting a good bath, and some clean clothes; then, as he went in imagination to the dining-room, his eye would grow brighter and his voice louder. He would call over the bill of fare. Biscuit and butter and "shore-enough" coffee were mentioned in loving tones, and ham and turkey or chicken-pie were dwelt upon with a rising inflection, and so on his voice grew in volume until he reached the dessert, and puddings, pies and cakes, with abundant fruit, were shouted out in tones to be heard in the next brigade; and he wound up with, "Glory, won't that be a happy time!"

But one day I heard a voice as to eating that went to the opposite extreme. Jim O. was a liberal feeder when he could get provender. As we were marching along the dusty roads of Mississippi, in the campaign around Vicksburg, we were very hungry, and some of the boys were particularly vivid in describing the pleasures they used to derive through the stomach and its food supply. Jim was silent and sad. At last he broke into the flow of talk with, "Oh, hush, boys; a fellow might as well have no belly as for all the good it does him here!"

When [Confederate] General Hood started on his campaign into Tennessee, in the fall of 1864, the sorghum was just ripening through Georgia, and we passed daily great fields of the sweet cane. We found it delicious to the taste, and so great quantities of it were chewed up, swallowing the juice, and leaving thousands of dry quids of the stalk spit out by the way. Steve E. was our commissary sergeant, and had peculiar advantages for gathering the sorghum. Every day he furnished me with a good supply of the stalk, and I marched and chewed, and threw aside the quids all along the way. Steve declared that "the parson had chewed a streak a hundred yards wide through the State of Georgy."

After the war was over Steve was riding along with an old comrade in Dickson County, Tennessee, when they passed a ten-acre field of sorghum in fine condition. The companion said: "Wouldn't we have enjoyed that during the war?" "Yes," said Steve, "but if you'd turn the parson in on it he'd chaw it up in a night."[33]

THE SLEEPY CHIEF JUSTICE
☛ A report that Chief Justice Taft was dead started newspaper telephones ringing and sent reporters scurrying out to the Taft residence. "So far as I know," said the Chief Justice sleepily from a window, "the report is without foundation." Then he went back to bed.[34]

BOB & MIKE
☛ Bob H. was a fine soldier—a mere boy when he enlisted. He was

brave, kind, good humored and quaint. One day, after he had been away from home for three years and more, he was talking in a reminiscent way of the folks at home, and especially of one of the H.'s with whom he used to be very familiar. I asked him the question, "Bob, is he kin to you?" His answer, with a queer drawl, was, "Well, parson, I don't know; I haven't *seen* him in a *long* time."

One of Bob's closest friends and his messmate was Mike M., also full of fun and free from care. In our marches he had frequently called my attention to a very tall, slender, red-headed man, over six and a half feet high, belonging to one of the regiments of our brigade. Looking along the line, this figure, wearing a little skull cap, a jacket and trousers both too short for him, and often barefooted, was certain to be seen either before or behind us. As we were tramping through North Georgia under Joe Johnston, one rainy day, Mike seemed unusually depressed. After a while he stooped down on hands and knees to take a drink from a little branch that crossed our way. Just as he was about to drink the long soldier straddled the branch right by his head. Looking up, Mike was just about to "tell him what he thought": but when his eyes reached a height where a man's head ought to be he saw no face. With wonder he ran his eye up the man's anatomy until he saw his full length; then, with a laugh, "Why, hello old *thunderpole*: where did you come from?" He did look like a lightning-rod.

It is said that at the beginning of the war Mike's father was opposed to his enlisting because he was too young. One evening he sent the boy out to bring a log of wood for the fire. Mike didn't return just then, but went on to Camp Cheatham. Four years afterward as he came home he passed by the woodpile, and bringing in a log of wood threw it on the fire, saying, "You see it took a long time to find it."[35]

BATTLE FUN

☛ This story was told a friend by Celsus Price, son of the [Confederate] General [Sterling Price]:

"It was during Price's hurried exit from his raid into Missouri. [U.S. General] Pleasonton's Cavalry had made a splendid charge, breaking our lines, capturing lots of prisoners, and we were going to the rear on a dead run, in silence, when a loud laugh was heard ringing above the roar of a thousand horses' feet. This sounded sacrilegious—like a church dog-fight during prayers. Looking around, Arthur McCoy, one of our most reckless dare-devils, with empty revolver and blowing horse, was shaking with jollity. 'Arthur, you—fool, what're ye laughing at?' 'I was thinkin' if we—had the yanks like they've got—us, wouldn't—it—be—f-u-n?' And that laugh was better than a reinforcement. We re-formed at once."[36]

A CONCISE SPEAKER

☛ The following story illustrates the advantage of compression in speech. A little girl had been asked to tell the story of Elisha, and she gave it thus: "Elisha had a bear and the children mocked him, and he said: 'If you mock me, I will set my bear on you, and it will eat you up.' And they did, and he did, and it did."[37]

A SENIOR MARRIES HER 8TH HUSBAND AT BEAUVOIR
☛ "If the Lord keeps on taking 'em, so will I," was the sentiment of Mrs. Mary Sanders, seventy-four years old, seven times a widow, who was married to her eighth husband at the Beauvoir Confederate Home. The bridegroom, A. B. Fuller, is ninety-six years old. Six of her former husbands were Confederate soldiers. "Uncle" Pat McLoughlin, a bachelor, one hundred and four years old, and also a Confederate veteran, was best man at the wedding.[38]

VIVID ACCOUNT OF BODY LICE IN CAMP
☛ G. G. Buchanan, now of Belcher, Texas, who was of Company A, Palmetto Sharpshooters, sends to the *Confederate Veteran* special inquiry for his comrade and friend, Bob Greer. He relates some thrilling experiences they had together, and especially a time when they were in the trenches by Petersburg. He tells an interesting story of how he and Bob went down to a running creek for a bath one July morning in 1864, and how the yankee gunner cut his fuse for their great discomfort. They were between the lines of battle, and had gone to the creek through great peril, but they were in need of a change from some "jayhawkers" that "could climb a fellow's leg the straightest, stick the closest, and scratch the hardest of any crawling thing on earth." He says: "Bob and I were having a good time. O yes, we were down under the hill, as we thought, out of sight; but mind you, blind things can travel in dark places. We had taken off our old shirts and began to splash them down in the water, thinking we would, by concussion, kill or shake off a few of those critters and that some of them might run across the lines to see how a good fat yankee would taste. But let me tell you, if that water business had been the only way to get rid of those things, I am sure we would have to have been half-soled before this time. When we got in a good way with our washing a doleful sound came at us saying, "Where is you? where is you?" And they kept coming, and getting closer and closer. Bob took up his linen and struck off in a long trot, saying, "Come on Buck; this ain't no good place." But neither of us were hurt, and here I am, August 25, 1893.[39]

SHE WAS WORSE THAN HE TOOK HER FOR
☛ At the end of three weeks of married life, a Southern darky returned to the minister who had performed the ceremony and asked for a divorce. After explaining that he could not grant divorces, the minister tried to dissuade his visitor from carrying out his intention of getting one, saying: "You must remember, Sam that you promised to take Liza

for better or for worse." "Yassir, I knows dat, boss," rejoined the darky, "but—she's wuss dan I took her for."[40]

THE MORAL OF PLAYING POKER

☛ One winter poker playing was fashionable in the Missouri Division. General Parsons called up Major _____, who had been promoted for bravery, and charged him with playing cards with his men, to the utter subversion of good order and military discipline. "Yes, general, it's true. But, you see, they were big men at home, and it's an honor for me to play with them. There's _____ [who] was a judge on the bench, _____ was county clerk, and _____ owns the biggest farm in the county, while I'm only a common blacksmith. And they play a good game too!" And there was a moral in this reply which some of the martinets could never see.[41]

THE BATTLE OF THE IRONCLADS.

APPLE DUMPLINGS

☛ I was a [Confederate] prisoner at Camp Douglas, and slowly dying of starvation. A young man from my neighborhood was a fellow-prisoner, and quite a number from our county were enduring the same hardness as good soldiers. My friend's father was a man of wealth, and determined to send succor to his son if it could be done. This determination was made known to my father. After some delay for correspondence and compliance with red tape regulations, the checks came, one for $35 and one for $25. We felt rich! What now? said my friend. A dinner, was the reply, and all the boys from our county invited. Good, just the thing! To the sutler we went and bought a generous supply of meat, bread, butter, sugar, coffee, flour, lard, and a half bushel of green apples. All these things we carried to my kitchen and instructed the cook to cook them all, and to make all the apples into dumplings. You should have seen the dumplings—two large sauce-pans full! Not one was left. To this day I have never had such a feast nor seen nor tasted such dumplings. Of course I cannot give the sauce which made the reminiscence so enjoyable from the narrator, but I enjoyed the dumplings . . . Such is the story of Rev. T. J. McGill.[42]

HOW THEY STOOD PICKET

☛ This story is by one of Forrest's scouts: One day in 1864 orders came to the regiment for a detail for scout and picket duty, and the instructions accompanying the orders were for the detail to proceed along a certain road until the enemy was discovered, then stop, hold him in check if possible, but under all circumstances to inform the General of the whereabouts and strength of the enemy. All know that when "old Bedford" [Forrest] issued orders he intended them to be obeyed, and promptly, too. So worn out as the men were it was not long before the party, under command of Lieut. Garner, started on what might prove a wild goose chase, and was just as likely to prove a tiger hunt, with lots of tiger in it. Of one thing the men were sure, they would go until they found the enemy if he was on that road.

Every old soldier knows that on such expeditions he always picked out a mate. One if the men, Burns, a youngster in point of years, but an old soldier, and one of the best that Forrest had, picked out Dick Townsend for his chum. Townsend was riding a gray, almost white, horse. This part of it Burns did not like at all, but decided he would rather risk Townsend with a white horse than any other man there, with a less objectionably colored horse. But I'll let Burns tell the rest.

We had ridden ten or twelve miles when, just after dark, we came up to an old fellow's house and asked him if there were any yanks about, and he told us that they were camped just across the creek about half a mile ahead. We went on quietly, keeping a good lookout, and sure enough, when we got near the creek we could hear dogs barking. They always had dogs about their camps; why, we never could tell, unless it was because the negroes followed them and the dogs followed the negroes. At any rate, the dogs were always there. We halted, and could distinctly hear them talking; and after listening long enough to be sure that we had accomplished our mission, we fell back down the road about a quarter and put out a picket. It came Townsend's and my turn to go on late, and we went to the top of the hill with a lot of orders, mostly "nots"—namely, not to talk, not to smoke, not to make the least noise, and not to shoot, if possible to avoid it, and not, under any circumstances, to dismount, but to sit quietly on our horses and watch. I do not know how long I had been there when I got so sleepy it seemed to me I should fall off of my horse. I leaned over, and in a whisper asked Townsend if he was sleepy too. He said he was nearly dead. Finally, we could stand it no longer, and got down off our horses and began walking back and forth in front of them as far as the halters would let us, but this didn't do any good. Looking around I saw that the road was raised—that is, it was higher than the ground on either side of it. I told Townsend that I was going to sit down on the ground and rest. We both sat down, putting our feet in the ditch. There were plenty of weeds growing close up to the side of the road. I leaned over and put my head down on my hands as they rested on my gun. I did not expect nor intend to go to sleep, but I was completely fagged out. I don't know how long I had been in the position described when something passed by through the weeds with a whisk, [a] whisk that waked me instantly. It was right under my nose when I saw it, and I tell you the truth when I say it nearly scared the life out of me. It scared me so bad I yelled, "hellfire, what's that?" as loud as I could, and then I saw it was nothing but a coon. Almost instantly we were on our horses listening, but the yanks never heard a word, or if they did they made no sign. As soon as we found we hadn't alarmed them we got to laughing, and really after the scare was over it was about as funny an adventure as any that happened to me during the war. It shows how little it takes to scare a fellow almost to death when he is tired out and expecting to be scared anyhow. Just before day we withdrew, but Townsend and I laughed all day over that terrible fright.[43]

A CLEOPATRA JOKE
☛ First Englishman: "Charlie, did you hear that joke about the Egyptian guide who showed some tourists two skulls of Cleopatra, one as a girl and one as a woman?"
Second Ditto: "No; let's hear it."[44]

STORY OF THE FOUR SCOTSMEN
☛ There is a story of four Scotsmen, which is declared to be the best story in the world and the most searching test of humor. Two Scotsmen were talking about a third. Said the first to the second: "He has no sense of humor at all. He wouldn't see a joke if you were to fire it at him out of a pistol." "But," objected the second, "you can't fire a joke out of a pistol." The first Scotsman went away depressed, and, meeting a fourth Scotsman, told him the second Scotsman's remark. The fourth Scotsman thought for a moment, and then said, with a short laugh: "Ay, he had ye there."[45]

THE MAN WHO HATED THE SMELL OF GUNPOWDER
☛ The [C.S.] conscript officers were after every man that could fire a gun, and my friend's husband was among the recruits taken up. He came to Mr. Morgan in great distress, and asked him to write a note to Dr. Paul F. Eve, stating his inability to do service. He said he knew Dr. Eve was his friend, and anything he would write him would have its influence. He was very patriotic, but he didn't like the smell of gunpowder. My husband told him he was not a member of the medical board, and he didn't see how he could write him a paper of disability. He had a holy horror of going into the army if there was any way to prevent it, and had his heart set on the note, and said: "Write anything you think will help me, and I believe Dr. Eve will release me." Mr. Morgan still declined, not knowing what to state; but he would take no denial. So the note was written to this effect: "Dr. Eve: Having known this gentleman and family intimately for eighteen months while in Marietta, I think that I can safely say that I do not think he is good for anything in the world." He read it over, and said: "O my friend, I will never forget you while I

live. I thank you most heartily." I think that he was the first man I ever knew who thanked another for calling him a fool. Dr. Eve was a man of keen perceptions, and saw the joke and enjoyed it immensely. He gave him a letter of disability, and as long as the doctor lived he laughed over this funny incident.[46]

SOME LAUGHS AT THE LEE-CUSTIS MANSION

☛ For the first time since the war period a squadron of [U.S.] cavalry was recently [circa 1892-1893] quartered near Washington, on the old Lee estate, "Arlington." One of the companies halted near a farm-house, and the captain, in conversation with the owner, remarked that he was going to the Bull Run battle-field, and would remain there over Sunday. The farmer's daughter, seated near by on the piazza, began to laugh, and when asked for an explanation said: "Well, Captain, yours will be the first Union soldiers who have stayed there that long."[47]

WANTED TO BE FLATTENED OUT

☛ When a [Confederate] company of home guards on the Mississippi River had fired upon a [U.S.] gunboat the boat acknowledged by opening on them with shell. The guards immediately got down close to the ground, and one of them said, "Boys, if I ain't flat enough won't one of you please get on me and mash me flatter?"[48]

MADE ONE OF 'EM HOLLER

☛ In the Spring of 1868, at Cochran's Cross Roads, in North Mississippi, we engaged in a lively skirmish with Grierson's Federal cavalry. At first they gave way before us in a very satisfactory manner, but being reinforced they sent our boys back on the reserve after the latest improved double quick style. A red-headed corporal named Tom Murray dashed by me, and as he halted exclaimed, "Well, Captain, we made one of 'em holler." "What did he say, Tom?" the Captain inquired. Tom looked up, squinted his gray eyes and replied, "He said, 'Forward, skirmishers.'"[49]

THE WRONG PLACE TO WEAR A STOVE PIPE HAT

☛ As Ferguson's brigade of cavalry was marching through Mississippi in 1864, on a country road, we met an infantry Colonel in full uniform, with the exception that instead of the cap or soft hat usually worn he had on a silk hat, or, as the boys would say, a "stove pipe." You may imagine the result. One would ask it he had stoves to sell, another if he was moving his bees, or if he had honey to sell, and shouts of laughter would roll out all along the line. The Colonel was in a buggy with his wife, and had to leave the road and take to the woods to escape the fun.[50]

TOO MUCH CROW

☛ As my command, Perrin's regiment, Mississippi Cavalry, Ferguson's brigade, was moving from Mississippi to Georgia, spring of 1864, a soldier by the name of Crow had a pass to go by his home and join the command as it came by. Crow's house was immediately on the road by which the command marched, and he had his family and neighbors present to see the command, at this time a large one. As we passed in front of the house the boys of Company "D" recognized Crow, and they all began cawing, and you would have thought the crows of Mississippi had all gathered in council as the cawing passed from company to company of the regiment. Our comrade Crow wisely beat a retreat.[51]

HEAVEN OR HELL?
☞ An old negro woman stood by the grave of her husband, and said mournfully: "Po' Rastus! I hope he's gone where I 'spec he ain't."[52]

THE SIDE OF HIS HEAD SHOT OFF?
☞ A company of cavalry of this section of Mississippi was on duty on the Tennessee River. Privates John W. T. and a man named Gamble were on out-post picket; it was night, dark and wet, and the reserve picket were making themselves as comfortable as possible, when two shots rang out, and following closely after the shots they heard a horse coming rapidly down the road, and in a few moments G. came up and reported that John W. T. was shot and the enemy was advancing. But in a minute or two another horse and rider came tearing in, and John was the rider. He said, "Captain, I am shot." The Captain asked him where, and he said, "The side of my head is torn off." The Captain put his hand to John's head and felt it and said, "It is true, take him back to the hospital." But when day came the wound on the side of John's head proved

THE "KNIGHTLY HORSEMAN OF THE VALLEY," CONFEDERATE GENERAL TURNER ASHBY.

to be mud and water. The facts, as developed afterward, were, that John and his friend had fired at a farmer's mule, and John's horse had thrown him, and as he went off his carbine had slapped him on the side of the head, and as he hit the ground his head went in the mud and water. Poor John has gone now, but he never relished this story, but it was true.[53]

NOT A SENSATIONALIST
☞ Here is a story of infantry to match the cavalry incident. Private H. was on picket when he saw what he thought was a [U.S.] battery moving up. He rushed back and said, "Captain, I am no sensationalist, but the enemy are planting a battery on the hill over there." The Captain

immediately ordered out the company and advanced in skirmishing order, to attack the supposed battery. On getting in good view the battery proved to be an old-fashioned cart which an old negro had driven up and turned around with the tail-board toward the camp. Our friend to this good day does not like to hear any one say, "I am no sensationalist," as he thinks it is personal.[54]

STAMPEDE AMONG TEXAS HORSES AT ROME, GEORGIA

☛ A friend of mine, now living here in the drug business, was stationed during the war at Rome, Ga., and tells this incident: A Texas regiment of cavalry came in town and halted in front of the hotel, and the officers and many of the men scattered around town, but the majority of them remained mounted and took the easiest positions they could in their saddles, many of them sitting sideways with one leg thrown across the saddle. It was about dinner time, and the negro waiter came out with one of those Chinese copper gongs, and giving it one tremendous rap, made it rattle with that nerve-shattering noise so well known to passengers at railway depots. The result was fearful. Horses reared, plunged, and, turning like goats, stampeded in all directions, leaving many riders on the ground, and creating more excitement than the fire of a Federal battery of six guns would have done. But after a few minutes the officers of the regiment came up to see what was the matter, and hearing the cause told the proprietor of the hotel to hide his negro out, as his men would surely kill him if they found him. And so sure enough, in a few moments they came on the hunt for him, but the negro had been safely hid away, and was not seen any more during the stay of that Texas command. Any soldier who met Texas cavalry during the war knew that they were superb riders, and to throw them was no easy matter, but this Chinese gong dismounted more of them than a charge on infantry would have done.[55]

THE DAY A. P. HILL COMMANDED GEN. LEE & PRES. DAVIS

☛ No soldier bore a more conspicuous part or won more laurels in those great battles than [C.S. Gen.] A. P. Hill. He especially distinguished himself and covered with glory his "Light Division" in the battle of Frazier's farm, where alone at first and afterward supported by Longstreet, he made a fight and won a victory which Gen. Lee had designed to make complete by having Stonewall Jackson cross Whiteoak Swamp and strike the enemy in flank and rear—a movement which Jackson, for once in his brilliant career, pronounced "impracticable," and failed to execute. It was during these movements that an incident occurred of which President Davis told with evident gusto. The President was reconnoitering at the front when he met Gen. Lee on the same business and remonstrated with him, saying, "This is no place for the commander of the army." The General gently explained and rejoined, "It seems to me that this is clearly no place for the

Commander-in-chief of all our armies." "Just then," said Mr. Davis, in telling me the incident, "gallant little A. P. Hill galloped up and exclaimed, 'What are you two doing here? This is no place for either of you, and as commander of this part of the field I order you both to the rear.'" "We will obey your orders," was the laughing reply, and they moved a little to the rear and became absorbed in a consultation about the situation, when Hill again galloped up and exclaimed, "Did I not order you away from here, and did you not promise to obey me? Why, one shot from that battery over there might deprive the Army of Northern Virginia of its commander, and the Confederacy of its President."[56]

AN EMBARRASSED COMMAND
☛ Col. W. C. R., of Columbus, Miss., tells this: His command was ordered to the front, and had to cross a creek, and the men were ordered to take off their shoes and lower garments and wade the stream. The line of march was down a lane, and just as they approached the creek a man and woman in a buggy crossed. There was no chance to dodge, so the command was given to "open ranks" and let the buggy go through. The lady had on a veil, and in silence the buggy passed along. When they had proceeded about half way through the line the ludicrousness of the scene struck the boys and a shout of laughter rang along the line, and the Colonel says, as he turned in his saddle to look back, the man and woman were shaking with the contagion.[57]

A FAKER & TWO "SISTERS"
☛ A long train of soldiers traveled in the Carolinas from Charlotte to Columbia. There were two ladies in the rear, a passenger car. It was crowded, and many of the soldiers had to stand up. One sallow-faced fellow begged a gentleman to let him have his seat, and they exchanged positions. It was concluded by the gallant young fellow, afterward, that he had been imposed upon, and when he asked the fellow in his seat to change back, and he declined, comments were in order, and he told the fellow who was playing off sick that he was a "tar-heel." Gossip of such nature continued until the lazy fellow, in a sort of whining tone, said: "He's climed simmon trees; you can tell from the seat of his breeches that he's climed simmon trees." All the passengers roared, and the two ladies cast off all dignity and participated with the men in hearty laughter. The ladies looked like sisters. They were very attractive, and were much honored in the tedious journey. I journeyed with them the next day to Charleston. Just before the train arrived at the station I told the senior that I had seen them almost constantly for two days, and would he glad for their cards. She wrote. "Mrs. Ed. Means and daughter."[58]

SAMMY, KEEP YOUR SHIRT ON

☛ On a march at night [C.S.] Gen. [Samuel] French's division was moving when those tiresome and exasperating halts occurred so often that the men became worn out with the oft-repeated command to "move up." Gen. French was trying to get his Quartermaster to push the headquarters team to the front, as the enemy was dangerously near in the rear. The men having dropped down by hundreds in the road to sleep it was almost impossible to get a team through without running over the men. Gen. French became impatient and rode forward to see for himself. He began to order the men out of the road with an occasional oath. In the midst of his career a thin, sharp voice, just off the road, sang out, "O Sammy, keep your shirt on; don't burn your shirt." The General was furious, and rising up in his stirrups said: "I will give fifty dollars to know the man who said that." It is needless to say he did not find out, but laughter was heard along the line for some distance.

[Another] . . . story recalls a night march down Sand Mountain, Ala., as Hood came to Tennessee. [Benjamin Franklin "Frank"] Cheatham's command had been halted for some time, and he was working his way to the head of the column to extricate a wagon from the mire. The soldiers were very tired, and lay asleep in the roadway. "Mars Frank" could not get along except in the middle of the road, and his aids pressed the men to give way. By and by Cheatham, impatient but affectionate as well, said, "Damn it, boys, you know I don't want to ride over you."[59]

VIRGINIA F. DOYLE, POET LAUREATE, UNITED CONFEDERATE VETERANS.

WHAT WE REALLY MEAN

☛ "Two or three" always means at least three, or three and upward. "One or two" seldom if ever means one. "In a minute" means anywhere from five to fifty minutes. "That reminds me of a story" means, "Now you keep quiet while I tell my joke." "I hold no brief for _____" means "I am now going to defend _____." "While I do not wish to appear critical" means, "But I am going to have my say anyhow." "Of course it's no business of mine" means, "I am simply devoured with curiosity." "My conduct calls for no apology and needs no explanation" is the usual introduction for an apology or an explanation. "No one could possibly have mistaken my meaning" is what we say when some one has mistaken it.[60]

CHAPTER TWO

THE BLANKET ELEVATED HIM TOO MUCH

☛ Every old soldier who has hugged the ground under an artillery fire will appreciate the following anecdote of the war, told by [C.S.] Capt. W. W. Carnes, of Memphis, who commanded Carnes' battery of light artillery in Cheatham's famous division of Tennesseans:

In front of Murfreesboro, on Friday morning after the main fight of Wednesday, a position in front of bend of Stone[s] River was held by Chalmers' Mississippi brigade, then commanded by Colonel Smith, supporting Carnes' Tennessee battery of Cheatham's division. Instruction had been given the artillery not to open fire in response to any artillery shots directed against them, but to remain quiet as a masked battery and use the guns only in repelling an assault upon the position by an infantry charge. Occasionally some officer commanding a federal battery, in line across the open fields between, would take a notion to develop the state of things in the Confederate position there, and a sharp artillery fire would be opened on it. With orders to stand still and take the fire without replying, the [C.S.] artillerymen could only protect themselves as well as possible, the cannoneers getting behind the trees, and the drivers, who could not go away from their teams, lying down by the side of their horses. There had been rain the day and night before, and the ground was uncomfortably wet to lie down on. After one of the periodical shellings from across the way one of the veteran drivers on the wheel team of a piece was seen to prepare himself for more comfortable lying down. He had placed his own blanket, for more convenient carrying, on top of his saddle-blanket, and under his saddle, and this he proceeded to take out and spread on the ground where he had to lie down by the side of his horse. The First Lieutenant called the Captain's attention to it, and remarked, "Matthews is going to make himself as comfortable as possible, even under fire. He is a cool fellow; look at him now." The soldier referred to had just thrown himself down at full length on the blanket with a laugh, and remarked that he was tired of getting up and down, so he was fixed to stay during the performance. Soon after this the artillery opposite us commenced again a furious cannonade, which lasted several minutes and caused our men to "lay low" for protection. As soon as this was over the man Matthews sprang up, and shaking out his blanket, preceded to put it back into its former position. Seeing this, the Lieutenant said to him, "What's the matter, Matthews; is your blanket getting too wet on the ground?" The soldier shook his head slowly, and then, with a serio-comic expression on his face, answered, "Oh no, sir; I was not considering the good of the blanket, but of myself. When those things are flying over my head like that I want to be as close to the ground as possible, and just a minute ago that blanket seemed a foot and a half thick."[61]

AMUSING INCIDENTS AT SPOTSYLVANIA, VIRGINIA

☛ On the 12th of May, 1864, the hard, all-day struggle, when brigade after brigade had been rushed in to regain the ground lost early in the morning; on the spot where dead and wounded men, horses, and disabled artillery told of the deadly strife; where a man, after trying it awhile, if not killed or wounded, looked anxiously for the next relief to come up; late in the evening our (Humphreys) brigade was rushed in to relieve another that had served its time. While passing along the line of low earthworks to take our allotted position, one of the men in front of us, who had been sorely pressed, and was thinking seriously of the rear, cried out, "Are you all fresh troops?" After repeating the question several times, getting louder and louder every time, Pat Burns, a cool, brave Irishman of my company, yelled back at the fellow, "Yis, we niver was in a fight before." A few minutes later, when we were ordered to take our places in the shallow trenches, we found them occupied by dead and wounded, and among them a big six-footer lying prone on his

LAST MEETING OF LEE AND JACKSON.

face, as still as a mouse, seemingly dead, and in the place that then belonged to Pat. The Irishman was nonplussed. He did not want to molest the dead or wounded. But soon the very position of the man aroused his suspicion, and, jumping astride of him and grabbing him by the shoulders, jerking him up and down, said, "Are you dead?" When the fellow rolled up the white of his eyes, showing he was "possoming," Pat hauled him out and started him to the rear. It created a laugh, though in the midst of extreme danger. W. Gart. Johnson.[62]

CURING A SERVANT OF AN UNWANTED HABIT

☛ [Here's how] . . . a Southern woman . . . cured her negro marketman of bringing the family a turkey daily for dinner because he had speculated in them and they were cheaper than other meat. She invited him to "stand on the gallery and gobble a little." This ludicrous performance deterred him from a repetition of his offense when more serious remonstrance had proved fruitless.[63]

SOME JOLLY CONFEDERATES & THEIR HATS
☞ As we had no way of disposing of . . . [Yankee] prisoners [at the time], they were kept with the command on our march for several days, and our boys became quite well acquainted with them. They were as jolly a set as I ever saw, and seemed to enjoy everything in the way of a joke, and swapping hats had become a source of much amusement. Every Confederate who came near them, if a better hat was found on a prisoner than he had, a swap was at once made, the prisoner as often as otherwise making the proposition. The sentiment that prevailed was, that as the Federals were to go South and the Confederates were going North, the latter should have the best hat; consequently, any Confederate passing who had a worse hat than was to be found among the prisoners, an exchange was made, and without regard to the fit, especially as far as the prisoner was concerned, and it was often the case that a 6¾-hat was seen on a 7¼ head, or a 7¼-hat on a 6¾ head.[64]

DODGING LEAD & RABBIT FOR SUPPER
☞ There was a Colonel in our brigade who, in marching his regiment into the battle, commanded, "Heads up! Eyes to the front and stop your dodging." At that time a grapeshot came flying by and the old man, turning to his men, said, "Dodge the biggest of them, boys." We had held the yanks at bay about five hours, when we got orders to fall back in good order—which we did—to our fortifications at Mills Spring. A funny incident on the field: We had orders to lie down, and did it; one of our Lieutenants lay so that his overcoat collar was sticking up, and a rabbit run down his back. "Cousin Ike" pulled it out, and told the Lieutenant to "hush hollering, it is only a rabbit, and not a cannon-ball." Colonel Miller, of our regiment, ordered him to turn the rabbit loose, and he told him he could not let it go for he was out of meat, so he carried it back to camp and we had rabbit for supper.[65]

JOLLY SPIRITS KEPT US GOING
☞ I was a private in Company G, 12th Tennessee Cavalry, under Forrest. The greater part of our company were boys from sixteen to twenty, and we were a jolly set. German Tucker took a [hard] Confederate cracker to show to some ladies living near camp, and they wanted to know how we ever got them to pieces. He told them that we put one corner of the cracker in our mouth, placed the chin on a stump and got some one to hit us on top of the head with a maul. Bill Combs, when discussing the crackers as an article of food, said, "I can get full of the 'dad gum things, but can't get enough."

Late one night we were cooking rations for one of our Middle Tennessee raids. Two of the boys, one in the 14th Tennessee Regiment on another hill, and one of my company, were "jawing" at each other, when the 14th man yelled out, "You go to hell." Our man answered, "There's no way of getting there now, the yankees have burnt the bridges." Fourteenth answered, "They did a good thing for you, then."

While on that raid we marched and fought for days and nights in succession. Late one dark night we were on the march, it was raining, and we were all wet, cold, tired, sleepy and hungry. We were hunched up in a creek bottom waiting for those in front to cross the stream. Not a word was being spoken. Old sore backed horses were trying to rub their riders off against some other horse. We knew we would have fighting to do as soon as day broke, and we had the blues. All at once Joe Leggett said: "Boys, I have become reckless; I've got so I don't care for nothing. I had just as soon be at home now as to be here." The effect was magic. While the skill and bravery of our Generals and the fighting qualities of our soldiers could not have been excelled, if it had not been for those jolly spirits to animate others the war would have come to a close much sooner.[66]

THE DOCTOR WHO WAS NOT A GOVERNOR

☛ Adjut. E. O'Brien of Berwick, La., tells a funny story of his mistake in calling Dr. J. B. Cowan, of Tennessee, who was medical director of Forrest's Cavalry through the war, the Governor of Texas. The Doctor told him that he killed two men at Birmingham for calling him a "Hogg." The two Confederates had a pleasant journey over the battle ground of Chickamaugua, and the Louisianian realized much benefit through Dr. Cowan's familiarity with the battle.[67]

TOMBSTONE ERECTED TO THE WRONG MAN

☛ The question is often asked about why it is that I [W. C. Nixon of Dyersburg, Tenn.] have a tombstone, and am still alive. I was wounded and captured at Murfreesboro on the 2nd of January, 1864, was carried to Nashville with others and put in the penitentiary, from which place I made my escape the 22nd day of February; but being too weak from my wounds to travel, I was recaptured near Triune, at Mr. William King's. I was regarded as a suspicious character, and was sent to Camp Boyle, at Louisville, the meanest district prison in the United States. After being robbed of everything I had (which you know must have been a great deal), I was photographed and placed under strict guard pending examination. I was so scared that I determined to escape or die in the attempt. I suddenly got so "sick" that I had to be sent to the hospital, hoping that some other idea would present itself. The hospital ward was a long hall with a door at each end; the beds or bunks were placed on either side of the walls, perhaps forty on each side. There was put on the headboard the name, company, and regiment of each patient. My bunk was next to Rufus Hawkins, of Georgia, who was very sick and died the night of the second day after I was sent there. The dead were taken out only in the morning; so after the ward master had left, and everything was quiet, by the assistance of my old friend, Jack Glimp, I moved Hawkins from his bunk to mine. Then for the attempt. There were no windows, and only two doors, which were barred and guarded on the outside. The slop chute was a square hole cut in the floor and boxed up from the ground, making a passage about 18 inches by 6 feet through which all the slops were emptied. When everything was still, and the time had come, I told Jack. I went into the hole feet foremost. My feet struck the ground first, and I slipped so far and so fast that I feared I would slide through the L. and N. depot before I could stop. I was not on my feet when I had finished my greasy slide. There was no one present to laugh with me but it was very funny. I went to the house of Mr. Burns, who had clothing ready for me. After I had washed and dressed, Mr. Burns and two young ladies held a council and

JEFFERSON DAVIS AND HIS SECOND WIFE VARINA HOWELL, CIRCA 1845.

decided that I should remain concealed in the house. Mr. Burns was to act as spy at headquarters, one of the young ladies watch the servant, who only came to prepare meals, and the other young lady to attend to the burial of Hawkins. My name was used instead of his. So the next morning both guards were locked up for neglect of duty, and detectives given the description of Hawkins. After the war the Ladies' Monumental Society erected at Hawkins' grave a slab, and copied the inscription on the pine board at his head:

W. C. NIXON,
Co. G., 4th Tenn. Reg., Strahl's Brig.
Died March, 1864.

Hawkins has the grave, but I have the headstone [1894].[68]

THEY HONORED HIS GRANDFATHER

☛ The First Arkansas Infantry was sent to the defense of Richmond early in the war, and placed with Bate's First Tennessee, in Holmes' Brigade, at the mouth of Aquia Creek, near the memorable city of Fredericksburg. Captain, afterwards Colonel, Robert W. Crockett, a grandson of the heroic Davy Crockett, commanded one of its companies. That fact was made known along the route, and crowds assembled to greet Captain Crockett, the grandson of the famous backwoodsman, whose picture had illuminated the almanacs of nearly a century ago. Captain Bob had an exhaustless fund of humor and anecdote, and enjoyed a joke. Seeing that the admirers of his grandfather were dubious of him in his trim uniform and modish appearance, he got somewhere an old coon-skin and shaped it into a rude cap, with the tail hanging down behind, and on suitable occasions produced it as his grandfather's, to the immense delight of the spectators, saying, "Those old fellows had larger heads than are fashionable at this time," as the cap came down over his ears and eyes, and flowing, black locks. At Fredericksburg he soon became a social as well as military lion. Dr. Blackman, a hospitable old citizen, took a great fancy to this grandson of the Tennessee Congressman and hero of the Alamo. He went around with him, always introducing him as such, and invariably adding that "he knew his grandfather intimately." On one occasion Captain Bob introduced one of his men to Dr. Blackman as "Mr. Crusoe, grandson of Robinson Crusoe." The good old Doctor greeted young Crusoe with his accustomed warmth, remarking that "although he did not know his grandfather personally, he had read about him, and was proud to make the acquaintance of his patriotic descendant."[69]

FRIDAY AIN'T UNLUCKY
☛ Friday is considered an unlucky day, but it was on Friday that Washington was born, Shakespeare was born, America was discovered, the Mayflower Pilgrims landed, Queen Victoria was married, Napoleon was born, Julius Cesar was assassinated, the battles of Bunker Hill, Waterloo, and New Orleans wore fought, and the Declaration of Independence was signed. So it wasn't such a bad day after all.[70]

THE GREATEST THINGS
☛ The greatest sin—fear.
The best day—to-day.
The greatest deceiver—one who deceives himself.
The most beautiful woman—the one you love.
The most expensive indulgence—hate.
The worst bankrupt—the soul that has lost its enthusiasm.
The cleverest man—one who always does what he thinks is right.
The best teacher—one who makes you want to learn.
The best part of anyone's religion—gentleness and cheerfulness.
The meanest feeling—jealousy.
The most important training—training in democracy.
The greatest need—common sense.
The best gift—forgiveness.[71] [Frank Crane]

CHARACTER
☛ Build it well and build it straight,
Strong enough to buffet fate,
Stanch enough to bear the blow
Life compels us all to know;
Have it rugged, have it clean,
Nowhere false and nowhere mean.
Whatsoever be your post,
Make your character your boast;
Build your character to be
Fit for every eye to see;
Never let some secret sin
Or some shameful thing creep in;
He gives power to his foe
Who must hide what he may know,
But who keeps his record true
Has no foe who may pursue,
Spite of loss or spite of gain,
Let your character remain
Free from blemish, free from guile;
Let it sing and dance and smile;
Keep it cheerful, keep it kind,
Big of heart and broad of mind;
Then, whatever may befall,
You may triumph over all.[72]

RUNNING THE BLOCKADE
☛ While in Richmond I [Confederate Colonel John W. Overall] was commissioned by the Confederate government to take charge of all the straggling companies that were reported to be entering New Orleans and muster them into the public service. New Orleans fell, not by the hands of [U.S.] Gen. Butler, of Massachusetts, but by the Tennessean, [U.S.] Admiral Farragut. That put an end to my instructions. Nevertheless, as my family and my brother were within the enemy's lines, I determined to enter New Orleans and rescue them if possible. With permission of [C.S.] Gen. Lovell, at Jackson, Miss., I launched on a Lake Pontchartrain sloop under the guns of the Federal war vessel *New London*, and found my little family debating how to provide for the immediate future. That was soon arranged, for I had plenty of South Carolina money, which I exchanged for greenbacks.

You will understand that I took my life in my own hands when I entered the lines of Butler. The danger of being arrested as a spy and the specter of a halter, however, did not deter me. At that time Gen. Butler was rapidly developing into a second Caligula. I had left my commission of a Confederate colonel and what arms I had in the hands of a sympathetic lady in Madisonville, on the other side of the lake, but this was known to more than one person who were fellow-passengers on the little sloop. This story of Opie Read's will illustrate the situation.

A man was arrested for stealing a mule and killing the owner, who had attempted to rescue his property. It was when, under carpetbag and negro rule, ignorant black men were made justices of the peace.

"I's a special justice, sah, and de Supreme Court can't undo what I do do, sah. I hab two laws, de Texas law and de Arkansas law; which will you take, sah?"

"Well, Judge, I think I'll take the Texas law."

"Berry well, sah. In dat case, made and pervided, I'll hang you for stealin' de mule."

"Well, Judge, that's hard. I think I'll take the Arkansas law."

"Berry well, sah. In dat case, made and pervided, I'll hang you for killin' de man!"

So, in New Orleans if you escaped hanging, you were sent to Ship Island if Gen. Butler got hold of you.

There was one man that Gen. Butler was afraid to hurt: Father Mullen, the most popular of the Irish Roman Catholic priests. One day Butler sent for him. "I understand, Father Mullen, that you refused to officiate at the burial of one of my soldiers." "That is a mistake," replied Mullen, "for I would gladly bury, according to the ceremonies of my Church, every one of your soldiers." The good old Confederate priest was not molested.

I found [U.S.] Gen. Weitzel Mayor of New Orleans. Gen. Butler had sent Mayor John T. Monroe to Port St. Philip, because he would not take the ironclad federal oath. The baby boy of Monroe, named for him, lay at the point of death. Mrs. Monroe sought Butler in her frantic grief. The General agreed that if Monroe would take the oath he should be reinstated in the Mayor's chair and brought to the city to see his sick son. Mrs. Monroe repaired to the prison of her husband, sixty miles below on the Mississippi, and on her knees besought him to agree to Butler's terms of release. Big tears rolled down his cheeks as he thought of his dying baby boy, but he said: *"I will not take the oath!"* He

UNITED DAUGHTERS OF THE CONFEDERACY'S CROSS OF HONOR, AWARDED TO WORLD WAR I VETERANS WHO DESCEND FROM CONFEDERATE SOLDIERS.

had been imprisoned because he had refused to pull down the Confederate flag on the city hall, and had placed himself at a window of the building directly facing the Federal flagship *Hartford*, when Farragut threatened to bombard the city if the flag was not taken down and furled. Monroe was a Roman. Is it any wonder that when they made him bear a ball and chain he still refused to succumb, and that, weary of him, the Federal authorities sent him into the Confederate lines from Fort Pickens, and when he visited Richmond President Davis threw his arms around him?

I had left George McKnight, the genial humorist known as "Asa Hartz," at Madisonville as provost marshal. Maj. McKnight told me that just before leaving the fortifications at Chalmette, below New Orleans, the Federal fleet shelled them. A negro valet picked up a section of an exploded shell, and, after examining it with much trepidation, said in a trembling voice: "Fore de Lord, Marse George, deys shootin' smoothin' [clothing] irons at us!" But I found another genial humorist in New Orleans, Harry Macarthy, known as the "Arkansaw Comedian," the author of that ringing song, "The Bonnie Blue Flag," and also of "The Volunteer," and "Missouri." Mr. Macarthy was a small, handsome man, and brimful of the humor and the pathos and impulsive generosity of the Celtic race. Gen. Butler had seized and burned his "Bonnie Blue Flag" and other music, and he was in daily peril of being sent to Ship Island. His wife was with him—a pretty, modest, and talented singer, who accompanied him in such duets as "The Volunteer." Soon after my arrival, I invited Macarthy to my house. It was a warm June night, and all the windows were open. He sang the "Bonnie Blue Flag," with piano accompaniment. Men and women flocked around the house and loudly applauded the patriotic air, as I they did "The Volunteer," which recited the heroism of the Confederates at Manassas. Seeing a policeman making his way through the crowd to my door, I advised the singer to sing a sentimental air, and he sang, "We'll All Be Happy Yet." Fortunately this episode passed without harm to any of us.

It took me three weeks of incessant work, together with the influence of several friends, to obtain permission to leave New Orleans for Mobile. The Federal authorities were, during this time, greatly excited over the alleged insult of Mrs. Phillips to a funeral escort of one of their soldiers, and which called forth Gen. Butler's undeservedly condemned proclamation. At length Gen. Weitzel, who had been an engineering companion of [C.S. Gen.] Beauregard on the Southern coast, amended an order of Gen. Butler, allowing myself and family to leave on the last trip of the truce boat, used as a flour boat, plying between New Orleans and Mobile. No examination of baggage was to be made. Gen. Weitzel said to me:

"You must not take anything out that is contraband."

"What is contraband?" I asked.

"O," said he, laughing, "powder and shot."

"Well," said I, "we'll send you plenty of that."

"Thank you," he replied, good humoredly.

The Confederates were indebted to Gen. Weitzel for many previous favors. It was he who obtained the order of permission for me, and he will always be gratefully remembered.

I carried out with me on the truce-boat my wife, daughter, and brother; Mrs. Macarthy, under the name Mrs. MacMahon, a member of my family; Harry Macarthy, disguised as a deck hand; and a negro manservant, who bore Macarthy's banjo. In the gulf we were boarded by a Federal man-of-war, but permitted to go on. When at some distance away, Mrs. Macarthy whipped out from her skirts a full-size Confederate flag and flung it to the breeze. It was a daring act, and so thought the commander of the Federal vessel, who prepared to bear down upon us. *But our little boat flew like a bird over the waters.* Every timber creaked as her speed increased. Running for life, she was soon under the guns of Fort Morgan, over which floated the stars and bars of the newborn Confederacy. Thenceforward echoed the strains of the "Bonnie Blue Flag" and "Dixie," cheering the Spartan men and Spartan mothers, wives, sweethearts, who said to them in the old Lacedaemonian way: "Take this sword for our defense; take this shield for your defense, and bring it back to us with honor or be borne back upon it."

The culmination of that hard and bitter struggle was the compensatory legacy of the grandest figure in modern history: Robert E. Lee.[73]

AS MUCH TRUTH AS POETRY
☛ Spending and lending and giving away
Are the easiest things you shall find in a day;
But begging and borrowing and getting your own
Are the three hardest things that ever were known.[74]

A FINANCIAL QUESTION
☛ "I called for a little light on the financial question," said the man in the rural editor's sanctum.

"Well, you've struck the right place," returned the editor. "If there is anything we are light on, it is the finances."[75]

TOO COOL
☛ "Tell me," said the lady to the old soldier, "were you cool in battle?"
"Cool?" said the truthful veteran, "why I fairly shivered."[76]

MIKE KELLY
☛ He was an Irishman by birth and a blacksmith by trade, but gave up his bellows and tongs to follow his gallant countryman, [C.S.] Gen. Pat Cleburne, into the Confederate Army, and become a gunner in a battery that was organized by that peerless soldier. In many of his characteristics Mike was strikingly like his Captain. Though possessed of a rich vein of Irish wit and humor, he did not have that volatile, bubbling overflow of spirit so natural to his people; on the contrary he was quiet, and rather retiring in his disposition, even to apparent timidity. His only form of dissipation was tobacco. I well remember his dirty little cob pipe, black

with age and tobacco, with a stem of the same color and from the same causes, not three inches long. Every old soldier who saw much active service in the field, in thinking of the close places he has passed through, will recall vividly the sunburnt face and form of some comrade, friend or acquaintance conspicuous for his courage, brave where all were braves, but he the bravest of them all. In this light dear old lion hearted Mike Kelly always appears to me. With the courage of a game cock, the modesty of a woman, and a sunny temperament, he was a lovable companion, and when by your side in action made you feel as if you had two right arms and a double pair of eyes. It is not, however, to speak of his courage, but some ludicrous incidents that happened to him after he "jined the cavalry," that I write.

Mike was torn nearly in two by a canister shot at Shiloh, and as soon as he was able to stand the journey his surgeon sent him home to Helena, Ark., to die, which Mike, with an Irishman's perversity, refused to do, but which he explained to me afterward in a half apologetic tone for not doing, that the shot didn't damage his "in'ards." It, however, incapacitated him for service in the infantry, and as the yankees by that time had the river as far down as Vicksburg, he could not well get back to his old command, so he reluctantly joined the cavalry. I say reluctantly because while he knew every bone and nerve in a horse's foot, and was perfectly at home when he had that article between his knees tacking on a shoe, put him on a horse's back and he was as helpless as a new-born babe. I doubt if he was ever on a horse a half dozen times in his life before he joined Capt. Ruf. Anderson's company of scouts, of Col. Dobbins' Regiment and Walker's Brigade of Arkansas Cavalry, of which I was at that time a member. Seeing him one day shortly after he had joined hesitate on the bank of a little stream as if debating with himself which would be wiser, to ride across or to get down and wade and lead his horse, I called out to him, "Grip him with your knees, Mike, and your back will keep dry." "Grip him with me knase, is it," he replied; "thin b' jimminy I'll wade, for I'm as bowlegged as a barrel hoop; its me grub and not me back I want to kape dry."[77]

WHY HE WOULD BE A CONFEDERATE

☛ [The following is the] story of a little Southerner with his mother in a Brooklyn theater, when the play was "Held by the Enemy."

During a brief intermission he asked: "What did the Yankees fight for, mother?"

"For the Union, darling," was the answer.

Just then the curtain fell, and the orchestra struck up "Marching through Georgia." An expression filled with painful memories, brought up by the air, swept over the sad face of the mother.

After a brief pause the little fellow asked: "What did the Confederates fight for, mother?"

The second question was hardly asked before the music changed, and the ever-thrilling strains of "Home, Sweet Home" flooded the house with its depth of untold melody and pathos.

"Do you hear what they are playing?" she whispered. *That* is what the *Confederates* fought for, darling."

Then he asked quite eagerly: "Did they fight for their *homes?*"

"Yes, dear; they fought for their *homes.*"

Was it the touch of sorrow in the mother's voice? was it the pathos of the soft, sweet notes of "Home, Sweet Home?" or was it the *intuition of right?* No matter. The little boy looked up at his mother with adoring eyes, burst into a flood of tears, and, clasping his arms around her protectingly, sobbed out: "O mother, I will be a Confederate!"[78]

MAIDENS DISGUISED AS YANKEES

☛ I too was a member of the old Laurel Brigade, and often acted as scout through different parts of Virginia. I was a member of Company D, 7th Regiment, Virginia Cavalry, Captain Sommors's Company in [C.S.] Col. Turner Ashby's Regiment. I went one night in company with a comrade to call on some young ladies, and as the country at that time was infested with the boys in blue, we agreed to stand guard alternately while the other fellow went in and chatted the young ladies, and I noticed, too, that my comrade was very willing for me to take the first turn in the house, although he acknowledged he was hungry as a wolf. I was very much in love with one of the young ladies of the house and I thought that she reciprocated. When I walked into the house my best girl met me at the door, and took me into the parlor. I asked the question, "Where are your sisters?" She said they had gone to a neighbor's to stay all night. I was pleased with that, for, as my comrade's best girl was gone, he would not object to standing guard all the time.

"THE THREE GENERALS," L-R: STONEWALL JACKSON, JOSEPH E. JOHNSTON, ROBERT E. LEE.

"Now, Ben," said my lady love, "I have been looking for you to drop in to night, and I have ready the nicest supper I could prepare; so just give me those cumbersome pistols, that you may eat with some pleasure."

I had left my saber in my saddle. "No, I thank you Miss Nannie. I cannot part with my pistols: there are too many yanks around here." But her bright eyes and lovely smiles disarmed me. She just wanted "to have the honor of holding them" while I ate supper, but she slipped my pistols in a sideboard drawer and turned the key on them. As I finished a good supper two blue coats opened a door on one side of me, and two entered by another door behind me, and all four of them leveled their pistols at me and commanded me to surrender. To make the matter more real, my girl threw herself on her knees at my feet, put up her hands to the yankees, and begged pitiously for them not to shoot me, and one of the bluecoats said: "Well, Miss, for your sake we will not shoot him, but you must be responsible for his good behavior while we eat our supper." Then one of them said: "Your arms, sir, quick!" I explained that I was already disarmed. One of them leveled a pistol at me and said: "No fooling now, Johnny; give up your arms." And then Miss Nannie said: "O Mr. Yankee, please do not shoot him! I will get his arms for you." And off to the sideboard she flew to get my arms. During this stage performance my comrade stood on the outside on the gallery looking through the window. I saw that he was shaking his sides with laughter, and in a second it occurred to me that I was not being taken prisoner by real yankees. So I made a break for him, running over the yankees; but he knew what was coming, and jumped off the gallery, and hid. By the time I got back to the dining room the yankees had disappeared, and my best girl met me with a smile and said: "Forgive me, Ben; the girls forced me into this." I told her she had better take to the stage, for it was the best "forced" performance I had ever witnessed. The yankees were her sisters and a young lady neighbor, who had dressed themselves up in Yankee uniforms and laid a trap to capture me. I very cooly told my best girl that she could have made the capture without any assistance whatever.

There is but one of those girls living to-day, and my comrade too has crossed over the river, but many persons yet living in Page Valley remember it well, for it was many a long day before I heard the last of it. The boys used to try to tease me about the matter. I would turn them away with the remark that I would not give a cent for a soldier who would not surrender to four pretty girls. He was no soldier if he did not surrender. Many hundreds of miles separate me now from those four long years I followed Stonewall Jackson, J. E. B. Stewart, and Gen. T. L. Rosser, through all those stirring scenes . . .[79]

WHAT IS NEEDED
☛ It isn't buildings of steel and stone
That the world needs most to-day;
It isn't fame and it isn't gold,
It isn't the knowledge that textbooks hold—
    That's the smaller part—

It's the kinder smile and friendlier hand,
The love that knows no creed nor land,
But speaks from heart to heart.[80]

TWO CONFEDERATE GENERALS TEASE ONE ANOTHER

☛ An episode connected with Bentonsville: The 18th and 45th Tennessee Regiments, [C.S.] Col. Searcy commanding, about nightfall charged through the yankee lines and we gave them up as captured. Several days afterward we were surprised to find them report back, having wandered for miles in getting back. In [C.S. Gen.] Bate's speech to his troops I remember, as a boy, this little piece of humor. Says he: "Fellow soldiers, when I was at Nashville, [C.S. Gen.] Govan's Brigade chanced to pass my brigade. Govan's men hallooed out: 'Lie down, Mr. Bate, Mr. Govan is gwine to pop a cap.' The other day at Bentonville my brigade chanced to pass Govan. I made my men halloo out: 'Lie down, Mr. Govan, Mr. Bate is now gwine to pop a cap.'"[81]

GENERAL LEE'S SHARPSHOOTERS

☛ Gen. Lee was informed of every move by some fleet-footed [Confederate] sharpshooter, while others were before, or behind moving columns of the enemy, and like sleuth hounds, never lost sight of them. A number developed into valuable scouts, and often, in case of necessity, penetrated to the very heart of the Federal Army. But for the watchful sharpshooters, Gen. Lee could never have met every advance of Gen. Grant in the memorable campaign from Germania to the Appomattox. So annoying were they and so accurate their information, that Gen. Grant issued a special order concerning them. By their bold bluffs they often delayed the advance of the enemy until Gen. Lee could bring up troops. When an attack was decided upon, they were sent forward to clear off every obstacle to the enemy's line of battle, taking places with their command in the charge.

The fatality was fearful, and their depleted ranks had to be constantly recruited. There was, however, a bright side to their lives. They bore the relation to the army that a drummer does to the wholesale trade in business.

They always had a fund of good humor at hand. In their exposed positions, games of draw poker were often played. The new jokes generally originated with the sharpshooters.

When it was quiet along the lines they became well acquainted with the fellows on the other side, swapping tobacco for coffee, or, perhaps, the best poker hand would take the pot. An underground railway was established by them with the Federal pickets opposite. Many letters found their way to anxious parents by this means, and many a coy maiden's heart was made glad by news from her bold soldier lover passed across the lines by the sharpshooters. Strong friendships were sometimes formed between men on opposing lines, and not one instance of treachery, either personal or to their respective armies did I ever know.

The night was never too dark or the storm too fierce for them to hesitate when called on. They could go to sleep in a minute, and were so well trained that they could wake at any moment.[82]

WHEN YOU HEAR "LIE DOWN, ROCKSY!" . . .

☛ The writer went to school in a country village, and at the opposite side of the campus from the boys' department there was an Institute for girls, and he was so in love with them that he was always on his dignity when in that vicinity. Not so with big John England, who would roll his trousers above his knees, and in the foot race go as near the groups of pretty girls as the lax rules allowed. England was not considered among patriots, but he enlisted and endured the hardships and perils of the Confederate soldier in the 41st Tennessee. He rarely swore outright, but he would affirm "By Gads" and with other similar expressions peculiar to himself. His nickname was "Rocky," and he was certainly the author of "We'uns and Yu'uns." "Rocky," or "Rocksy," was prudent against shot and shell, and the saying, "Lie down, Rocksy!" would be echoed from regiment to regiment throughout the entire brigade.[83]

A BOISTEROUS THEATERGOER

☛ [The following occurred] at the Broad Street Theatre in Richmond in June, 1862. It was just before the Seven Days Battles. The city was full of citizens and visitors from all over the South, and the army, being camped near by, hundreds of [C.S.] soldiers were there, also, on short leave. Among the latter on that particular night was quite a number of us from Barksdale's Brigade. An Indian play was on the boards in which there was a battle, shooting, killing. In the last scene, when the shooting began and the Indians began to fall here and there on the stage and the vast audience in breathless silence was intent on hearing and seeing everything, one of our boys, Newt Helm, of Company K, of Jackson, seated up in the gallery, unable to hold in any longer, yelled out at the top of his voice, "Bring up the litter corps!"

That brought down the house. The police seemed anxious to take him out, but they dared not touch him. Brave, generous, noble Newton Helm, descended from the Helms of Kentucky, in whose veins ran some of the best blood of the old South, laid down his life in the next battle; and his body was never found by his friends.[84]

I AM THE CHURCH

☛ I am the Church. I am human, but also divine. I am far more than men have yet made me, I am potentially all that God means me to be.

I am commissioned to bow men in prayer, to lift them in worship, and to knit them together in love.

I am to be the house of God's gifts, the altar of penitence, the mercy seat of forgiveness, and the temple of aspiration.

I am to become the home of truth, childhood's school of the spirit, youth's academy of the ideal, and manhood's prophetic armory.

I am called to be the herald of Jesus the Christ, and the heart power of his everlasting gospel.

I am summoned to supply the key-men of the kingdom of God, to bind the evil, to release the good, and to send peace on earth.

I am to be at once the soul of brotherhood and the genius of crusading righteousness.

I am set to be the watchtower of the heavenly hope, and the harbinger of immortality.

I am to become the world's dayspring, and history's dynamic.

I am the Church. God keep me humble with the sense of my limitless need, but also audacious in the strength of my more than conquering faith.[85]

A CONFEDERATE WOMAN TAUNTS A YANKEE GENERAL

☛ In March, 1862, when the news came that [U.S. Gen.] Buell's army would pass through Franklin [Tenn.] the next day, everybody was intensely excited and awaited with eagerness its approach, as none had ever seen a "live Yankee" and wondered what they would do when he came.

Bright and early the next morning the cry was heard, "The Yankees have come!" The cavalry had arrived, but found no Confederates lurking behind. Soon after came the infantry, thousands upon thousands, well dressed in new uniforms, bands playing and flags flying—an imposing sight.

While the troops were passing, an officer of pompous mien, with dangling sword and waving plumes, rode up to a group of ladies standing on the steps of the old Dempsey house, at the foot of Main street, and asked one of them, Miss Winnie Nichols, then a blooming lass, but now a dignified matron, "What beautiful stream is that?" referring to [the] Harpeth River. She instantly replied: "That, sir, is second Bull Run, and you are now on your way to second Manassas." At the reply he became furious and livid with rage, but his fellow officers, who heard the repartee and appreciated the wit, exploded with laughter at his discomfiture, and in turn, saluted the young lady, doffing their caps to her. She is even now [1895] an enthusiastic worker for the "Lost Cause."[86]

SWINDLING A PIE-SELLER

☛ Capt. Dicks tells a funny story of how a Confederate, while en route to a northern prison, shrewdly swindled an old woman selling pies at twenty-five cents each. He took advantage of her confusion, slipped his hand under a fat one, raised it up, and said: "Old lady, give me my change." "How much is it, honey?" was replied; and he told her fifty cents. She handed him the quarter, and he soon gave it for more pie.[87]

WHY THE SOUTH LOVES GENERAL FORREST

☛ Maj. Chas. W. Anderson, who was Gen. Forrest's Chief of Staff, illustrates his nobility of character among noncombatants:

Every living soldier of Forrest's West Tennessee Cavalry remembers the 6th Tennessee Federal regiment, commanded by [U.S.] Col. F. H. [Fielding Hurst], of Purdy, McNairy County, Tennessee, a regiment of [Union] cavalry unknown to fame by any gallant deeds or meritorious conduct on the battlefield, and one which the war records of the rebellion alone have preserved from merited oblivion. It may be truthfully said of this [U.S.] regiment that it did more plundering, burning, robbing, and running and less fighting, than any regiment in the Federal army. Fifth Tennessee Federal Cavalry only excepted.

On one of Forrest's campaigns, from Mississippi into West Tennessee, and soon after leaving Corinth, he learned that H. [Hurst] and his regiment had evacuated Purdy, and that before leaving they had laid in ashes the homes of absent Confederate soldiers, also those of a number of citizens who were known to be in sympathy with the South.

Wilson's 16th Regiment, of our command, and Newsom's, also, were composed of men from McNairy and adjoining counties, and Forrest knew that unless timely steps were taken to prevent it there would be trouble when he reached Purdy.

When within a few miles of that place he directed me to take a sergeant and five men from his escort, dash on into Purdy, and place a guard around the residence of [U.S.] Col. H. [Hurst].

On entering the town, blackened wall's, lone chimneys, and charred remains of buildings gave abundant evidence of H's. cowardly vandalism. Learning from a citizen that his residence was in the suburbs, and directly on our line of march to Jackson, we were soon at its front. Dismounting and entering the portico of his dwelling, I tapped lightly on the door with the hilt of my saber. In a moment or so it was opened by a lady, when I asked, "Is this Mrs. Col. H. [Hurst]?" She tremblingly answered, "Yes, sir."

I noticed her agitation, also that on opening the door her countenance quickly changed, manifesting on the instant both surprise and alarm.

"THE GOD OF WAR," CONFEDERATE GENERAL NATHAN BEDFORD FORREST.

Hastening to relieve her apprehensions, I said, "We are not here to harm you, but have been sent for your protection. Although Gen. Forrest has not reached Purdy, he is aware of the ruin and devastation caused by your husband's regiment, and has sent me in advance of his troops to place a guard around your house. This guard is from his own escort, and will remain with you until all of our command has passed, and I assure you that neither your family or anything about your premises will be disturbed or molested."

Giving the officer of the guard instructions, I turned to her, and was in the act of raising my cap before mounting my horse, when, brushing away tears she could no longer repress, she said, "Please, sir, say to Gen. Forrest, for me, that this (referring to the guard) is more than I had any right to expect of him, and that I thank him from my heart for this unexpected kindness. I shall gratefully remember it and shall always believe him to be as generous as he is brave."

Returning to the town, I rejoined the General as he was entering the public square, where he halted and was soon surrounded by citizens of the place, among them the venerable father of Col. D. M. Wisdom, of our command, who said, "You see, General, the marks of Col. H's. last visit to our town, and you are also aware that a large number of our citizens are Union people, and they are greatly alarmed for fear of retaliation on the part of your command."

Forrest's reply was characteristic and stripped of his habitual way of emphasizing matters: "I do not blame my men for being exasperated, and especially those whose homes have been laid in ashes, for desiring to revenge such cowardly wrongs, but I have placed a guard around the home of H. [Hurst], and others need feel no uneasiness. Orders have been issued to my command that no Union citizen of this town must be insulted, much less harmed, and this order was accompanied by my personal request that it be obeyed to the letter, and I am sure no soldier of my command will disobey the one, or disregard the other. Of one thing, however, the Union friends of H. and his cowardly [U.S.] regiment of Tennessee renegades may rely upon. If we ever are so fortunate as to find them just once in my front, I will wipe them off the face of the earth. They are a disgrace to the Federal army, to the State, and to humanity."

Ever after this, whenever it was known that Forrest was on the move, that command stood not on the order of its going. They well knew that whenever they confronted Forrest there would be a long account to settle.[88]

A YANKEE GENERAL'S FIRST FIGHT

☛ A funny story is reported of [U.S.] Gen. Carr, who died recently, in connection with his *first* engagement against the South. It was at Big Bethel. He commanded the 2nd New York, and had halted his men for refreshments, in a pleasant shade, when the Confederates opened fire upon them. Excited, even to bewilderment, he rode up to a group of [U.S.] officers and exclaimed, "They are firing upon my regiment! My God! what is to be done?"[89]

AN OLD WOMAN KEEPS A CONFEDERATE CAVALRY AT BAY
☞ Ward McDonald, Captain of 4th Alabama Cavalry, Powderly, Texas:

Many incidents crowd my memory of the old war days. I write of events that transpired while the army was at Bowling Green, Ky. This was near where I first saw light, in 1841.

I joined the [C.S.] Buckner Guards of sixteen members soon after the arrival of the army. Our only officer was Lieutenant Thomas H. Hines, who distinguished himself in contriving for Morgan's escape from the Ohio penitentiary. We stayed at [C.S.] Gen. Buckner's headquarters, ready to go as scouts or guides upon expeditions into any part of the country. On one occasion I made a visit to three Federal camps, Jimtown, Tompkinsville, and Glasgow. After reporting things as I saw them, an expedition was sent to Jimtown, consisting of about one hundred Cavalry from the 8th Texas (Terry's Rangers), and I served as guide. Jimtown was a village about forty miles nearly east of Bowling Green. The country is rough. The people, generally, were ignorant, and decidedly Unionists [Yankee sympathizers]. Many of them looked upon the [C.S.] Texas Rangers as devils incarnate.

"THE LITTLE REBEL," LOUISE C. CLARK.

Nearly all the men, and many of the women, who lived by the road, fled to the woods when they heard of our approach. On the second day of our march, our men stopped at every house on the road to get buttermilk, etc. Even Terry's men were "Buttermilk Rangers." At only two houses in a long distance were the occupants found. A woman, whose husband had run away, had the hardihood to remain at home. She soon tremblingly gave the men all the buttermilk she had, and would have given them anything on the place. Her surprise was manifest when one of the men politely thanked her and handed her the pay. At the next house, about half a mile farther on, there were two old men, an old woman, and some children. The two men went out to the fence, but the old woman remained on the porch with a pistol in her lap and knitting in her hands, seeming to take little notice of us. When some of the men dismounted to go in, the old woman looked up with a face full of defiance, and called out, "I will shoot the first man that comes in!" The men halted, and a general laugh broke through the ranks.

The old lady kept up her warlike attitude, with pistol in hand and the knitting by her side on the floor. Presently a woman entered the back yard, came hurrying up toward her, exclaiming, "Mother, mother! Treat those men right, they are perfect gentlemen; they came to my house and never hurt a thing!" "It don't make any difference. I'll shoot the first man that comes in!" Many a laugh did we have at the boys who started to go into the yard. They were bluffed away by the old woman.[90]

SUCCESSFUL BUSINESSMEN
☛ An army travels on its stomach, said Napoleon. Many a young business man gets there on his gall.[91]

A CLEVER WAY TO STIMULATE CHURCH OFFERINGS
☛ A clergyman, taking occasional duty for a friend in a remote country parish, was greatly scandalized on observing the old verger, who had been collecting the offertory, quietly abstract a fifty-cent piece before presenting the plate at the altar rail.

After service he called the old man into the vestry and told him with some emotion that his crime had been discovered.

The verger looked puzzled for a moment. Then a sudden light dawned on him.

"Why, sir, you don't mean that old half-dollar of mine? Why, I've led off with that for the last fifteen years!"[92]

THE USEFULNESS OF CHICKENS
☛ "Chickens, sah," said the negro sage, "is de usefulest animal dere is. You c'n eat 'em fo' dey is bo'n an' after dey's dead."[93]

FUN TIMES IN FORREST'S OLD REGIMENT
☛ I note a little incident that happened at [a fight at La Grange, Tenn.] After the yankees had retired from the field, Forrest ordered me to pursue them with the battalion, which I did at a gallop. Coming to a short bend in the road on a hill, I saw the enemy formed in line of battle, evidently preparing to charge us. I caught Forrest by the shoulder, saying: "General, they have got us; they are going to charge!"

He checked his horse and asked: "How many men have you?"

My reply was, not more than thirty; that the most of the men had stopped to pillage the yankee wagons.

His orders were: "Bring them into line at a gallop," which was instantly done.

By the time the lines were formed, he asked, in a loud voice, for a white handkerchief. A man answered from the ranks that he had one. Forrest then, in a loud voice, said to the man: "Put it on a stick and go down there and tell them yankees that if they do not surrender I will kill the last one of them."

The man started, and so did the yankees, on a perfect stampede. We actually caught some of them. Certainly no man but Forrest would ever have thought of playing such a trick on the enemy. We were at that time in their clutches, if they had but known it. A bold charge at the time by that yankee command would have captured Forrest. We could not possibly have escaped. But the charge was not made, and we rode away to fight them again at Moscow, where we forced our way through them and saved our recruits and supplies, taking all into Mississippi.[94]

HOW GENERAL EARLY VIEWED SOUTH CAROLINA SOLDIERS
☛ Old [C.S. Gen.] Jubal Early was a character in Virginia. He was drawn up into a hard knot with rheumatism, and had a face like a hickory nut. His voice was pitched on a very high key, and he was a compound of shrewdness and sarcasm in equal parts. He was very strongly opposed to secession at the beginning of the war, although he fought valiantly when fighting was inevitable. In the Virginia Convention of 1861 he attacked the conduct of South Carolina bitterly. After the war had actually begun he had in his brigade a South Carolina regiment. It was observed that old Jubal was always sure to put that regiment in the most ticklish place when the brigade was under fire. During one of the battles around Richmond Early's brigade was ordered to the front, and, as usual, Early made the South Carolina fellows head the column, squeaking out at the top of his voice as he rode up to them: "Yes, I'll send you to the front, and I'll keep you there, too! You got us into this fix, and, hang you, you've got to get us out!"[95]

MISS ELIZABETH HANNA, SOUTHERN PLAYWRIGHT, 1910.

CHAPTER THREE

MY FIRST EXPERIENCE AT THE FRONT

☛ J. W. McKinney, Greenwood, S.C.: After leaving the camp of instructions we were ordered to Sullivan's Island, near Charleston. Our regiment had no number, but was called the Orr Rifles, as it was organized by James L. Orr, our first colonel. He was elected to the Confederate Congress, and Foster Marshall was promoted to his place. Our regiment numbered 1,400 as fine looking men as could be found in any country. We remained on the island nine mouths, and some of us were so anxious to get to the front that we got up a petition asking the colonel to resign and let us get a colonel who would carry us to the front. I was one of the committee appointed to present the petition. "Old Forty," as we called him, looked at it, and told us if we did not get back to our quarters he would have us bucked and gagged, so we all sneaked back.

THE MOUND BATTERY RESISTING AN ATTACK OF THE YANKEE FLEET AT FORT FISHER.

The long-looked for orders came at last, about the last of April, 1862. The colonel had the orders read at dress parade, and made a speech in which he said he had been trying to get to the front ever since he had been colonel, but he was a subordinate and had to obey his superior officers, and all he asked of his regiment now (when they got to the front) was to follow Foster Marshall. We gave him three cheers, and moving commenced. We had been quartered in good houses and had everything usually kept in a well-regulated family, and as we tried to take all with us, it took four big wagon loads to move our company to the boat, and the other companies had about the same. When we landed in Richmond and moved upon Main street the citizens would ask what brigade it was, and judging from the amount of baggage you would have thought it was a division. We had not been there long before a little [C.S.] officer, dressed in artillery uniform, with patent leather boots, came around. He reminded me of one of those little bantam roosters more than anything I can think of just now. He curtailed our baggage to one oven and gave one wall tent to ten men. My hat box, paper collars, teapot, looking glass, blacking brush, and all the rest of my things were sent to the rear. We came very near rebelling, but "Old Forty" said we must be quiet, we were at the front now.

We were put on the train to run down to Guiney Station, four miles above Fredericksburg, and camped in an old field, with not a stick of wood and no fire. It was getting warm on the Island at that season of the year, but that night the mercury in the thermometer went away down. Tom Puckett and I concluded that we would not sleep in the tent with the rest, as we were gentlemen and did not want to be crowded, so we got a pole and tied one end to a pine sapling and put a fork under the other, stretched a blanket over it, and made down our bed.

It was cloudy and the wind was blowing from the north, and it soon began to sleet. It was awful cold. I had to take the position of a person with a first class case of cramp colic, and by that means I could get my feet under the blanket. Tom was very tall and was not so fortunate. Do his best, there was about two feet of his legs outside. We had not made a ditch around our tent, and the water commenced running under, and our teeth began to rattle. I got up and went to the wall tent and asked the boys to let me in. They said, "No, you have seceded from us, and set up on your own hook." I went back and sat up a while. Everything was still. I could not hear anything but the sleet and Tom's teeth rattling. After ruminating a while, I yelled out: "Oh Sullivan's Island, how I long for thee!" "Old Forty" was quartered just behind me, and I heard him ask who was that. Lieutenant Colonel Ledbetter told him it was "that big mouthed McKinney." Then he laughed and said, "I reckon he will sign another petition to go to the front."

My blood had been hot to get to the front, but that sleet had cooled it down, and right there and then I would have signed a contract to keep Cothran's old mill on Hard Labor Creek for the rest of my life.[96]

THE CONFEDERATE ARMY'S DESCRIPTION OF A MULE

☛ The army mule used to be described as "Without pride of ancestry or hope of posterity."[97]

CONFEDERATE FINANCIAL WISDOM
☛ Making money doesn't make people better. Merely saving money doesn't make people better. Spending money upon ourselves doesn't make us better. About the only way you can deal with money so as to make you a better man or woman is to do good with it.[98]

MARITAL ECONOMY
☛ Mandy: "I'se decided to leave mah husban'." Hannah: "How come? Is you beginnin' to economize?"[99]

THE REAL CAUSE OF DIVORCE?
☛ Leonore: "What is the cause of so many divorces?" Elizabeth: "Marriages."[100]

SOME NOMENCLATURE OF THE CONFEDERATE ARMIES
☛ The North Carolinians are called "Tar Heels;" South Carolinians, "Rice Birds;" Georgians, "Goober Grabbers;" Alabamians, "Yaller Hammers;" Texans, "Cow Boys;" Tennesseans, "Hog-Drivers;" Louisianians, "Tigers;" Floridians, "Gophers;" Virginians, "Tobacco Worms;" Arkansians, "Tooth-picks;" Missourians, "Border Ruffians;" Kentuckians, "Corn Crackers;" and Mississippians, "Sand Lappers." The Cavalry, "Buttermilk Rangers;" Infantry, "Webfoot." A regiment of deserters from the Federal Army, kept behind by us to build forts, "Galvanized Rebs." The Federals called us "Johnnies;" we called them "Yanks" and "Blue Bellies."

See a fellow with a Bee Gum hat ride down a line, "He's a gentleman from the States." The soldiers guy him with such remarks as "Come out of that hat. I know you are thar; see your toes wigglin'." If boots are long and big, they will say, "See your head stickin' out." In passing a troop in camp, a number will look up a tree and halloo, "Come out of that tree. See you up thar." This attracts, and then the laugh comes. In camp, when all is still, the monotony is broken by some forager making a hog squeal. His fellows cry out, "I'll kill any man's hog that bites me." A cavalryman, passing infantry, is accosted with "Jump off and grab a root." A by-word of the soldiers—"I havn't had a square meal for three days." Soldiers in camp say to soldiers going to the front, "You'd better gim me that hat; you'll lose it out thar."

Cavalry tantalization to Webfoot: "If you want to get buttermilk, jine the Cavalry." Old Webfoot replies: "If you want to catch hell, jine the Webfoot." One of the staff, in drilling a Brigade, told them to dress up in the center about half an inch. As he would pass afterward, they'd begin, "Boys, there goes half-inch." Fun, to be sure, but it worried him shamefully.

I got hold of a silver crescent on the Dalton Campaign, placed it on the left side of my hat, put on a biled shirt and a paper collar, and rode down Division line. They began on me, "Ahem! Umph! Umph! Biled shirt! Ladies' man! Parlor ornament! Take him to his ma!"

On the march to Tennessee, the officer who would get them out of the sorghum patches caught it. They'd say, "Boys, there goes old Sorghum."

In Cavalry, Number Four invariably held horses in battle. It was such a delightful number that when it fell upon a soldier, he would say, "Bully!" Col. Paul Anderson changed the mirth by saying, "Boys, Number One will hold horses, and you 'Bullies' will dismount." One night, one of Col. McLemore's Captains formed a line of battle by saying: "Boys, you can't see me, but dress up on my voice." Col. Anderson would say, "Dress up on my friend Brit." These things got to be by-words in those commands. Instead of "Blow the Bugle," it was "Toot the Dinner Horn." That takes me to some of our greenhorns in the drill. When we first started, a fellow in East Tennessee began drilling his Company thus: "Men, tangle into fours! By move forward! Put! Wheel into line! By turn around! Git!" A Middle Tennessee Captain, wanting his Company to cross a creek on a log, said: "Attention Company! In one rank to walk a log! Walk a log! March!"

It carried you back to old times to hear the guards around a regiment halloo out, "T-w-e-l-v-e o'-c-l-o-c-k and a-l-l-'s well!" The rude and untrained soldier would play on that and say, " T-w-e-l-v-e o'-c-l-o-c-k, and as sleepy as Hell!" When a soldier goes out foraging, it is called "Going on a lark;" when he goes stealing, it is "Impressing it into service;" when a Quartermaster wants to shield his rascality, he has a favorite abstract called "L," which is used, and means "Lost in the service;" when a squad runs from the enemy, it is "Skedaddling;" the ricochetting of a cannon ball is "Skiugling"—words whose origin began with this war. Let a stranger or soldier enter camp and call for a certain company—say, Company F. Some soldier will say, "Here's Company F!" By the time he can get there, another will cry out at the far part of the regiment, "Here's Company F!" Then the whole command will take up the refrain, until the poor fellow in vexation will sulk away. Let an old soldier recognize a passing friend, and say, "How are you, Jim?" a marching division will keep it up, with "How are you, Jim?" until the poor fellow swoons.

In the army we have some of the finest mimics in the world. Let one cackle like a hen, and the monotony of camp is broken by the encore of "S-h-o-o!" Then other cacklers take it up, until it sounds like a poultry yard stirred up over a mink or weasel. Let one bray like an ass, others

CONFEDERATE GENERAL GEORGE W. GORDON.

take it up until the whole regiment will personate the sound, seemingly like a fair ground of asses. As mimics they are perfect; as musicians, also. I met one once who said, "If you'll give me a jigger, I'll give you some 'chin music.'" He put his hand to his chin, and with his teeth made a sound like rattling bones, keeping time to his song and pat. Some of the finest singing I ever heard, and some of the best acting I ever saw, are done by the soldiers. In camp it is so delightful to hear the brass bands dispensing music in the sweetest strains. Near Atlanta, a Dutch Battery entertained us every fifteen minutes, and whilst we kept our eyes open to the music of the shells, from far away would beat upon our ears the music of the enemy's brass bands; our bands would tune up and make us oblivious to the roar of that old Battery. I tried once in the progress of battle to assimilate it to music. The sound of a minie ball—Zip! Zip!—I dubbed the soprano; the roar of musketry, the alto; the lingering sound of battle, the tenor; the artillery, the basso. Now, intersperse it with the interlude of an old Rebel yell, and you've got it. As to the wit and sarcasm you hear in camp, I'd defy the world to beat it. Anyone attempting to be consequential, or unnatural, is the character to work on, and the gravest of the Chaplains cannot look upon their ridicule without smiling.[101]

AN UNRECOGNIZED FORREST GETS SCOLDED

☛ After a skirmish in late June of 1863, Forrest and his men, then fighting under General Bragg, found themselves retreating into the Cumberland Mountains through the small town of Cowan, Tennessee. Riding along at the rear, Forrest heard a commotion up ahead.

Drawing closer he saw a woman castigating some of his soldiers for not "whipping back the Yankees." As Forrest himself rode by, the angry Confederate female shook her fist at him and yelled: "Oh you big, cowardly rascal! Why don't you turn and fight like a man, instead of running like a cur? I wish old Forrest was here. He'd damn well make you fight!" Apparently she did not, or could not, see the officer's stars on his collar.

Wanting to avoid any further abuse, Forrest spurred his horse into a run, laughing out loud as he charged down the road. Later, in retelling the incident, he said: "I would've rather faced Yankee artillery than that fiery dame!"[102]

SPEAKER CONFEDERATE GENERAL FITZHUGH LEE

☛ Gen. Fitzhugh Lee at the Chicago [War Reunion] Banquet said: "The country seems to be safe to-night. I find myself surrounded on every-side by the flag of the United States. I had a similar experience about thirty years ago (laughter) at the little village of Appomattox, and I remember sleeping that night after I had received my parole between two major generals of the United States army. I had not felt so safe for many of the proceeding days—both my flanks were well protected.

(Continued laughter and applause.) History in a measure repeats itself. To-night the mayor of what he terms the greatest city in the world—it is evident he has never been to Richmond, Va.—sits here quietly, serenely smoking his cigar, between two rebellious rebel generals of cavalry, Wade Hampton and Fitzhugh Lee, and he is not afraid." (Laughter.)[103]

GENERAL JACKSON & AN ALL TOO LITERAL ORDER

☛ On the 11th of the month, the Texas Brigade was ordered to Staunton to reinforce Stonewall Jackson. The day after reaching Staunton, however, it marched back across the Blue Ridge toward Charlottesville. Early in the day Gen. Hood halted each regiment in turn, and gave his orders. To the 4th he said: "Soldiers of the 4th: I know as little of our destination as you do. If, however, any of you learn or suspect it, keep it a secret. To every one who asks questions, answer, 'I don't know.' We are now under the orders of Gen. Jackson and I repeat them to you. I can only tell you further, that those of you who stay with the command on this march will witness and participate in grand events."

Such an address, such orders and such a prediction, not only astonished the soldiers, but inflamed their curiosity to the highest pitch. Many were the conjectures—some sensible, some ludicrous, but none probably near the truth. There were many [moonshine] stills in the sequestered nooks of the mountains, and by noon many of the men were in an exceedingly good humor—a few staggering—and apple jack and peach brandy could be had out of hundreds of canteens. To prevent the men from getting liquor, Gen. Hood authorized a statement, which was industriously circulated and really believed, that smallpox was raging among the citizens. Whether true or not, it had a good effect; I did not straggle.

Riding along by himself, half a mile in rear of the Brigade, General Hood discovered, lying in the middle of the road and very drunk, a soldier of the 4th. Checking his horse, the General asked, "What is the matter with you, sir? Why are you not with your company?" The stern and peremptory voice sobered the man a little, and rising to a sitting posture and looking at the General with drunken gravity, he said: "Nossin' much, I rekon, General—I just feel sorter weak and no account." "So I see, sir," said Hood, "get up instantly and rejoin your company." The victim of John Barleycorn made several ineffectual attempts to obey, and some men coming along just then. Hood ordered them to take charge of him and conduct him to his company. But as they approached with intent to carry out the order, the fellow found voice to say between hiccoughs, "Don't you men that ain't been vaccinated come near me—I've got the smallpox—tha's wha's the masser with me."

The men shrank back in alarm, and the General, laughing at the way his own chickens had come home to roost, said: "Let him alone, then—some teamster will pick him up," and rode on.

Gen. Jackson gave strict orders against depredating on private property. Apples were plentiful, and it was contrary to nature not to eat them. Jackson saw a Texan sitting on the limb of an apple tree, busily engaged in filling his haversack with the choicest fruit. He reined in his old sorrel horse, and in his customary curt tone, asked: "What are you doing in that tree, sir?" "I don't know," replied the Texan. "What command do you belong to?" "I don't know." "Is your command ahead or behind you?" "I don't know." And thus it went on—the same "I don't know" given as [the] answer to every question. Finally, Jackson asked: "Why do you give me that answer to every question?" "Cause them's old Jackson's orders," replied the man in the tree, and the officer had to ride on, disgusted at a too literal obedience of his own orders.[104]

THE STINGIEST MAN
☛ The stingiest man was scoring the hired man for his extravagance in wanting to carry a lantern in going to call on his best girl. "The idea," he scoffed. "When I was courtin' I never carried a lantern; I went in the dark." "Yes," said the hired man, "and look what you got."[105]

A GOOD BARGAIN!
☛ Dealer (bargaining for the cow): "How much milk does she give?" Farmer (warily): "I don't rightly know, sir. But she be a darned good-natured cow, and she'll give all she can."[106]

ADVICE IGNORED BY LEFT-WING HISTORIANS
☛ A plea for the unbiased teaching of history in schools as one of the best means for promoting world peace was voiced by Sir Auckland Geddes, British Ambassador in the United States, addressing the American Academy of Political and Social Science, Philadelphia.

"Let the history which is taught be fair to all the nations concerned," he said, "fair to those who once were enemies, but not too fair; fair to our forefathers, but not too fair."[107]

A YANKEE BAND SERENADES THE SOUTH
☛ That was a touching scene upon the Rappahannock when the Confederate and Federal armies confronted each other on the opposite heights of Spotsylvania and Stafford. One beautiful evening there came down to the northern bank a magnificent Federal band, and begun to discourse sweet music. Large crowds of soldiers of either army gathered on the opposite banks, the friendly pickets not interfering. First they played United States National airs, such as "Star Spangled Banner," "Hail Columbia," "Yankee Doodle," and the like, and as one of these would cease the "Boys in Blue" would give their measured "Hip, Hip, Hurrah!" And then, in compliment to their friends across the river, the band played "Bonny Blue Flag," "Dixie," "My Maryland," and others of our Southern melodies, and as one of these ceased the "Boys in Gray" would

give their indescribable but never-to-be-forgotten "old Confederate yell."

But presently the band struck up in sweet strains that were wafted across the beautiful Rappahannock, "Home Sweet Home," and as these notes died out there went up a simultaneous shout from both sides of the river, and the "Hip, Hip, Hurrah!" of the men in blue mingled with the "Confederate yell" of the men in gray.

The music had struck a chord in response to which the hearts of even enemies—enemies then, friends now, thank God!—could beat in unison, and those hills, which had so lately resounded with hostile guns, echoed and reechoed the glad acclaim.[108]

OLD CONFEDERATE DAYS: SOUTHERN WOMEN IN WARTIME

☛ Mrs. F. G. de Fontaine gives reminiscences that will recall to our Veterans and their helpmeets some of the tribulations of war as well as some of its humor. Even misfortune has its funny side. These illustrations of war times will be vivid to many readers:

Before me is an old memorandum book, crumpled and torn. Its cover is of stiff wall paper; its inner leaves of the coarse, dingy paper manufactured in the Confederacy during the war. Among other things, it contains the following entries of household expenses: One sack of flour, $75; 1 ham, $40; 10 lbs. brown sugar, $60; 4 yds. of shirting, $40; soap, $10; 4 lbs. coffee, $120; 3 chickens, $20; lot of mackerel, $125; 12 yds. cambric, $144; half bushel of rice, $14. 50; watermelon, $5; 1 lb. butter, $6.80; beef, 2 lbs., $4; lard, $5; 1 lb. tea, $65; 12 yds. flannel, $150; mending shoes, $10; 1 calf skin, $80; bottle port wine, $45; bottle brandy, $75; bonnet frame, $8; 2 yds. cloth for coat, $120; 2 calico dresses, $108; pair of trousers, $175; coat, $200; cutting hair, $2; corset, $50; shoes, $150; and so on.

Curious old figures these, but they belong to the class that "don't lie." It used to be said in those days that a woman went shopping with a wheelbarrow to carry her money in and brought home her purchases in her pocketbook. Dear old days! They are far enough removed to have

RARE PHOTO OF A GROUP OF CONFEDERATE SOLDIERS STATIONED NEAR CHARLESTON, SC, CIRCA 1863.

gained a perspective, and to borrow the hues of romance from the distance. How their memory clings to us. We triumphed and wept and lived a great deal in those four eventful years.

Time and again it has been written, and with much truth, that the heroism of the Southern women prolonged the conflict several years, and that the efforts of the men in the field were sustained by the courage of the women at home.

Not only were they brave and hopeful, but as the war progressed, they became expert in devising "ways and means" whereby their supplies which every day were growing less, might be eked out. "The boys at the front" were their first consideration. After their wants were supplied, only what was left would be utilized by those at home. To do without, was part of a Southern woman's religion. During the war many a sick and wounded soldier was brought back to life by their tender nursing and the home delicacies of which they were only too glad to deprive themselves.

The subject of clothing soon became a problem. Old garrets were ransacked for discarded garments that were brought out and given a fresh lease of life in new characters. Bonnets were made of old black silk dress waists, lined with red or blue satin from the lining of old coat sleeves, and trimmed with goose feathers. New hats were constructed from discarded ones, trimmed with old velvet coat collars and cock's plumes, cut from the roosters in the yard. Palmetto and corn shucks were also forced to do duty in like manner.

A lady in Columbia, South Carolina, was fortunate enough to receive through the blockade a beautiful imported bonnet. The first Sunday that she made her appearance in the church with the startling revelation on her head, there was not a woman in the congregation, I venture to assert, who heard one word of the sermon; and the following week that bonnet had more visitors than any ten of the most fashionable women in the city.

Our jackets were made of our father's old-fashioned cloaks, those of the style represented in the pictures of John C. Calhoun, doing splendid service by supplying all the girls in the family at once. One velvet jacket came out triumphant at the close of the war, having done heroic duty for five girls of the family on all festive occasions.

If there were two girls in the family, we went out singly, in order that the same dress might do double duty. We borrowed, loaned, patched, lengthened, shortened, turned and twisted our garments until there was nothing left of them.

One Richmond belle laughingly told, after the war, of going to a party in a borrowed dress so short for her that she was ashamed to walk across the floor. Usually, the gayest among the gay, she was asked on the evening, in question why she was so quiet—why she was not dancing?

"Dancing!" she said, "Good heavens, I'm only too thankful that I can breathe. I don't even dare to laugh, for I should burst this girl's dress to pieces and it's all she has."

Some of the situations were ludicrous in the extreme. We made a journey once with a worn-out pair of Confederate mules, and while the distance was only thirty miles, it necessitated camping out for the night. In the morning our ablutions were performed in a stream near by. One of the party pinned her hair switch to the back of the wagon preparatory to the arrangement of her toilette after returning from the water; but lo, and behold! the switch had disappeared. Primus, the [black] driver, was questioned, but the only satisfaction to be gleaned from him was: "I dunno nuffin 'tall 'bout no switch mam; I bin see dat black mule chaw 'pon sump'n dat look like a hoss tail. I specs dat' w'ar yo' har don' gone, missis."

Picture it! Think of it! A woman blessed by nature with only slight hirsute adornment, thus suddenly bereft of her "crown of glory" without the remotest possibility of replacing it and the prospect of a protracted war before her.

It was not an uncommon sight to come suddenly upon a bevy of pretty girls sitting tailor fashion making and mending shoes, the material for the purpose being rabbit or squirrel skins. The neatest fitting gloves were made of old silk stockings that had been raveled; and I knew of a dainty pair of shoes being made for the baby of the house out of an old morocco needle book that had been ripped up for the purpose.

Buttons being out of the question, and pins five dollars a paper, a substitute was made by boring holes in persimmon seed and sewing them on the children's clothes. An old colored mammy was the first to devise this clever substitute.

Old men and little boys helped to wind thread and hold brooches, and even knitted on the soldier's socks, after the mystery of "turning the heel" had passed. As the merry spinning wheel went round, you could frequently hear the strain of a patriotic songs like the following:

"Our wagon's plenty big enough,
The running gear is good;
It's stuffed with cotton round the sides
And made of Southern wood.
Carolina is the driver,
With Georgia by her side,
Virginia'll hold the flag up,
And we'll all take a ride."

A favorite night employment was making envelopes. Letter writing was one of our luxuries. White paper could not be wasted on the outside of a letter that had to bear our messages of love to our dear ones in the camp or on the battlefield. Wall paper and sheets with pictures on one side served for the purpose of envelopes. These were stuck together with gum from peach trees, and goose quills supplied our pens.

Many of our private missives were written by torchlight. Blessed pine trees! What a resource you proved to be in our emergencies! The Confederates were all "Fire-worshipers." Women wrote letters to absent lovers, knitted, read and sewed by the bright flames of pine knots. Matches were very scarce; a factory was started in Richmond, but the matches furnished were poor, having a habit of going out before the candle was lighted, making it always safer to trust to a coal of fire or a lightwood knot.

Candles! Ah, these were the things on which the women tried all their ingenuity. They were sometimes made of tallow and beeswax, mutton suet and wax, while very swell green candles were the product of myrtle berries. The great trouble with them was to get the candles strong enough to stand alone when lighted, most of them having a way of lopping over like the Tower of Pisa as soon as the wick was ignited, and depositing arabesque designs in grease on every article within reach of their "continual dropping."

Our coffee was made of various substitutes, such as rye, wheat, rice, potatoes, peas and peanuts. Tea was a decoction of blackberry or sassafras leaves. Think of it, ye devotees of five o'clock teas! Your favorite beverage made of blackberry leaves sweetened with sorghum or molasses.

Vinegar was manufactured from persimmons; shoe blacking from Pride of India berries boiled with water, soot and mutton suet. Ink was made of sumach berries; salt was distilled from the water of the ocean, and frequently from the earth in the smokehouses where meat was cured.

Being an agricultural and not an inventive people, we were often sorely tried for the want of the most insignificant articles. The trouble with us was that we had always depended upon the North for everything from a hair pin to a tooth pick, and from a cradle to a coffin, and to be thus suddenly cut off from our source of supplies with our ports blockaded was not a pleasant situation. This condition of things was not however, without its good results, as the number of factories and machine shops on Southern soil now demonstrate.

Nearly all of the smaller towns and villages in the Confederacy that were not within the Federal line of march, were filled with refugees from the beleaguered towns and cities. This was especially the case in South Carolina. Every inch of space was occupied. Many of the first families of the State lived in discarded baggage cars along the lines of the railroad. It was not an unfrequent thing to hear the sound of a harp, piano, or guitar from these homely abodes, which were fitted up with all the elegance that refined taste could dictate.

Our diversions during the war consisted of nothing more exciting than concerts for the benefit of soldier's hospitals, sewing societies for making soldier's clothing, surprise parties and prayer meetings.

Some of the most laughable incidents occurred in these sewing circles. In one instance where an old spinster was in charge of the "cutting and giving out" department, she inadvertently put but one leg of a pair of drawers in a bundle of clothing that was taken home by a young girl who was enthusiastic on the subject of sewing for the soldiers. She made up and finished the odd drawers leg and returned it to the society. At the next meeting, the unique article was held up before the assembled members by the spinster who, in her bitterest tones said, "Who made this?" "I did," said the young girl, blushing deeply, "I thought it was intended for a one legged man."

In the absence of the men, the women undertook to perform their duties, and many a fine crop was planted and harvested by fair hands unused to anything more laborious than a lesson on a harp or piano. Some of them became expert hair-cutters, and one girl had the honor of having shaved her father with a pair of embroidery scissors, the work being so cleverly done that the old gentleman remarked: "Sallie, I do believe that if you had a pair of scissors large enough, you could build a house."

One Winchester maiden did paint the outside of her house, and while mounted upon a ladder dressed in an old homespun dress and split bonnet, with paint pot in hand, received a call from two of her most fashionable neighbors. Descending the ladder and assuming the air of a servant, she invited them to enter the house; then hastening to her room, she changed her dress, came in and greeted her friends in the most graceful and cordial manner. During the visit however, she did not fail to observe vague little punctuation marks in the corners of her visitor's mouths, and an occasional twinkle in their eyes that said as plain as words, "You have not fooled us a bit," but they were not sufficiently acquainted to reveal their knowledge; and it was only through a third party that the young painter learned that her incog had been discovered.

MRS. ST. JOHN ALISON LAWTON OF SOUTH CAROLINA, PRESIDENT GENERAL, UNITED DAUGHTERS OF THE CONFEDERACY, 1925.

It is the glory of two Georgia women however, to have done what no other woman in the world was ever credited with doing: that is, to clean out a well; and the work when finished would have done credit to a first class well-digger.

It was during these years of hardships and privations that Southern women showed their true worth. With husbands and brothers in the army, in many instances, prisoners, often without home or money, and starvation staring them in the face, they were uncomplaining, cheerful, helpful and hopeful; and when the end came, it was these women who had endured all these hardships that encouraged the men and kept them from despair. They put their shoulders to the wheel and did not look back, and the brave fight which they have since made with fate, has often given proof of valor worthy of the Spartan days.

In regard to the loyalty of the slaves, be it said to their eternal credit, no race was ever more loyal and helpful than they, during those four years of bloody strife. They took special pride in the feeling that they were the only protectors of the mistress at home during the absence of her natural protector and guardian. A certain lady was told that her negroes were holding nightly meetings in her kitchen, and it was suspected that they were making arrangements to desert [to] the [Yankee] enemy. One night, a low, earnest sound was heard from that locality. Creeping softly along to hear what the conspiracy might be, the mistress found the entire group of negroes on their knees, while one of them was offering up an earnest petition to the "Fader in Hebben," and praying Him to "bress missis and de chillun, an pertickler de young masters in de wah."

A ten dollar Confederate bill is now kept as a memento of an old [black] nurse who, after the war, brought it to her mistress to "he'p 'er ter git along."

An old negro man who had been his master's body-servant, brought a store of provisions and laying it before his former owner, said: "Marster, it mos' breaks my heart to see yo' an' ole miss in dis yere shanty, but 'would break 'tirely to know yo' was hongry an' couldn't git nuffin to eat."

His master, brushing the tears from his eyes, said: "Tom, I can't take these things from you and leave you and your children to starve."

The faithful old man replied: "No danger o' dat, Marster; Tom is used to helpin' hisself, but you an' ole miss nebber could do dat."

The master, greatly touched by this show of affectionate gratitude, said: "Tom, we have fallen upon evil days, but perhaps I may live to repay you for your kindness."

"Lord, Marster," replied the old man, "You's done dat time an' agin fur all dese years, an' I'se sho' it's my time to tek keer o' yo' an' ole miss."

The negresses would sell any of their home products for finery. A veil with these dusky dames would bring any amount in butter, eggs or chickens; the blacker the skin, the more ardent the desire to "dress like de white folks."

When the Federal Army was leaving Columbia, a number of the negroes followed, some of them going in their Masters' carriages. One old dame thus seated, dressed in all the finery she could lay her hands on—including a white lace veil—and fanning herself vigorously with a huge palmetto fan, although it was February, was met by an acquaintance, who hailed her after this fashion, "Hello, Aunt Sallie, whar yo' gwine?"

Nodding her head with a patronizing air, she answered, "Lor',honey,

I'se gwine back inter de Union." And she got there. In less than six months afterwards, word came back to Columbia that she was "doing time in a prison for pilfering from her Northern mistress."[109]

PUTTING AN ARROGANT YANK PRISONER IN HIS PLACE
☛ A wounded [Confederate] Irishman, at Shiloh, refused to be carried to the rear, saying that he wanted to see "the prasoners." He took out his short pipe, filled it up, struck a light and began to puff like a loyal editor. As the [U.S.] prisoners filed past, including [U.S.] General [Henry] Prince, he kept inquiring, every minute, "I say, boys, what State are you from?" No one deigned a reply. All strode along, in sullen, not to say majestic, silence. At length one of our Northern brethren, being led along, in durance vile, turned upon Patrick, and, cursing him bitterly, said: "I'm from Ohio, you impertinent Irish Rebel." Pat, without taking the pipe out of his mouth, and without a moment's hesitation, answered: "And a good deliverance it was to the State of Ohio when you joined the Yankee army."[110]

HOW HE PASSED THE EXAMINATION
☛ A city business man was very keen on having proficient clerks in his employ. Before a clerk could enter his office he was required to pass a written examination on his knowledge of business. At one examination one of the questions was: "Who formed the first company?" A certain bright youth was a little puzzled at this, but was not to be floored. He wrote: "Noah successfully floated a company while the rest of the world was in liquidation." He passed.[111]

THOMAS JEFFERSON'S FLOWER GARDEN
☛ Thomas Jefferson, President of the United States, wished his little grandchildren to share his love of gardens and all things beautiful. He had a way of his own with the tulips and hyacinth bulbs that was really enough to make those bulbs laugh with the children. President Thomas Jefferson gave them names as they were planted. He used to call his grandchildren and introduce them to a bulb as if the bulb were a person; then, not to get these friends mixed in the garden, he put a stick into the ground beside each bulb, on which the bulb's name was plainly written.

They tell us that it was amusing in the springtime to see these children go visiting their garden friends and to hear one call out: "Come, Grandpa, come! Marcus Aurelius has his head out of the ground."

While another sweet child would say: "The Queen of the Amazon is coming up!"

Happy times they had in that long ago, those little children of Virginia, with their garden-loving grandfather![112]

WHERE GOD IS NOT
☛ An English clergyman once said to a bright little girl in his Sunday

school: "If you will tell me where God is, I will give you an orange." "If you will tell me where he is not," promptly replied the little girl, "I will give you two."[113]

NOTHING
☛ A Scottish farmer, being elected a school manager, visited the village school and tested the intelligence of the class by this question: "Now, boys, can any of you tell me what nacthing is?" After a moment's silence a small boy in a back seat rose and replied: "It's what ye gied me the other day for holding yer horse."[114]

THE FEROCIOUS LOOKING BULL & THE MAIDEN
☛ Bertie and the girl of his heart, while taking a country walk, had just encountered a ferocious looking bull and had retreated behind a high gate. "But I thought, dear," ventured the maiden, "that you always said you'd face death gladly for me." "So I would," the swain assured her, "but that bull isn't dead."[115]

COMICAL INCIDENTS AT FREDERICKSBURG
☛ It was, I think, on the 14th that our Brigade was lying—presumably on its arms—in a forest of tall timber, but near enough to get into line at a moments notice. A blanket had been spread on the ground and four or five men were seated around it playing poker. A hand was dealt and Bill Smith felt happy; he held four sixes. Two of his companions were also lucky, and when one of them bet fifty beans—they were playing cent ante—the other raised him two hundred. Confident of winning, for two hands of fours are seldom held in the same deal, Bill, with a fine pretence of bluffing, looked over his cards long and anxiously and finally said, in a trembling voice, "I see your bets, gentlemen, and go you five hundred better." Scarcely were the words out of his mouth, when a shell from a long range cannon struck the dead limb of a tree near by, and sent a piece of it against Bill's breast with such force as to knock him backwards, sprawling to the ground, the cards flying from his hands, each in a different direction. Jumping to his feet instantly and glaring wrathfully on everybody in sight he exclaimed: "Damned if I can't whip the cowardly whelp who threw that chunk—now's his time to cheep, if he's got any sand in his craw." But no one cheeped; Bill meant every word he said and was well-known as a man who could not be insulted with impunity. And it took quite a while, and considerable argument to persuade him that the person responsible for his loss was on the other side of the Rappahannock, fully two miles away.

The battle of Fredericksburg has been no exception to the rule in furnishing us with a feast—lots of pure coffee and unlimited quantities of desiccated vegetables. Soup made of the latter has been the first, last, and, sometimes, middle course of every meal I have eaten for a week.

Confident that the Yankees will be in no hurry to risk a repetition of the drubbing they have received, we are making preparations for the winter. Snow has fallen to the depth of several inches, but wood is plentiful, and most of us drew an extra supply from the Yankees in the way of blankets. I sleep in a tent with our Adjutant, but mess with my German friend, Webber. He is not only a good and economical cook, but is willing to act in that capacity without relief, and this last consideration appeals strongly to my keen sense of the fitness of things. While our alliance as messmates began only a few days ago, our friendship dates from the retreat from Yorktown. He is the happy possessor of a huge pipe as German as himself, the bowl of which, lined with iron, holds fully an eighth of a pound of tobacco. For facilities of transportation, as well as because he loves the weed, the pipe is always hanging from his mouth on the march, and within reach of it when he lies down to sleep. Coming up from Yorktown, everybody's tobacco, except Webber's, got wet, and Webber refused peremptorily to divide with several who at different times applied to him.

LIVING CONFEDERATE FLAG (MADE OF FLOWERS) AT THE STATUE OF ROBERT E. LEE, RICHMOND, VA.

It was a case of wet or dry tobacco with me, and I schemed. Catching the old fellow off to himself, I said, "Give me some dry tobacco, Webber, please; mine is wet and won't smoke." He glanced around at me quickly and suspiciously and answered gruffly, "I giffs not mooch tubacca avay." "I know you don't" said I, "and I don't blame you for refusing to divide with everybody; but give me some now, and when we get to our knapsacks, I'll give you half of mine." "Veil, den," he replied opening his heart and tobacco pouch simultaneously, and beaming upon me with the first smile I ever saw on his face, "Dat vash goot." And not only then, but until I had a chance to dry my own tobacco, Webber's pouch was constantly at my command. Of course, I made my word good when I got to my knapsack, and since then tobacco is common property between us.

"Why did you join the Confederate Army, Webber?" I asked one day. "It vash my beezness," replied he: "I vas been a solcher in Charmany all ze time." "You would have joined the Northern Army then if you had been in the North, wouldn't you?" I asked again. "Oh, yah," he answered. "Vot ish der defrance? Vat ish got to coom, vill coom anyvay, und to be a solcher vash my beezness."[116]

ANOTHER HUMOROUS OCCURRENCE AT FREDERICKSBURG
☛ While I write, some of my comrades are exchanging compliments with half a regiment of [C.S.] Cavalry that is marching by, which incident reminds me of another [amusing incident]. One day on the trip from Winchester, while our Brigade was encamped near Culpeper Court House, a lone Virginia cavalryman came wandering in an offensively lordly way through the camp. Had he come afoot, little attention would have been bestowed on him and he would likely have been suffered to depart in peace and happiness. Presumptious enough, however, to bestride a gallant steed whose hoofs stirred up more or less dust, he promptly became the cynosure of all eyes. About the strongest feeling infantry and cavalry have for each other is that of contempt; down in the bottom of his heart the foot soldier nurses an idea that his mounted comrades lack a great deal of doing their whole duty in killing and taking the chances of being killed, while from his elevation on the back of a horse, your cavalryman feels himself a superior being and looks down with an air of humiliating pity upon an arm of the service which must depend on its own legs for transportation. When, therefore, it appeared that this particular gentlemen had no other object in view than to gratify an idle and impertinent curiosity concerning a people of whom he had heard the most wonderful tales, the Texans, not being in holiday attire or in the humor to be closely inspected by strangers, determined to trade a little upon their reputation for bloodthirstiness.

A fair opportunity was given them, for it happened that for the purpose of solving some doubt which a cursory view failed to settle or remove, the visitor came to a temporary halt in the middle of the camp and proceeded to look, at his leisure, on the strange surroundings. Immediately surrounded by a dozen or more Texans, several of them with their guns, others with pistols belted around their waists, and all wearing, either naturally or intentionally, the most reckless and dare-devil airs imaginable, he suddenly lost his look of unconcern and began to glance uneasily around in search of an avenue of escape from his admirers. One fierce looking fellow stepped to the side of his horse, and assuming the manner of a sick man just out of the hospital, laid his hand on the Virginian's scabbard and, in a whining voice, asked: "Couldn't you pull your jobber out for a minute Mister, just to please a sick man?" The laugh that followed the request caused a flush of anger to overspread the countenance of the horseman, and he was about to make an angry reply, when his attention was arrested by a colloquy between two of his entertainers, which, although not at all personal in character, was not calculated to be reassuring to its hearer and object, the tone, manner and looks of the speakers indicating something more than mere idle banter.

"How much is it, Tuck," asked the one, with a significant glance at the Virginian, "that Longstreet offers for the body of a dead Virginia cavalryman?" "A thousand dollars in gold," answered Tuck, "and if a feller was'nt partickerly squeamish, it'd be powerful easy to git the body." "Why, Tuck," protested the first speaker, "you would'nt think of killing one yourself, would you?" "Why not?" replied Tuck, looking at his gun, apparently to see if it was capped. "That's the only way I know of to git the money, fur none of these damned cavalry fellers ever git close enough to a live Yankee to be killed."

The gallant Virginian lost not a word or a movement of the participants in this conversation, and, knowing Texans only by repute, deemed it prudent to work himself and steed to the edge of the surrounding crowd, experiencing just enough difficulty in this undertaking to increase his very natural apprehensions of bodily harm. Once there, he bestowed a hurried but tremulously polite "Good mawnin,' gentlemen," on the party assembled in his honor, and went off at a brisk trot. He was allowed to reach the outskirts of the grove without molestation—then a gun cap snapped behind him, and even his iron nerve could not restrain him from glancing back and—when he discovered Tuck on his knees, gun in hand and hurriedly fumbling in his cap box for another cap—from clapping both spurs and whip to his steed and disappearing in a cloud of dust amid the derisive shouts and jeers of the Brigade.[117]

PARENTS & TEACHERS

☛ The following are samples of notes from parents to teachers: "Dear Miss Smith: Please excuse Rachel; she had to fetch her mother's liver." "Dere Miss: Please excuse Mary be'en late she has ben out on a herring." "Dear Madam: Jane has had to stop home as I have had twins. It shan't occur again."[118]

TOO CRUEL A PUNISHMENT

☛ "I hear that you have given up singing to prisoners?" "Yes. They complained that it wasn't in the penal code."[119]

UNIQUE METHOD OF GETTING A FURLOUGH

☛ Sometimes it pays to be original. A marine on furlough wired in as follows for an extension, and got it: "Nobody sick. Nobody died. No train wrecks. Everything fine. Still got a lot of money. Having a good time and going strong. Request extension."[120]

THE DILEMMA OF A TEXAN IN HOOD'S ARMY

☛ But alas! the present can only be an interlude between the acts of this terribly real and bloody tragedy of war. Another may never come to me, and, to make the most of this, I devote a part of it to your entertainment. Don't imagine that because I am so happily situated, I am not on duty; for I am. Ostensibly, I am protecting the premises of an F. F. V.—a gentleman of the old school, the paternal ancestor of a pretty and vivacious daughter, and the host of a prettier and more vivacious friend of the daughter. Under the humanizing influence of the fragrant roses that bloom in the yard and those animate flowers who, flitting from room to room and from piazza to porch of the house, come within range of my greedy eyes whenever I raise them from the table, my warlike spirit has been tamed into the peacefulness and timidity of "Mary's little lamb," and, were it not for the conflict between obligations that distress my tender conscience, would be as sportive. The trouble is this: In exchange for three substantial daily meals, and for the blessed privilege of flirting *ad libitum* with the young ladies and sleeping at night in the front yard, I am expected to protect my host's roasting-ears, watermelons, pumpkins, apples and the like, from the depredations of my gallant comrades, encamped three miles away in the direction of Fredericksburg. At the same time, my duty to these comrades is to afford them every possible opportunity to follow the advice of Jim Sanders of the 5th. Catching sight of a terrapin one day, he captured it, saying, "A man orter vairegate his eatin' every chance he gits." Considering that Jim has been a man of mark ever since he awarded to the Enfield Rifle the

"THE LITTLE GENERAL": ROBERT E. LEE IV (GREAT-GRANDSON OF GENERAL LEE) IN HIS CONFEDERATE UNIFORM.

palm of superiority over the Mississippi Yager, on the sensible ground that the "chronic" ball carried by the former was so much more destructive than the round ball of the latter, the Texans are not to be censured for following his wise counsels. This granted, I do not feel called upon to be an obstacle to "vairegation" as long as I can keep myself out of the sight and hearing of the boys.[121]

THE LATITUDINAL WALKER

☛ Crossing the Potomac on a pontoon bridge, at noon we halted in the outskirts of the town of Williamsport, Md., and, *mirabile dictu*, drew rations of whiskey. There was only about a gill to the man, but as the temperance fellows gave their shares to friends, the quantity available was amply sufficient to put fully half the brigade not only in a boisterously good humor, but in such physical condition that the breadth of the road over which they marched that evening was more of an obstacle to rapid progress than its length. At an early hour, John Brantley, of my company, became so exhausted by his latitudinarian tendencies as to prefer riding to walking, and perceiving that Col. Key was in an excellently good-natured condition, took advantage of a momentary halt to approach that gallant officer and, slapping him familiarly on the leg, remarked: "Say, Kunnel! I'm jus' plum' broke down; can't you walk some an' lemme ride a while?" Bending forward over his horse's neck and grasping the pommel of his saddle with both hands to steady himself, the old Colonel looked pityingly down at Brantley and, between hiccoughs, replied: "I'd do it in a minute, ole feller, damned if I wouldn't, but I'm tired as hell myself, ah sit tin' up here an' ah hol'in' on."[122]

CIRCUMSTANCES ALTER CASES
☛ "When de Jedge he say t' me is I guilty," said Charcoal Eph, ruminatively, "I says if yo' all kin prove hit, Jedge, I is; but I'f'n yo' all got any doubt about hit, not guilty, Jedge, not guilty!"[123]

HERE'S MY HUSBAND—TAKE 'IM!
☛ During the war, [U.S.] Army Headquarters received the following:
"Deer United States Army: My husband ast me to rite you a reckmend that he supports his family. He kaint read, so dont tell him. Just take him, he aint no good to me. He aint done nothing but drink lemmen essence and play the fiddle sence we married eight years ago. Maybe you can get him to carry a gun. He is good on squirrels and eating. Take him and welcome to him."[124]

SENSIBLE ALLIGATORS
☛ The Florida beach and blue sea looked inviting to the tourist from the North, but before venturing out to swim he thought to make sure.
"You're certain there are no alligators here?" he inquired of the guide.
"Nossuh," replied that functionary, grinning broadly. "Ain' no 'gators hyah."
Reassured, the tourist started out. As the water lapped about his chest he called back:
"What makes you so sure there aren't any alligators?"
"Dey's got too much sense," bellowed the guide. "The sharks done skerred dem all away."[125]

THE FINAL TEST
☛ Old age is the final test of a man's genuine sincerity. It shows where he has really lived in his soul. Life's motives are so mixed through the years that not until old age removes many of them can it be determined what a man truly cherishes in the inner citadel of his being.[126]

THE IMPORTANCE OF BACON
☛ Just after crossing the boundary line into Pennsylvania, I went to a

farmhouse in sight of the road and inquired if the owner of it had any bacon for sale. Answered in the affirmative, I asked the price and was told "fifteen cents a pound." Reflecting that in Virginia the price was two dollars for the same quantity, and bacon almost impossible to buy at that, I determined to lay in a good supply. So selecting from his well-filled smoke house two sides which weighed exactly eighty pounds, and were streaked with lean and fat in exactly the right proportion to be exceedingly toothsome, I tied them together with a piece of old rope and, throwing them across the loins of my horse, handed the farmer a twenty dollar Confederate bill. "Oh!" said he, as he took it gingerly between thumb and fore-finger and eyed it as if suspicious that it were

unclean, "I can't pass this kind of money here in Pennsylvania." "Yes, indeed you can, my dear sir," said I, speaking with the fervor of absolute conviction. "Can't you see from the army passing by that we intend to take possession of this little neck of the woods? You will need our money to pay taxes and for many other purposes, and you had better begin to get hold of it." "But I can't change this bill, for I haven't got any of the same kind," he whined. "Oh! that's a small matter," said I; "just give me greenbacks—I ain't afraid of them." "I'll see what I can do," he answered, after a moment's hesitation, and walked into the house. In less than a minute I heard

ALABAMA'S CONFEDERATE TWINS: W.T. AND E.J. WEISSINGER, OF DALLAS COUNTY, CIRCA 1924.

the shrill voice of an angry woman scolding vigorously and, guessing that the farmer was encountering opposition that might interfere with the trade, deemed it prudent to mount my steed and be prepared for emergencies. I had scarcely settled myself in the saddle when the farmer appeared and, extending the bill toward me, said: "Here, Mister, give me back that bacon and take your money—I can't make the change, for I aint got eight dollars in the house." Fully equal to the imperative demands of the occasion, I resolved not to suffer such a pitiful trifle as eight dollars of Confederate money to spoil a good trade, and, assuming the most lordly Southern air of which I was capable, said: "Then just keep the change, sir," touched my weather-beaten hat with the politeness of a Chesterfield and, giving free rein to my horse, soon overtook a wagon and unloaded my prize into it.

There are men in the 4th Texas endowed with as keen a scent for food as any animal, and Dick Skinner, of Company F, is one of them.

Excepting the driver, whom I swore to absolute secrecy, not a soul saw
me put that bacon into the wagon, and yet, within twenty minutes after
we went into camp near Greencastle, Dick approached me with as bland
a smile as he wears when asking a comrade to hold his gun while he takes
a drink of water, and said: "See here, Joe, I haint had a bite to eat for
three days and I'm gettin' too weak to serve my country. Can't you lend
me about ten pounds of that bacon you got this evening? I'll make it even
with you within the week." Devoting one minute to wondering how in
the world Dick had learned of my purchase, I gave another to rapid
reflection. While the fellow lied like a trooper about his starving
condition, he was obviously too hungry to be a good Christian and obey
all of God's ten commandments, and especially those against
covetousness and stealing; therefore, solely out of regard for his moral
welfare, I placed temptation out of his reach by lending him the bacon.
But, although I abjured him with tears in my eyes not to think of making
things even until he could buy as I had, I am satisfied that when, two or
three days later, he settled the account by sending me a couple of fat
chickens, somebody's henroost had been robbed.[127]

MONUMENT TO CONFEDERATE MAJOR HENRY WIRZ,
ANDERSONVILLE, GEORGIA.

CHAPTER FOUR

MISSING THE JOKE BY A COUNTRY MILE

☛ Several Americans and an Englishman were touring the Pacific Coast in an automobile. The Americans were much amused at a roadside sign, which read: "Three miles to San Francisco. If you can't read, ask the blacksmith."

When nearing San Francisco, the Englishman burst out laughing, saying that he had just caught the joke. When the Americans asked what it was, he said:

"Suppose the blacksmith wasn't at home?"[128]

MILKING HORSES IN ENEMY TERRITORY

☛ Horses were needed to move the artillery and, to obtain them, the non-combatants of the Q. M. [Quarter Master] Department were ordered to scout through the country and pick up as many as possible. Always ready to serve our country in its time of need, we set out as blithely as schoolboys on a frolic, our cheerfulness wonderfully increased by timely information that we would not be expected to penetrate the mountain fastnesses where guerillas were supposed to be lying in wait for the unwary, but, on the contrary, were to confine our researches to the open country between Longstreet's Corps and Ewell's, then far up the Susquehanna toward Harrisburg. Shortly after noon of the first day's scout, we caught sight of two colts feeding on a

FIGHT BETWEEN THE CSS *ALABAMA* (RIGHT) AND THE USS *KEARSAGE*, (LEFT) OFF CHERBOURG, FRANCE, JUNE 19, 1864.

hill, a mile to the right of the road. Knowing their dams must be near them, we cut across the country and, tied to a hedge, found two splendid young mares. I took the bay, while Capt. Cussons (or Cozzens) of Gen. Law's staff, who had joined our party, took the sorrel. The poor animals kept up such a constant and increasing racket over the separation from their offspring that when night came, and we encamped in a grove some

distance away from any road, an expert at milking was in demand. Far away from the protection of friendly infantry, in an enemy's country and armed only with pistols, we felt unpleasantly lonesome, insecure and forlorn; it was recklessly imprudent, therefore, to run the risk of having our presence betrayed to passing foes, as it might be, unless the uneasiness of our captives was speedily allayed. Having graduated in the art of milking when a boy, I lost no time in practicing it on the animal chosen by me. Capt. Cussons, however had more difficulty. It was his first essay as a milkmaid and, although under my laughing tuition he finally succeeded, it was at the cost of infinite travail and labor, and he carried away in his eyes and mouth, and on his face, long flowing beard and new uniform far more milk than fell upon the ground.[129]

A PENNSYLVANIA FAMILY FEEDS A CONFEDERATE TROOP
☛ An old Dunkard gave us such an early breakfast next morning that when at noon we halted before a large and elegant mansion, surrounded by beautiful grounds, we were as hungry as bears. It fell to my lot to ask for entertainment, and, dismounting, I rapped gently at the front door. Waiting a reasonable time and hearing no sound from within, I rapped again a little more vigorously than before, and after another interval of absolute quiet, a third time. Then a well-preserved lady of fifty opened the door and, her face as white as a sheet, looked silently at me. Raising my hat in acknowledgment of her presence, I stated my errand. Not a word fell from her lips until she had first looked at me from head to foot and then glanced in the direction of my companions; then she said in a tremulous voice: "You are rebels, are you not?" "That is what you call us, madam, I suppose, but we call ourselves Confederates," I explained. "Orders have been published," said she, "prohibiting citizens from giving any aid or comfort to the Confederates." "I shall regret very much, Madam," I rejoined, "to have the orders obeyed in our particular case, for in that event we will have to ask elsewhere for food, and we are quite hungry, I assure you." "That alters the case," she replied quickly, smiling for the first time. "The Bible commands us to feed the hungry, and it is of higher authority than the orders of man. Ask your friends in—I will give you dinner." The smile and the spirit of genuine Christian hospitality, which spoke in the lady's sweet voice and shone in her still bright eyes, captivated me, and I suggested carrying my party around the house to the back door rather than have them tramp through the spotlessly clean hall. She smiled again gratefully this time—saying: "Thank you, sir. You have been trained by a careful mother, I see. It will please me very much to have your friends conducted directly to the back porch—they will find water, towels and a comb and brush there, should they need them."

To make a long story short, within half an hour, eight Confederates sat around a long table in a spacious dining-room, eating huge slices of light bread, cold ham, corned beef and roast mutton, interspersed liberally with sweet pickles, jam, jelly and apple butter, drinking genuine coffee and the richest of milk, and, between sups and bites, chatting as merrily with our hostess, her three handsome daughters and an old gentleman whom the girls called "Uncle John," as if they were acquaintances of long and intimate standing. Stray whithersoever he might in the delightful fields of literature, prose, poetry, the arts and the drama, the disputatious, critical and sarcastic Capt. Joe Wade, of the 4th Texas, found his match in the well-informed, bright-minded elder sister; for every one of our many crude essays at wit or humor, Capt. Walter Norwood, of the 5th and your humble servant, the writer, received an ample *quid pro quo* from the next in age of the girls, and Capt. Mills, of the 1st—a Chevalier Bayard *sans peur et sans reproche*, although quite an old bachelor—and the others of the visitors, found ample entertainment in lively, laughing converse with our hostess, her youngest daughter and "Uncle John."

We sat there fully three hours; then Capt. Mills suggested departure, and, calling me to one side, quietly dropped a treasured five dollar gold piece into my hand, saying in a low voice: "Here, Joe, pay for our dinner with this. They have been too kind to us to be offered Confederate money." Turning to the hostess, I offered the coin and asked if it would satisfy her for her trouble. "Yes, sir, it would were I willing to accept pay," said she, drawing back rather indignantly. "But I am not. We have heard horrible stories of the treatment we might expect from Confederates, but if all are gentlemen like yourselves, I will make them as welcome to my house and table as you have been. Won't you stay longer? It is early yet." The invitation declined, each of us expressed our thanks for her hospitality and took leave. It was my youthful appearance, I reckon, that gained me the compliment, but when I said good-bye, she clasped my hand warmly and, looking at me with eyes that reminded me of my own good mother in far away Texas, said: "Good bye, my dear boy, and remember if you get sick or are wounded and will only let us know where you are, you shall be brought here and nursed until you are well again."[130]

IT WAS A GOVERNMENT JOB
☛ They were looking down into the depths of the Grand Canyon.

"Do you know," asked the guide, "that it took millions and millions of years for this great abyss to be carved out?"

"Well, well!" ejaculated the traveler, "I never knew that this was a government job."[131]

ARGUMENT FOR INDUSTRY
☛ Old Hen: "I'll give you a piece of good advice."
Young Hen: "What is it?"
Old Hen: "An egg a day keeps the butcher away!"[132]

ONE OF THE GREAT CONFEDERATE FEASTS OF THE WAR

☛ Rejoining the Brigade late that night at its camp near Chambersburg [Pennsylvania], and being very tired, I laid down near the wagons and went to sleep. Awakened next morning by Collin's bugle, and walking over to the camp, I witnessed not only an unexpected but a wonderful and marvelous sight. Every square foot of half an acre of ground not occupied by a sleeping or standing soldier, was covered with choice food for the hungry. Chickens, turkeys, ducks and geese squawked, gobbled, quacked, cackled and hissed in inharmonious unison, as deft and energetic hands seized them for the slaughter, and, scarcely waiting for them to die, sent their feathers like snowy clouds flying in every direction, while immense loaves of bread and chunks of corned beef, hams and sides of bacon, cheeses, crocks of apple-butter, jelly, jam, pickles and preserves, bowls of the yellowest butter and demijohns of buttermilk were in confusion, all around. The sleepers were the foragers of the night resting from their arduous labors—the standing men, their messmates who remained as camp-guards and were now up to their eyes in noise, feathers and grub. Jack Sutherland's head pillowed itself on a loaf of bread and one arm was wound caressingly half around a juicy-looking ham. Bob Murray, fearful that his captives would take to their wings or be purloined, had wound the string which bound half a dozen frying chickens around his right big toe; one of Brahan's widespread legs was embraced by two overlapping crocks if apple butter and jam, while a tough old gander, gray with age, squawked complainingly at his head without in the least disturbing his slumber; Dick Skinner lay flat on his back—with his right hand holding to the legs of three fat chickens and a duck, and his left, to those of a large turkey—fast asleep and snoring in a rasping bass voice that chimed in well with the music of the fowls. . . . The scene is utterly indescribable, and I shall make no further attempt to picture it. The hours were devoted exclusively to gormandizing until, at 3 P.M., marching orders came, and, leaving more provisions than they carried, the Texans moved lazily and plethorically into line—their destination being the fateful battlefield of Gettysburg.[133]

A LETTER PROVING STONEWALL'S SENSE OF HUMOR

☛ I should like for those people who claim that General Jackson was lacking in humor to read the following letter, which he wrote to his sister announcing his engagement:

"Lexington, Va., 1857. My Dear Sister: I don't know whether you have yet returned from your visit to Aunt's, but I will write to you now, as I have the time, and might not have so much leisure a few days hence; and I will begin by stating that I have an invitation for you, and what do you think it is? And who from? For it is not often that I am authorized to send you invitations, and especially pressing ones. And I suppose you begin to think, or may think, well, what does he mean? Why doesn't he tell me at once and be done with it? Well, you see I have finished the first page of my letter, so if I don't tell you soon, you will hardly get it at all from this sheet. Well, now, having cultivated your patience a little—as all women are said to have curiosity—I will tell you that Miss Mary Anna Morrison, a friend of mine, in the western part of North Carolina, and in the southern part of the State, is engaged to be married to an acquaintance of your's living in this village; and she has requested me to urge you to attend her wedding in July next. To use her own words, she says: 'I hope your sister will come. You must urge her to do so. I should be very glad if she could come.' The wedding is not to be large. I told her that I would give the invitation, and, having done so, feel that I am freed from all further responsibility in the matter. I told her that I didn't think you would be able to accept it, and if you can't, just let me know in your next, and transfer the invitation to your humble servant, and he will not decline, for he is very anxious to go, as he is much interested in the ceremony and the occasion, and the young lady is a very special friend of mine.

"Our weather is beautiful at present and I suppose that spring will rapidly advance now. Give much love to all. Your affectionate brother, Thomas."[134]

A KINDLY YANKEE VETERAN

☞ While attending the [SCV] reunion in Chattanooga [Tenn.] my thoughts reverted to boyhood days, so I decided to once more visit "Orchard Knob." On reaching the top I found a good old Union soldier in charge of that picturesque hill, now covered with Federal monuments by States. The old Yank was seated in an easy chair, and when I saluted him and said, "Good morning, sir," he gazed at me for awhile as if surprised, then he said: "Good morning, Johnny Reb." That surprised me, and when I asked why he designated me thus, he simply responded: "You are younger than I, so come and shake hands, and let's talk some." This I did, and during our talk he told me that during the war whenever he got sight of a Reb he at once began to fight like—everything, or else ran as fast as he could. "But," he added, "now it's all settled and you and I are forever friends." I thanked him for his Christian spirit, but again asked, "What made you insist that I was a Johnny Reb?" "O, I saw that Confederate flag on your coat lapel." But the flag was so small that I wanted to know how he could see it, and at last he said, as his face turned red: "I can see a Confederate flag, however small, farther away than anything in this world." We both laughed heartily, and I bade him good by.[135]

THE MOUNTAIN MOONSHINER

☞ As a private in the Army of Tennessee on advanced picket duty, I was waked one night out of a refreshing nap, not to take my turn on post, but with the whispered words: "Give me your canteen! Give me your canteen!" Next morning half the camp was intoxicated—must I acknowledge it? Even the sergeant of the guard was not as straight and dignified as he might have been. Solution: A mountain moonshiner, with the assistance of a mule, was trying to smuggle a barrel of his peculiar industry through the lines, and, not knowing the position of the picket, had been halted. Just how much of the moonshine reached market this deponent sayeth not. No report—no charges![136]

THE CONFEDERATE NATIONAL ANTHEM IN CALIFORNIA!
☛ Yesterday afternoon a man with a banjo and a woman with a violin stood on Main Street [in Los Angeles] playing snatches of old-time songs for the pleasure of passers-by. An elderly woman stopped, dropped a nickle in the collection cup, and asked: "Can you play the national anthem?" The musicians immediately struck up "Dixie," and the woman, together with other auditors, applauded.[137]

"YANKEE HUNTERS" & OTHER MISSISSIPPI TROOP NAMES
☛ Abe's Rejectors, Blackland Giddeonites, Brown Rebels, Buena Vista Hornets, Chunkey Heroes, Cold Water Rebels, De Soto Brothers, Dixie Heroes, Ellisville Invincibles, Fishing Creek Avengers, Hancock Rebels, Impressibles, Jasper Avengers, Kemper Rebels, Lafayette Rebels, Marion Men, Mississippi Rip Raps, Mrs. Body Guard, Oktibbeha Plow Boys, Plentitude Invincibles, Rankin Rough and Readys, Red Invincibles, Rockport Steel Blades, Secessionists, Sons of the South, Southern Sentinels, Sunflower Dispensers, True Confederates, White Rebels, Yankee Hunters, Attala Yellow Jackets, Buckner Boys, Buckner Rebels, Center Marksmen, Coahoma Invincibles, Copiah Rebels, Dixie Boys, Edwards Tigers, Enterprise Tigers, Gaines's Warriors, Helen Johnston Guards, Johnston Avengers, Kossuth Hunters, Loula White Rebels, Meridian Invincibles, Mississippi Yankee Hunters, Newton Hornets, Panola Patriots, Prairie Guards, Raymond Invincibles, Red Rovers, Scotland Guards, Sons of Liberty, Southern Farmers, Spartan Band, Tippah Tigers, Tullahoma Hardshells, Union Stars, Yankee Terrors.[138]

FOOD RATIONS MAY AFFECT ONE'S PATRIOTISM
☛ The battle of Chancellorsville has been fought and won, but it has cost us the life of Stonewall Jackson. It is the only great battle Gen. Lee has fought without Longstreet. McClellan, Pope, McClellan again, Burnside and Hooker, have each been pitted against our peerless chieftain. Who will be the next, is both an interesting and a vexed question with us Confederates. Confident of the superiority of our Commander over the very best material the Yankees can find, we prefer that he should meet a foeman worthy of his steel. But while there is little credit to be gained, either by army or commander, in opposing such vainglorious boasters as Pope, Burnside and Hooker, there are more rations, and these are getting to be a consideration of no small importance. Why we cannot be better and more regularly supplied is a problem beyond our solution.

Perhaps we are expected to live off of the enemy; if so, we protest. When fighting ceases to be a matter of pure, self-sacrificing patriotism, and degenerates into a mere business, we Texans will ask discharges. We are getting homesick any way, and nothing in the world increases the severity of that complaint more than hunger. Apropos to nothing, apparently, except the communings of his own inner man, a comrade said the other day: "I wish to God I was at home." "Oh, yes," I replied, "you want to see the girl you left behind you, don't you?" "No, indeed," he blurted out, "but I want something to eat," and, hungry myself, I unanimously acquiesced in the sentiment.

It is not so much at the quantity of rations we grumble as at the intolerable sameness of bread and meat. Such a limited variety gives us, by the rule of permutation, only two changes; if coffee were added to the menu, we could have nine, and if sugar also, no less than twenty-four. As Bill Calhoun says, "This thing of having bread for the first course one day, and meat the next, and so on, *vice versa* and alternately *ad infinitum et nauseam*, has an excessively depressing effect even upon a fellow's patriotism."[139]

CEREMONY AT THE WHITE HOUSE IN RECOGNITION OF THE RETURN OF SEVERAL CONFEDERATE FLAGS FROM THE STATE OF MAINE TO VIRGINIA, NORTH CAROLINA, AND TEXAS. A SUPPORTIVE PRESIDENT CALVIN COOLIDGE IS AT CENTER, CIRCA 1928.

THE CAMP THIEF

☛ Jim Mann was a private in the 12th Tennessee Cavalry and the prowling thief of the brigade. No night was ever too dark for Jim to "get in" his work. One night the brigade was temporarily in command of an ex-preacher, who was playing colonel, and knew very little of the play, as he usually misconstrued his orders or missed the right road, and this time the command was lost in West Virginia. The night was of Plutonian darkness and the rain was of the "pitchfork" order, and while the bewildered colonel took himself to a farmhouse near by, to inquire the way to the Confederacy, the men were enjoined to strict silence, which injunction they religiously obeyed until Irvine Shield broke the oppressive stillness by shouting: "Boys, what a good night this would be for Jim Mann's business!" A lusty shout followed, with the usual avalanche of smart sayings, and this brought the angry colonel to the front with an order to move on. When the Confederate camps became destitute of things worth stealing Jim deserted to the enemy.[140]

TEXANS OFFER TO BUY HOOD A GUNBOAT
☛ Writing of Bill [Calhoun] reminds me to tell you of his generosity at Suffolk, where, in order to accomplish any good, our men would have had to be amphibious. One day while the Brigade was there, Gen. Hood halted for a moment at the Fourth's camp to speak about some matter to Col. Key. While talking, the General noticed Bill standing a little way off, and, knowing his character and with a view to sport, said, in a voice loud enough to be heard by the whole regiment: "Detail an officer and twenty-five of your best men, Colonel, and order them to report to me at once at my quarters. I have set my heart on the capture of one of those gunboats down on the river, and I know that many men of the 4th can easily get it for me." Bill heard and accepted the challenge. Stepping to the side of Hood's horse and laying one hand on the animal's neck, while with the other he touched the brim of his hat in respectful salute to the rider, he said: "Now look ah here, General, if you've just got to have a gunboat, whether or no, speak out like a man and the 4th Texas will buy you one, but we don't propose to fool with any of them down yonder in the river. They say the darned things are loaded, and, besides, there's only a few of us fellers can swim."[141]

EATING A FISH DIET ON THE COAST OF NORTH CAROLINA
☛ Not being with the Brigade at Suffolk, I can tell you little of its performances there. I was more pleasantly engaged hunting for rations and forage in the section of North Carolina lying near the coast and between the Pasquatank and Chowan Rivers, where the only obstacle to rapturous enjoyment of life was the invariably monotonous diet of salted shad. Intensely Southern in sentiment and within the Yankee lines quite long enough to delight in the sight of a Confederate soldier, the people were lavish in their hospitality to us, and the young ladies everything that was kind and charming. But, while at first almost captivated, the exclusive fish diet demanded such watchfulness and operated so adversely against any indulgence of a naturally aesthetic temperament that I insensibly acquired the habit of looking more carefully for bones than for aught else. Indeed, toward the last, I not only began to feel fishy, but imagined that my entertainers regarded me with fishy stares. These, however, may have been caused by my strict and undeviating adherence to the soldierly principle of eating everything in sight—a course in which, by the way, I was ably seconded, if not outdone, by my comrades for the time being, Captains Jimmie Littlefield, Jimmie Rust and Walter Norwood, each of whom, and especially the last named, is a trencherman of unsurpassed capacity, spirit and persistence.[142]

THE REAL FEAR OF BATTLE

☛ [1862] Where we are going now, is a question concerning which a private soldier can only surmise. Camp rumor saith that the time has come to offer the Marylanders another chance to flock to the Confederate standard, but of the truth of the report or even of the probability of a movement at all, I must absolutely refuse to vouch. While protesting vigorously against the inaction which denies me access to the Federal Commissary Department, I have long ago gratified my once inordinate thirst for gore and glory. Sometimes I feel inclined to echo the desire expressed by Jackson's man, who, reprimanded by his General for running out of the fight "like a baby," broke into a big boohoo and exclaimed between his sobs: "I don't care what you say, sir, but I wish I was a baby, and a gal baby at that." Not for the world would I cast the faintest shadow of a slur upon the manly characters of my comrades here in the Army of Northern Virginia, but we are all human beings, and I honestly believe there is a whole lot of the bravest and most gallant of them who would at

"A TRUE DAUGHTER OF THE OLD SOUTH": MILDRED RUTHERFORD, HISTORIAN GENERAL, UNITED DAUGHTERS OF THE CONFEDERACY.

times be glad of a chance to return to babyhood, even at the risk of a change of sex. With their easy access to Europe, the plagued Yankees have such an ability and habit of outnumbering us, that we are not prompt to join in any severe censure of the 5th Texas Irishman, who, sent out on the skirmish line, came back on a treble quick, and when told by his Lieutenant, "I'd rather die, Mike, than run out of a fight in such a cowardly manner," fixed upon the officer a witheringly sarcastic look and replied: "The hail you would, Leftenent—the hail you would, sor, whin there was only a skimmish line of us boys an' two rigimints and a bathery of them."

Still their numbers furnish a certain class of our soldiers with grand opportunities for killing. Charley Hume, of the 5th, tells an amusing story about a member of that regiment, whose name he will not mention, but whom I will call Dick. Dick is something of a braggart and is wonderfully assisted at times by a vivid imagination. On the day after the Yankees recrossed the Rappahannock at Fredericksburg, Hume found him snugly and safely ensconced behind a huge rock on the South side of the river, apparently busy in death-dealing warfare. "What are you doing here,

Dick?" inquired Hume. "Doing?" repeated Dick, as if surprised at being asked so foolish a question; "What am I doing? Well, sir, I'm killing Yankees, if you must know. Don't you see those fellows over yonder on the side of that hill? I've just set here by my lone self and killed every son of a gun of 'em." Hume looked, and, sure enough, there on the hillside, half a mile away, were twenty or more bodies dressed in blue and lying silent and still. But while he was wondering at such wholesale destruction of human life and framing a suitable compliment to the fell destroyer at his side, first one and then another of the presumed dead rose to his feet, and, picking up gun and accoutrements, sauntered carelessly up the hill without once glancing behind to indicate that he was aware of having been shot at. Hume's wonder and admiration evaporated instanter, but when he turned to apprise his companion of the fact and suggest that the corpses were a little too lively to be those of dead men, Dick was out of sight and hearing.[143]

WHY THE SERVANT COULDN'T WORK
☛ "Can you come and help me clean house, Mandy?" "No'm, can't come. I's j'ined de 'Sociation ob de Folded Hands.'"[144]

CAUTION
☛ The rector's wife rather objected to the gardener being a single man, especially as he lived in a picturesque cottage. "You know," said she to him one day, "the first gardener that ever lived had a wife." "Quite true, ma'am," replied the gardener; "but I've heard tell, ma'am, that he didn't keep his job long after he got her."[145]

NEVER DEBATE A CONGRESSMAN!
☛ To make honors easy between me and Dick, I must relate a joke that I can now laugh at, but for obvious reasons, personal to myself, have carefully concealed from my comrades. While moving from Winchester to Fredericksburg last fall, I straggled one morning and, about nine o'clock, knocked at the front door of a handsome residence on the Orange Plank Road. It was opened by a hospitable old lady whose first inquiry was whether I had been to breakfast. Conscience prompted an affirmative and truthful answer, but appetite overruled it, and I replied in the negative and, for reward, was ushered into a spacious dining room and delivered over to the tender mercies of two young ladies, while my hostess gave necessary orders to the cook. One of these girls was a Texan, and both were so entertaining and witty that I was at once put fairly upon my best mettle, joining forces with the fair Texan in defence of our State against the jocular but vigorous attacks of the equally fair Virginian. After a long lingering breakfast of fried chicken, hot biscuit, fresh butter, and potato coffee, we adjourned to the sitting room, where two old gentlemen—the host and a visitor—were keeping themselves warm before a brightwood fire. Texas being still the subject of

conversation, the right of the Southern States to secede was incidentally adverted to, and, strengthened wonderfully by the breakfast, encouraged by the presence and bright smiles of my Texas compatriot, and foolishly presuming upon the ignorance of the gentlemen, I boldly asserted that Texas had a right to secede superior to that of any other State.

"Ahem!" said the host, straightening himself up in his chair and looking at me with the air of a man ready for an argument. "Upon what fact, sir, do you base that claim?" Surprised by the prompt challenge and disconcerted by the intelligent look of my interrogator, I forgot the reason generally advanced—that Texas was an independent republic when she entered the Union—and answered, "Upon the well known fact, sir, that when Texas became a State of the Union she expressly reserved the right to secede whenever she chose." I spoke so confidently that the Texas girl gave me an admiring look and an encouraging smile. But, to my dismay, my antagonist returned to the charge. "Ahem! ahem!" said he. "Really, sir, I fail to recall any such reservation, although I was a member of Congress from the time annexation was first proposed until it was consummated." And then, as if determined to rout me "horse, foot and dragoon," he turned to the other fellow, saying: "You were my colleague in Congress, Judge; do you recollect any such reservation?" "No, sir, I do not," replied the Judge emphatically, "I recall nothing of the kind. Our young friend is certainly mistaken, for I distinctly remember——." But I was too utterly vanquished to care to listen to reminiscences, especially when the Virginia girl seemed to take keen delight in my discomfiture and the Texas maid to have lost faith in me; so, seizing my hat and bidding the party a rather hasty and awkward adieu, I made my exit, vowing to myself never again to take part in a political discussion without first learning whether or not my opponents had been Congressmen.[146]

NO ESCAPE AT HOPKINSVILLE

☛ I recall an incident of the "Great War" which occurred in Hopkinsville, Ky. I was captured and taken there in the spring of 1863, and, among other Confederates brought there about the same time, I remember three men—Kelly, Knight, and an Irishman—belonging to Gen. Forrest's command, who made their escape at Hopkinsville. We were confined up stairs in an old hotel. The three men made their escape by climbing out through the chimney. Kelly started up, but was suffocated by the soot and came back. He then made a second and successful attempt, followed by Knight and the Irishman, who carried his boots under his arm. The next day a Yankee corporal came in with the Irishman's boots on, which I recognized.

I assisted in their escape and expected to make mine also, but the putting on of [Union] relief guards prevented. I was soon after taken to Camp Douglass, Ill.[147]

BLACK SOUTHERN WISDOM
☞ Br'er Williams says: "De man what gits dar don't wait for sunshine an' don't worry 'bout rain, an' he don't stop ter consider what he's done till he's done done it, an' even then it don't look like half enough ter him."[148]

THE LITTLE TRUSTING RABBIT
☞ After going into camp in the laurel thicket, I witnessed the performance of a strange feat by a sleeping man—he caught a live rabbit. It is a solemn undeniable fact, which I can prove incontestably by a hundred men who failed to catch the little animal. It was this way; the rabbit jumped out of a hollow in a stump that some soldier wanted for firewood, and the moment it was seen, an immense shout went up and half a thousand men began chasing and grabbing at it. It ran hither and thither, and finally jumped squarely on Dansby's breast, just as his hand, moving unconsciously, descended to rest on the breast. The two acts—that of the rabbit and that of the man—were so nearly simultaneous, that the rabbit evidently thought it had found a hiding place, for it made no effort whatever to escape. Dansby drew a long breath, opened his eyes with astonishment, looked a moment at the captive, and then sprang to his feet, saying with a smile of delight, "By gum—I'm hongry." In less than five minutes that little, trusting rabbit was stewing in a quart cup.[149]

CANNONADING THE MOON
☞ A party of my regiment—17th Mississippi—visited [the historic old city of Yorktown, Va.], by leave of absence from our post on the Warwick (Warrick) River, to see the monument where Cornwallis surrendered his sword to Washington at the last battle in our first revolution. Also to witness the fun with the Yankee balloonist who had been trying to spy our lines. Just before we arrived that evening, the balloon with the Yank in it had started up above the tree tops from the lines of the enemy, some mile or more in our front. The battery boys of the breastworks, however, made him slide down again very quickly when they fired a broadside at him. The crowd at the breastworks around the battery were anxiously awaiting the reappearance of this novelty. The gunner stood with his hand on the lanyard ready to let drive whenever the thing would rise again. Meantime night grew on apace—the stars crept out one by one, as if afraid of being shot by the reckless battery, and the scene was enlivened by the pickets of both sides rushing to and fro around the monument of marble standing sentinel between our lines, first one side and then the other desecrating it by talking shelter behind it. Presently the commander of the battery exclaimed, "There he is again, boys! give it to him good this time!" Bang! bang! boom! boom! roared the battery. The boys raised the rebel yell and waited for the smoke to clear away to see the damage done. Imagine

our chagrin when all we saw was the pale-faced moon riding serenely above the tree tops and looking calmly down on us. When we saw the joke our boys guffawed very coarsely at the artillerymen, which made the battery boys heartily ashamed of what they had done—had shot at the man in the moon![150]

HIS FIRST PATIENT
☛ The doctor's small son was entertaining a friend in his father's office, and they were looking with awed admiration at the articulated skeleton in the closet. "Where did he get it?" asked the small guest in a whisper. "O, he's had it a long time. I guess maybe that's his first patient."[151]

CURIOUS SURRENDER OF TWO YANKEE OFFICERS
☛ We were within two hundred yards of the Yankees, and I had noticed that as their line wavered, a squadron commander bravely exhorted his men to stand, but they broke away. He rode deliberately to our front with uplifted hand in token of surrender. Several revolvers covered him; however, there was no harm meditated and when near enough he exclaimed, apparently livid with rage, "I surrender. I had rather be a prisoner than command any such a damned set of cowards."

At that moment the 11th came out of the woods on a charge led by Major Ed. McDonald, and away we all went with a yell into the now broken ranks of the foe, wounding and capturing many in the rout. As we were scouring the timber through which the enemy fled, picking up prisoners, loose horses, and accoutrements, scattered on both sides of the road, my eye rested upon a Federal officer crouched behind a tree. I called upon him to come out, and he crept from his hiding place, cowering with fear. He wore the stripes of a lieutenant.

After taking his arms I called for the canteen, a newly covered and handsome trick. He hesitated and gave up the canteen with more reluctance than his arms. When the demand was repeated, he begged the privilege of taking "one more swag." I then discovered it contained fighting whiskey. The lieutenant was himself pretty well charged. I told him to take "one more," but touch it light, as

FLAG OF THE HAMILTON GUARDS OF KENTUCKY, HELD BY A MEMBER, CONFEDERATE VETERAN JAMES A. MCDONALD, AS WELL AS THE LADIES WHO MENDED IT.

he was then under its influence. He gave the mouth a prolonged kiss and handed it over. I delivered him to the prisoners' guard and saw him no more.[152]

U.S. GENERAL GEORGE ARMSTRONG "FANNIE" CUSTER

☛ Custer [of "Custer's Last Stand" fame] and [Confederate Gen.] Rosser were old classmates, and when the latter ascertained who confronted him [during that morning's bloody battle], he wrote a note which was left at a farm house when we [Confederates] withdrew, addressed to "Fannie Custer" (Fannie was his nickname at school, because he wore long yellow hair). The note was in effect:

"Headquar. etc., Dear Fannie: Come over to see me and bring your people. Rosser."

Custer's reply was substantially, "You return my call made this morning. Fannie."[153]

A CAPTURED YANK INTERROGATES HIS REBEL CAPTOR

☛ Apropos to the battle of Sabine the following was written by a Federal officer who was captured on that occasion:

The [Confederate] "commander of the fort" was a modest, retiring, boyish-looking Irish lad, nineteen years of age. I could not refrain from laughing in his face when introduced to me as "Lieutenant Dick Dowling, who is in command of the fort."

"And you are the shaughran" ["rogue"], I asked, "who did all this mischief? How many men and guns did you have?"

"We had four 32-pounders, and two 24-pounders, and forty-two men," was his reply, made with a blush.

"And do you realize what you have done, sir?" I asked.

"No," he said frankly, "I do not understand it at all."

"Well, sir, you and your forty-two men in your miserable little mud fort in the rushes, have captured two of our gunboats carrying sixteen guns, a good number of prisoners, many stands of small arms and plenty of good ammunition; and all that you have done with six popguns and two smart 'Quakers' [fake log cannons]. And that is not the worst of your boyish trick. You have sent three other gunboats, 6000 troops and a [U.S.] general out to sea in the dark. You ought to be ashamed of yourself, sir."

"What was the matter with your fellows, anyway?" he asked. "Why didn't they come up and take us, as we expected they would?"

"I am very sorry, sir, that you were disappointed. . . . My impression is that it was owing to a sudden attack of homesickness."[154]

DINING WITH CONFEDERATES

☛ By a masterly stratagem, a ragged private secured a seat at a table on which was spread a bountiful dinner, prepared especially for a pompous Confederate General. The officer made no objection, but wishing to be sure that the soldier knew what distinguished company was present, very condescendingly asked: "Do you know, Sir, with whom you are dining?" "Indeed I do not," answered the soldier, "I used to be particular about such matters, but now, so the dinner is good and abundant, I don't care a damn who eats with me."

You would have complimented me on my resemblance to that private had you seen me hobnobbing with [C.S.] General Jenkins last Christmas Eve. There was a symposium at his quarters, "a feast of reason and flow of soul," under the exhilarating influence of unlimited quantities of apple jack, and the Colonel and Inspector-General of the Division invited me and others of his old company to attend. After the third drink, a Brigadier-General sank in my estimation to the level of a private, and I sought and obtained an introduction to my host. He treated me with distinguished consideration, talked with me until I got sober enough to be ashamed of much that I had said, and invited me to call again. I alluded to a former interview with him concerning a hog that met death and destruction by my hands at Chattanooga, but he waived all further discussion of the subject, saying kindly: "That was official intercourse, Sir; this is purely social."[155]

A STORY OF THE LEES

☛ The visit of [C.S.] Gen. Fitzhugh Lee, says the *Louisville Courier Journal*, has started a story which he told on himself several years ago, and which is a good illustration of the love the Confederate soldiers bore toward Gen. Robert E. Lee. As it is well known, Gen. Fitzhugh Lee was at the head of the cavalry, and these were much envied by the infantry men, who had to walk through the mud and dust.

After Gen. Robert E. Lee had surrendered, Gen. Fitzhugh Lee rode away from Appomattox. While riding through a lane he met an old North Carolina soldier.

"Ho, there," cried General Lee, "where are you going?"

"I've been off on a furlough, and am now going back to join Gen. Bob Lee," replied the soldier.

"You needn't go back, but can throw your gun away and return home, for Lee's surrendered."

"Lee's surrendered?"

"That's what I said," said General Lee.

"It must have been that damned Fitz Lee, then. Rob Lee would never surrender," and the old soldier put on a look of contempt and walked on.[156]

CONFEDERATE GEN. WILLIAM WHITING & THE MUDHOLE

☛ [1862] We rested in the laurel thicket several days, during which the recruiting officers, who left us at Dumfries, rejoined the brigade, bringing batches of raw recruits and many letters from home folks. When the order came to march it was raining heavily and continued to rain until midnight. Troops were passing by for six or eight hours before we moved, and we were beginning to fear that Gen. Johnston proposed to make us a rear guard again. It was a great relief, therefore, to be marched a half mile further from the enemy and left standing in mud and water two full hours. Then we began a system of alternate marching and standing still until past midnight. By this time order and discipline were at an end. No one could tell who was next to him, the different commands having become inextricably intermixed in the darkness, rain and mud. Officers on horseback rode back and forth along the road, begging, praying and ordering the

EDMUND KIRBY SMITH, ONE OF THE EIGHT FULL GENERALS OF THE CONFEDERACY.

men to go forward as fast as possible and get across the Chickahominy Bridge. "If that's all you want me to do," thought I, "it shall be done," and, accordingly, I resolved myself into an independent command and set out for the bridge.

Near the bridge, and stretching from one side to the other of the road, was a terrible mudhole. Some provident fellow had hung a lantern near it, that disclosed not only its length and breadth, but a narrow way around it, and that way was being followed by the soldiers. [C.S.] Gen. Whiting and I reached the loblolly about the same time, but I was much the wiser man of the two. I followed the current, he endeavored to change it. "Go right through that place, men," he commanded. "It isn't deep." One of the soldiers, marching in single file around, said in the sarcastic tone so easily adopted in darkness and confusion: "You go through it yourself, Mr. Man, if you think it ain't deep." "Do you know, sir, that you are talking to Gen. Whiting?" angrily demanded the officer. "Maybe so," responded the unknown, now almost around the mudhole, and, at any rate, too far away to be identified, "but damned if I believe a word of it. You are more likely a courier, taking advantage of the darkness to order your betters around. If you are a General, you are a damned small one."

"Arrest that man!" shouted Whiting, furiously, so beside himself with rage that he spurred his horse into the hole and was splashed from head to foot with its contents. "Oh, dry up, you damned old fool," came back through the darkness, and in a moment more Whiting was laughing heartily at the ridiculous position into which he had put himself.[157]

"A MAIDEN FAIR" AT THE RETREAT FROM YORKTOWN
☛ [In May 1862, as my Regiment, 17th Mississippi,] was slowly defiling through the streets, away from the boom of cannon and the rattle of

small arms at the other end of town, "A maiden fair, with golden hair," rushed out from a splendid mansion and began to scold the soldier boys for going the wrong way. She cried, "Don't you hear the guns and the shoutings of the Captains, and don't you see they are pressing our boys hard in the battle? Turn back, men! turn back! and defend this old town, the cradle of American freedom!" and other fine things too numerous to mention. The boys trudged on, however, seemingly unmoved by the eloquence and ardor of this fair Amazon. Presently she sailed in again with "Turn back, men! turn back! and fight the Yankees as our forefathers fought the "red coats" along here! If your Captain won't lead you, I will be your Captain!"

Just at this juncture the command ran down along the lines: "About face and double quick!" Then arose the Rebel yell at the prospect of another tussle with the "blue boys." The fair heroine, all ablaze with excitement, rushed out of the gate to the head of the charging column, fully convinced that it was her patriotic appeal that had turned the tide backward in defense of her home. But all the ardor and enthusiasm was taken out of this Joan of Arc when one of the boys exclaimed "Oh no, sis, don't go—you might tear your dress!"

We left her standing mute and motionless, while the boys raised a yell in honor of "the girl we left behind us." She must have gray in her hair now, if she is still on this side of the River. Who she was I never knew—but here's to that dear woman in the "olden time and golden!"[158]

BILL CALHOUN AT 2ND MANASSAS

☛ [Oct. 1862] The day and night's work cost us the slight wounding of a few men, and the capture of Bill Calhoun, of Co. B, 4th Texas. This Bill Calhoun is an oddity of whom we are very proud. Always sad of countenance, there yet dwells in the recesses of his bosom a spirit of constantly effervescing drollery which now and then, and when least expected, bubbles over and explodes. His messmate and bedfellow is Davidge. Carrying out their plan of an equitable division of labor, Davidge, on the day we passed through Manassas Gap, was intrusted with the blankets, while Bill charged himself with the transportation of the provisions and limited culinary apparatus. Davidge straggled, and, when camp was reached at night, was *non est inventus*. Confident he would come soon, Bill prepared supper, and, Davidge still not appearing, ate it all himself, lighted his pipe, smoked and chatted a while; and, then remarking that Davidge would be along soon, stretched himself out on the bare ground to rest. But here in Virginia the nights are cool enough even in July to make covering acceptable, and though Bill endured the hardness of his couch, and the chilliness of the night with unbroken placidity until midnight, he could stand it no longer. Rising and standing erect in the midst of five thousand recumbent forms darkening the moonlit hillside, he broke into magniloquent apostrophe: "O, Davidge, Davidge! friend of my bosom and possessor of my blanket, where art thou, Davidge, this cold and comfortless night? Art thou indeed false to thy many professions—false to the sacred obligations of true and loyal friendship thou hast sworn—oblivious of duty, and forgetful of the friend who has confided to thee even the blanket on which he dependeth for protection from the chilling blasts of winter? Art thou now reclining peacefully and blissfully on some hospitable feather bed and dreaming of the joys that will come when this "cruel war is o'er," or, art thou beguiled and betrayed by the demon of intemperance, and a damnable thirst for apple-jack, wallowing like a hog in the dust before the door of some disreputable mountain stillhouse; while I, thy friend and messmate, thy boon companion in happiness and adversity, stand here alone—a homeless, houseless orphan, his wandering footsteps guided only by the pale light of yonder refulgent orb of night, his shivering body covered only by the blue canopy of the sky, and his restless slumber watched over only by the myriads of twinkling stars that shine in the heavens above me? Alas! Davidge, thou trusted friend, companion, and confidant of my youth and manhood, thou hast been weighed in the balance and found wanting. The surrounding and circumambient circumstances are proof strong as holy writ that I have been duped, deceived, outwitted, and ungratefully left to encounter the slings and arrows of misfortune alone and unsustained by any human aid." And dropping from the sublime to the ridiculous, Bill nudged the nearest man with his foot and said in a voice of entreaty that would have melted the hardest heart: "Say, Val Giles, let me get under the blanket with you; if you don't, I'll be a standing monument before morning of man's inhumanity to man."

I have told you this story to prepare you for that of Bill's capture, as related by a Confederate who was near enough to see and hear everything, but laid low and kept dark lest he, too, should be captured. It is so in keeping with Bill's unique character that no one doubts it. Bill was on the skirmish line, and, like myself, lost sight of his Confederate friends, and got too far to the front. Carrying his gun in both hands, with a finger on the hammer ready to cock it at the first glimpse of an enemy, he was suddenly brought to a halt by the harsh and totally unexpected command: "Surrender, you damned rebel; throw down your gun and surrender." Such language, followed as it was by the threatening click of half a dozen gunlocks, was not to be treated lightly. Bill's fingers simultaneously released their grip on his minie rifle, and it dropped, clanging to the hard, stony ground; then he looked to his right and saw, behind a clump of bushes he had almost passed, a squad of Yankees. They were within twenty feet of him, and one of them stood with cocked and leveled gun, directly at his breast. Bill was no fool; the enemy had the drop on him, and any appearance of hesitation on his part might be unhealthy. Therefore, he made haste to say, in a voice pitched at a key to be plainly heard: "Of course I surrender. Who the devil is talking about not surrendering?" The celerity with which the pun was dropped, the odd manner of surrendering, and the absurd question asked, set the Yankee to laughing at such a rate, that he forgot to lower his weapon, but kept it pointing in the general direction of the captive as warningly as his shaking sides would permit. Noticing this, Bill protested earnestly: "See here, mister; please quit pointing that gun at me. I've done surrendered, and the darned thing might go off unbeknownst to you." "O," answered the Yankee between bursts of laughter, but still failing to lower his gun, "I ain't a-goin' tor shoot you." "Mont as well shoot a feller at once as to scare him to death with a wobblin' gun," rejoined Bill. "Damned if I wasn't always afeared of a wobblin' gun; it's just as apt to hit as to miss."[159]

THE SOLDIER'S HYMNAL
☛ Reveille—"Christians, Awake!"
Prisoners call—"When the Roll Called Up Yonder I'll Be There."
Assembly—"Art Thou Weary?"
Inspection—"When He Cometh."
Setting up—"Here We Suffer Grief and Pain."
Route march—"Onward, Christian Soldiers."
Mess—"Come, Ye Thankful People, Come."
Fatigue detail—"Go, Labor On."
Lecture by officer—"Tell Me the Old, Old Story."
Retreat—"O Lord, How Happy We Should Be."
Lights out—"Peace, Perfect Peace."
Taps—"Sleep On, Beloved."[160]

FINK'S MARCHING CONFEDERATE GANDER
☛ A funny story told by a comrade was as follows: "[C.S. Gen.] Featherston's Brigade went into winter quarters at Snyder's Bluff, some miles back of Vicksburg, in the fall of 1862, and while there one day a soldier named Fink, who blew the trombone of the 3rd Mississippi's band, seeing a peddler with a gander and other fowls, bought the gander, so that his mess could enjoy a fat goose dinner. Fink, a tall, good-hearted German, had no idea of the age of the gander, so when he took it to his mess the boys told him that it was thirty years old. At last they made him believe this, so he concluded to keep the fowl. Next morning Fink went to his place of practise and began blowing his horn with usual vigor. He had fairly got 'down to business,' when he noticed his gander come wagging its body in a joyous way near his feet. The bird showed its admiration for music, and even quacked an accompaniment. Fink, much astonished, called his band fellows to him, and they all gazed at the bird's antics when the horn was blown. Toward the end of November, 1862, a grand review of all troops under [C.S. Gen.] Pemberton was held at Snyder's Bluff, and, among other bands that participated in it was the 3rd Mississippi's. When the reviewing officers came along the band filed out to precede them, and in front of all was Fink's gander doing the part of

drum-major in a style that can not be surpassed to-day by the best professionals in that line. The appearance of the gander, wagging its head and tail, quacking, and marching to time, started the men to snickering; the line of officers joined in, then came the staff officers, and at last even the generals were forced into roars of laughter. It became so general that the titter soon swelled into a continuous roar on the old-fashioned Rebel yell, and Fink and his gander were the heroes."[161]

COMEDY AMID TRAGEDY

☛ The dangers of a battle, and even the presence of death, never utterly destroy a soldier's sense of the ludicrous. Among the first men of the 4th to be wounded was Jim Summerville. A bullet struck the buckle of his belt, and barely penetrated the skin; but one's stomach is very sensitive. Jim dropped his gun, folded his arms across the front of his corporosity, and, whirling around a couple of times, gave vent to a long-drawn, emphatic groan with all the variations of the gamut in it, which provoked a roar of laughter from the regiment. It was not insensibility to suffering or lack of sympathy which caused the merriment, but an irresistible desire to extract a little comedy out of deadly tragedy. In such critical emergencies men have no time to waste in bewailing what has happened; what may happen is far more important. Sympathy given every unfortunate would unnerve those on whose coolness and presence of mind depend the fate of battle. The wounded soldier has taken his risk and lost; that of his comrade is yet to be run, and who knows but that it may be death?[162]

TEXANS WON'T BE "STATIONARY TARGETS"

☛ [Oct. 1863] The battle of Chickamauga was fought, as you know, on the 19th and 20th days of last month. The Texas Brigade got into position early on the morning of the 19th, and during the balance of that long and struggling day the booming of artillery and the roar of small arms on its right and left was incessant and terrific. Judging alone from the noise, it appeared to us that every man of both armies must soon be wounded or killed, and we wondered much why the sound of the firing seemed neither to recede nor advance, and why there was none of the yelling to which we had been accustomed in Virginia. And when at last it was learned that the opposing lines were simply standing two or three hundred yards apart, firing at each other as fast as guns could be loaded and triggers pulled, comments were many and ludicrous—the consensus of opinion being that such a method of fighting would not suit troops which in Virginia were accustomed to charge the enemy at sight. One brave fellow said, and voiced the sentiment of all: "Boys, if we have to stand in a straight line as stationary targets for the Yankees to shoot at with a rest, this old Texas brigade is going to run like hell."[163]

NOT THE ANSWER HE WAS LOOKING FOR

☛ Members of the naval board were examining young applicants for appointment to a naval college. "Well," said an old admiral to one of the youths, "what must an officer be before he can have a funeral with full naval honors." "Dead," answered the bright youth.[164]

YANKS PICKING ON BOYS FROM THE PALMETTO STATE

☛ . . . The Federals charge them [South Carolinians] with being the instigators and beginners of the war, and, as I am informed, always exclude them from the benefit of truces between the pickets. It is certainly an odd spectacle to see the Carolinians hiding in their rifle pits and not daring to show their heads, while not fifty feet away, the Texans sit on the ground playing poker, in plain view and within a hundred yards of the Yankees. Worse than all, the palmetto fellows are not even permitted to visit us [Texans] in daylight, except in disguise—their new uniforms of gray always betraying them wherever they go. One of them who is not only very fond of, but successful at the game of poker, concluded the other day to risk being shot for the chance of winning the money of the First Texas and, divesting himself of his coat, slipped over to the Texas pit an hour before daylight, and by sunup was giving his whole mind to the noble pastime. An hour later, a keen-sighted Yankee sang out: "Say, you Texas Johnnies! ain't that fellow playing cards with his back to a sapling one of them damned South Carolina secessionists? Seems to me his breeches are newer'n they ought to be." This direct appeal for information placed the Texans between the horns of a dilemma;

VARINA ANNE "WINNIE" DAVIS, DAUGHTER OF CONFEDERATE PRESIDENT JEFFERSON DAVIS.

hospitality demanded the protection of their guest—prudence, the observance of good faith towards the Yankees. The delay in answering obviated the necessity for it by confirming the inquirer's suspicions and, exclaiming, "Damn him, I just know it is," he [the Yank] raised his gun quickly to his shoulder and fired. The South Carolinian was too active though; at the very first movement of the Yankee, he sprang ten feet and disappeared into a gulch that protected him from further assault.[165]

CHAPTER FIVE

SHENANIGANS UNDER CONFEDERATE GENERAL MAGRUDER
☛ . . . while lying in winter quarters at Spradley's farm, on the banks of
the James River, near the town of Williamsburg, the Louisianians in the
battalion proposed to give the denizens of that region an idea of what a
Mardi Gras celebration was in the Crescent City. Materials were not
very numerous in that day, but, with the assistance of the citizens of
Williamsburg, some two hundred New Orleans boys got up a wonderful
procession, rigged out in as fantastic a manner as it was possible to
accomplish. The celebration closed with an entertainment given to Gen.
Magruder and his staff at an inn in Williamsburg by the members of the
battalion. [Confederate soldier] . . . Ned Phelps . . . was a leader in that
affair. Another member of the battalion from New Orleans, Billy
Campbell (who likewise passed away only a few, years ago), was a
splendid make-up of a young girl. Campbell was perfection in this
regard, it being almost impossible to detect that he was not a girl.
Leaning upon the arm of Ned Phelps, Campbell entered the apartment
where Magruder was dining in the Virginia hostelry, and was introduced
to the General by his friend Ned as Miss Campbell, of New Orleans, on
a visit to her brother, a member of the battalion. The scene was most
ludicrous to those who were acquainted with the joke. Magruder, with
that gallantry which always characterized him, placed "Miss" Campbell
on his right hand, who partook liberally of everything that was going,
including the liquors. How far this thing would have gone on it is
difficult to say, had not some of the boys ripped up a feather bed
belonging to the landlord of the hotel and permitted its contents to fall
through an aperture immediately above the dining room, calling out at
the same time: "This is a Louisiana snowstorm." During the snowstorm
Ned and "Miss" Campbell took their departure, leaving the General in
doubt as to whether he had been in the company of a live lady or a
spook.[166]

IRISH COUNTERSIGNING
☛ The demand for countersigns [code words and phrases] in war-times
often resulted ludicrously. . . . While Col. Gillam, with a Middle
Tennessee regiment, was occupying Nashville he stationed sentries in the
principal streets. One day an Irishman, who, not long enlisted, was put
on duty, kept a sharp watch. Presently a citizen came along. "Halt! Who
goes there?"

"A citizen," was the response.

"Advance and give the countersign."

" I have not the countersign," replied the citizen.

"Well, begorrah! ye don't pass this way until ye say 'Bunker Hill.'"

The citizen, appreciating the situation, smiled, and advanced to the sentry and cautiously whispered the magic words. "Right! pass on!" and the sentinel resumed his beat.[167]

BATTLE OF THE WASPS

☛ On that hot Sunday afternoon, July 21, 1861, three regiments which had been supporting the center were rapidly transformed to the Confederate left, which had no sooner been reached and the alinement perfected than they were ordered forward at quick time. The bullets of the enemy were whizzing past or knocking up the dirt in our front. The advance of the regiment to which I belonged was through a pasture with occasional bunches of persimmon sprouts, say two years old. Just as we received the order to double-quick a bunch of these persimmon sprouts was encountered by the first company to the right of the colors and in it there was a wasps' nest. The boys were hot, and the wasps were easily angered, and instantly at least fifty men broke ranks (without permission), and were running in every direction, fighting this new enemy with their hats. Our colonel, seeing the panic, rushed into the breach, and at once the angry wasps attacked his horse, and soon the performance was at its height. The colonel, being a large, portly man, although a fine lawyer, was a poor horseman. The scene was ludicrous in the extreme, and, as a comrade told me next day at Stone Bridge: "It beat a circus."[168]

DISAPPEARING PANTS

☛ Ben F. Loftin, who gave a leg to the Confederacy, writes . . . of the scenes that transpired around Fort Donelson, February, 1862: My Regiment (the 32nd Tennessee) supported Graves' Battery on the right, the left of the regiment being in the ditches under the guns. After completing our breastworks, I kneeled down in the ditch, with my head resting against a wheel of Graves' rifle, to take a nap. I had slept long enough for my clothes to freeze to the ground, when the cannon was discharged at a sharpshooter. I jumped up, minus part of my pants, wondering what was the matter. The boys had the laugh on me. Pants were scarce; after dark I drew another pair, but don't tell how I got them.[169]

THE FELLOW WHO SERVED AS A BRIDGE

☛ [After the close of a successful fight against the Yanks:] One poor fellow was too sore, downcast, and trampled upon to be joyful. He was a litter-bearer named D_____, six long feet in height and Falstaffian in abdominal development. His position in the rear gave him the start in the retreat and his avoirdupois enabled him to brush aside every obstacle to rapid descent. But his judgment was disastrously at fault. Forgetting a ditch which marked the division line of descent of one hill and ascent of the other, he tumbled into it broadcast. The fall knocked all the breath out of him, and he could only wriggle over on his broad back and make a pillow for his head of one bank and a resting-place for his number twelve feet of the other, so that his body appeared as the trunk of a fallen tree. Scarcely, however, had he assumed this comfortable position when Bill Calhoun came plunging down the hill with a velocity that left a good-sized vacuum in the air behind him. Noticing the litter-bearer's body, and taking it to be what it appeared, Bill took the chances of its spanning the ditch and made such a tremendous leap that he landed one huge

BUST OF CONFEDERATE GENERAL ROBERT EDWARD LEE, PRESENTED TO THE MILITARY SCHOOL OF ENGLAND.

foot right in the middle of the unfortunate recumbent's corporosity. The sudden compression produced a sudden artificial respiration, and, giving vent to an agonized grunt, D_____ sang out: "For the Lord Almighty's sake, man, don't make a bridge of a fellow!"

Bill was startled, but never lost his presence of mind, and shouting back, "Lie still, old fellow, lie still! The whole regiment's got to cross yet, and you'll never have such another chance to serve your beloved country," he continued his flight with a speed but little abated by the rising ground before him.[170]

THE BEE-LINE
☛ A private on picket duty, under orders to allow no one to pass inside the Confederate lines without giving the countersign, was approached by his brigadier-general, who asked: "What would you do, sir, were you to see a man coming up that road toward you?"

"I should wait, General," said the private, "until he came within twenty feet of me, and then halt him and demand the countersign."

"Very good, very good," commented the General; "but suppose twenty men approached by the same road, what would you do then?"

"Halt them before they got nearer than a hundred feet, sir, and, covering them with my gun, demand that the officer in command approach and give the countersign."

"Ah! my brave fellow," began the General in his most flattering voice; "I see that you are remarkably well posted concerning your duties. But let me put still another case. Suppose a whole regiment were coming in this direction, what would you do in that case?"

"Form a line immediately, sir," answered the private unhesitatingly and without a smile.

"Form a line? form a line?" repeated the officer in his most contemptuous tone. "What kind of line, I should like to know, could a single man form?"

"A bee-line for camp, sir," explained the picket.[171]

FEELING FOR A FURLOUGH

☛ . . . there was both sense and philosophy in the behavior of a Confederate at Chickamauga. When the battle was at its height and the bullets flying thickest he stepped behind a tree, and, while protecting his body, extended his arms on each side and waved them frantically to and fro, up and down.

"What in the dickens are you doing, Tom?" asked an astonished comrade.

"Just feeling for a furlough," replied Tom without a blush, and continuing the feeling process as if his life depended upon it.

While few soldiers actually seek wounds of any character, fewer still regard a parlor wound—that breaks no bones, yet disables one temporarily, and requires time, rest, and nursing to heal it—as any very serious misfortune. Such accidents necessitate furloughs, and these the ladies of the South, by their kindness to both the sick and the well, have made blessings to be hoped for, prayed for, and—within safe and patriotic limits—struggled for.

"Why, sir, that handsome widow and her curly-haired daughter couldn't have been kinder to a son or a brother. They gave me the pleasantest room in the house, brought my meals to it, fed me on chicken and sweet cream with their own hands, dressed my wound half a dozen times a day, and were always ready to play and sing for me or read and talk to me. I wanted to stay a month longer, but my darned old finger healed in spite of me." That, and a great deal more to the same purport, was said by Lieut. L_____ when he returned to duty after losing half the nail of his little finger at Sharpsburg, getting a furlough on the strength of it, and, fortunately, falling into the hands of a wealthy and patriotic Virginia lady. Can you blame a poor fellow if, after listening to such a story, he is a little inclined to "feel for a furlough?"[172]

INCIDENTS AROUND FLORENCE, ALABAMA

☛ Reporting to [C.S.] Gen. Gibson what we saw, it was proposed that I take a force out there and find out the enemy's movements without bringing on a fight, if possible. Next morning I moved out the Nashville pike with one hundred and fifty men—fifty each of the Louisiana, Georgia, and Alabama Brigades—with twenty-four hours' rations. When near the Wilson house I had the battalion to make a detour in the rear of the house and come out on the big road where the Yankees left it the day before, and I rode with some officers up to Mr. Wilson's to find out what they had heard about the chase. Mr. Wilson and his grandson, Willie, were delighted to see us, and said that the Yankees were badly put out by not charging on us when we were at the house, but they said: "We will catch that fellow yet." Willie said to them: "No, you won't; that is the man that drove you all out of Florence." They asked his name, but Willie had forgotten it.

We soon moved toward Shoal Creek, and lay on our arms all night, allowing no fires. Next morning the Louisiana squad was posted opposite the foot of the big hill, and about fifty to seventy-five feet to the right, in a dense undergrowth, completely hid from view. The other squads went with me toward Bailey Springs. When near there a young lady told me that the Yankees were barbecuing meat in a lot close by. I dismounted, and, with one man, crept as close to the lot as we could, and fired at, but missed, a picket. The report of the Enfield was enough, and away went pickets and cooks, leaving us in full possession of nice, sweet, barbecued mutton, pork, and beef, and we made requisition on all that we could carry away. Soon after this we heard considerable firing in the direction of the big road. Away we went at a double-quick, and, on reaching the Louisiana squad,

A "MOTHER OF THE CONFEDERACY": MRS. OLIVIA POOSER OF SOUTH CAROLINA (REAR CENTER), WITH HER DAUGHTER, GRANDDAUGHTER, GREAT-GRANDDAUGHTER, AND GREAT-GREAT-GRANDDAUGHTER. FIVE GENERATIONS OF CONFEDERATE AMERICANS, CIRCA 1924.

learned that a company of cavalry came down the road, just as on the day before, anticipating no danger, laughing and talking as they rode into the jaws of death. When in good range the infantry that lay in ambush opened a deadly fire on them, causing many to bite the dust, while their horses were taken possession of by the boys who were fortunate enough to capture them. Those who escaped went back to their camp and reported "the woods full of Rebels."

The shades of evening were drawing near, and, having had enough fun for one day, we started back to camp with a better supply of horses than we usually had and with more barbecued meat than generally falls to a soldier's lot. [173]

HOW YANKEE CIVIL WAR "HISTORY" IS CREATED

☛ "Strange," murmured the magazine editor, "that this anecdote about Lincoln in his early days has never been in print before." "It isn't strange at all," returned the contributor with some indignation. "I just thought it up last night."[174]

THE WIT & HUMOR OF GENERAL FORREST

☛ [1897] If one should examine current history and biography to obtain a correct estimate of Gen. Forrest's life and character, only the bitterest disappointment would result. A central figure in the great martial drama of the war between the states, as can be plainly seen in the multitude of reports and dispatches penned during the contest by the leading commanders of both armies, he has been neglected in a marvelous degree since its close by the busy so-called historians and biographers, in accordance with their own peculiar views.

In some of these volumes he is dismissed with slight mention; in others, as, for instance, a certain encyclopedia of American biography, he is pictured as an "illiterate cutthroat and butcher." And even in a leading school history, printed in the South and used in most of the educational institutions in this community, we find in the whole book only this historical tribute to the man whom [U.S.] Gen. Sheridan pronounced one of the most remarkable produced by the war on either side: "N. B. Forrest and John Morgan—famous for their raids in the West." And this the man whom Lord Wolseley, the commander of the British Army, thought worthy of the careful study of great soldiers, and to whose military career and skill he paid, in a long analytical article, a glowing tribute.

Only in a little volume entitled, *Campaigns of Forrest and Forrest's Cavalry,* published in 1867, by Gen. Thomas Jordan and J. P. Pryor, is there a fairly correct statement of Forrest's military career; and this book was written by gentlemen entirely capable, but who were not eyewitnesses of the great cavalry leader's achievements, and therefore loses greatly in graphic detail and description.

I therefore feel it to be a sacred duty of those who are familiar with any part of his career to contribute while still living their mites to rescue the story of this remarkable man from oblivion. The late lamented Maj. Rambaut, of Forrest's Staff, had undertaken this task for the Confederate Historical Association, of Memphis, but was cut off after his second article by an untimely death—a mishap greatly to be deplored, as he was an accomplished and accurate writer and a companion of the noted general throughout the war.

But to revert to my subject. Few people except advanced in life and who had met Forrest before his death, which occurred nearly twenty years ago [in 1877], have a correct idea of his personal appearance and distinguished presence; and of these few, only those who have seen him in battle have any adequate conception of the heroic mold and fiery energy of this equestrian son of Mars. Tall beyond his fellows, of herculean build, broad shoulders surmounted by a massive head, dark gray hair, keen gray eyes, which blazed when lighted with the fire of battle, he was instantly recognized, even by strangers, as the commander of his army, and was as well known by sight to Federal as to Confederate soldiers. His face was peculiarly intellectual and his features strongly marked, the expanding nostrils and massive jaw indicating impetuous energy and overwhelming will power.

In the company of other distinguished officers he showed to the greatest advantage. Grave, dignified, unobtrusive, he was ever alert, and, when his opinion was asked, the lightning was not quicker. His ideas were tersely, lucidly, and briefly delivered, and he at once relapsed into silence. He never resorted to argument. His manner, while respectful, was almost imperious at such moments. The incident at Fort Donelson is richly illustrative of the character of the man under such circumstances. He, then a colonel of cavalry, being called upon by the council of war for an opinion, pointed out that it was the duty of the three generals to withdraw their commands by a road which he indicated, instead of surrendering them to the enemy; and, his advice being rejected, he curtly told them that he would rather that the bones of his men should bleach on the hills than to surrender them. He strode from the room to withdraw his command from the fort by the route indicated, which he successfully accomplished without losing a man.

But to the rank and file Forrest was a delight. He was absolutely approachable at all times to the humblest soldier. When not absorbed in thought or engaged in combat he indulged constantly in playful familiarity and exchange of *badinage* with his men, as did also the great Napoleon. No general officer ever dreamed of taking liberties with his hair-trigger temper. No private soldier in his ranks ever hesitated for an instant to jest him about any trivial matter or to guy him about his personal appearance or unusual actions, even in battle.

On one occasion, at Richland Creek, Tenn., when the enemy's artillery was hurling shells like handfuls of marbles about us, the General coolly dismounted and stepped behind the only tree in the vicinity, a movement which all of us longed to make, but dared not in his presence. One of the men said to him: "Come out from behind that tree, General. That isn't fair; we haven't got trees." "No, but you only wish you had," laughingly replied Forrest. "You only want me out to get my place."

On another occasion, at Mount Carmel, Gen. Forrest dismounted under a hot fire of musketry, and sat down on a rock, an example which was quickly followed by the writer, who was attending him, and who took care to get down on the opposite side of his horse from the enemy. The General, who had begun feeding his warhorse, "King Philip," with some blades of fodder he found there, turned, and, observing my point of vantage, playfully said, "You had better get on the other side of that horse, bud, and stop the bullets. Horses are lots scarcer than men out here"—a suggestion, by the way, that was not followed.

But there were two liberties which no one, private or general, ever attempted to take with Forrest. One was to disobey his orders, and the other to abandon the field in the presence of the enemy. Either of these breaches of soldierly conduct instantly brought down upon the offender a wrath that was truly frightful. On one occasion he seized a piece of brushwood and thrashed an officer whom he detected running away from the field almost to the point of taking his life.

Col. D. C. Kelley, major of his first regiment, wrote: "The command found that it was his single will, impervious to argument, appeal, or threat, which was ever to be the governing impulse in their movements. Everything necessary to supply their wants, to make them comfortable, he was quick to do, save to change his plans, to which everything had to bend. New men naturally grumbled and were dissatisfied in the execution, but when the work was achieved they were soon reconciled by the pride they felt in the achievement."

SOUTHERN ICON CONFEDERATE GENERAL NATHAN BEDFORD FORREST, AFTER THE WAR.

Gen. Forrest always exhibited the profoundest regard for religion. Col. Kelley, then and still a preacher, relates that Gen. (then colonel) Forrest and himself were intimately associated in camp for the first year or more of the war, tenting together, during which time Col. Kelley continued his lifelong habit of holding morning and evening prayers. These services Gen. Forrest always reverently attended, though not at the time a member of any Church. However, he became a very devout member of the Cumberland Presbyterian Church some years after the war.

After returning from his successful expedition into West Tennessee, in May, 1864, he immediately issued the following most unusual General Order No. 44: "Headquarters Forrest's Cavalry Department, Tupelo, May 14, 1864. The major-general commanding, devoutly grateful to the providence of Almighty God, so signally vouchsafed to his command during the recent campaign in West Tennessee, and deeply penetrated with a sense of our dependence upon the mercy of God in the present crisis of our beloved country, requests that military duties be so far suspended that divine service may be attended at 10 a.m. on to-morrow by the whole command. Divine service will be held at these headquarters, to which all soldiers who are disposed to do so are kindly invited. Come one, come all. Chaplains in the ministrations of the gospel are requested to remember our personal preservation with thanksgiving, and especially to beseech the throne of God for aid in this our country's hour of need. By order of Maj.-Gen. Forrest. W. H. Brand, Acting Assistant Adj.-Gen."

To ladies Forrest was instinctively knightly and deferential. A man of singular purity of life and absolutely temperate, he held woman in the highest regard, and lavished a degree of affection upon his devoted wife altogether unusual in a man of his fiery temperament. Only under peculiar circumstances did he seem to become oblivious of the presence of ladies, and that was during those fits of intense absorption in thought into which he so often lapsed when working out the great military problems which engaged his attention. On these occasions his staff discreetly withdrew to a distance and left him undisturbed. As soon as he had arranged matters in his mind he would rejoin his staff and at once proceed to chaff them in a vein of pleasantry. Once, while thus absorbed on a railroad car, as related by Maj. Rambaut, a lady, against the protest of the staff, insisted on going back and interviewing him. In a moment the stately dame returned in a towering rage, declaring that the General was not a man, but a bear. A few moments later he came forward, and with cleft politeness not only pacified, but captivated the offended matron. Presently, struck by a peculiarity of his appearance, she suddenly asked: "General, why is it that your hair is so much grayer than your beard?" As if with some faint recollection of his recent misbehavior, he quaintly replied: "I don't know, madam, unless it be that my mouth is always shut when my head is working."

On another occasion, as related by the venerable Mrs. John McGavock, of [Carnton Plantation at] Franklin, during the storm of the great battle there, Gen. Forrest rode rapidly up to her door, where she had gone to meet him, and, without so much as seeming to notice that she was there, strode by her into the hall, up the stairway, and out on the balcony, where he gazed intently through his glass for ten minutes at the enemy's position, and then returned in the same way to his horse, without paying the slightest attention to her presence, and rode rapidly away.

But another incident, related by Col. D. C. Kelley, vividly exhibits Gen. Forrest in another mood. When campaigning with his regiment in the vicinity of Fort Donelson the men captured some Federals who were known as bushwhackers by our men, as they operated in the country where they enlisted. The wife of one of these prisoners, seeing her husband in captivity, rushed out to where Col. Forrest was standing and, falling on her knees, appealed to him for his release. Col. Kelley witnessed this incident from a distance, and, observing the woman spring from the ground and clap her hands, questioned Col. Forrest about the unusual scene when he came up. The Colonel replied with rather unsteady voice: "They can have their husbands if I've got them—that is, if they will make them behave."

When in camp Forrest's restless mind was ever busy with the details of organization. Nothing escaped his attention, and no one, since the days of Napoleon, could more quickly equip an army or form a powerful military force out of raw recruits. In speaking of this marvelous power of organizing his raw West Tennessee volunteers later in the war, Gen. Thomas Jordan says: "In that short time (sixty days) he had been able to imbue them with his ardent, indomitable spirit and mold them into the most formidable instruments in his hands for his manner of making war."

Another characteristic of the man was his boundless fertility of resource when in close places. On one occasion, on crossing the Tennessee River, he found himself in a rough, rocky country, with unshod horses. At once he was at a standstill, for the horses could not march on the sharp rocks, and there was no material with which to make shoes. Encamping for the night, he at once sent details throughout the country to bring in all the old wagon and buggy tires that could be found at the farmhouses and barns around. Putting his smiths to work with this material, by morning he had all his horses splendidly shod and resumed the march without delay.

On another occasion, when on his rapid march of one hundred miles to attack Memphis, in August, 1864, he learned, when nearing Coldwater River, that that stream was out of its banks and that no bridge or ferry existed. Without apparent hesitation details were made, with instructions to scatter through the country, take up the heavy plank floors of the ginhouses, and meet him at the river with the planks, which the troopers carried on

THE "BOY HERO OF THE CONFEDERACY," SAM DAVIS.

their horses. He then hurried forward with some axmen, felled the telegraph poles near by and the large trees on the river bank, and, rolling the logs into the stream, secured them with such ropes as he had, supplemented with grapevines, and, laying the planks first as stringers and then across, soon had a substantial floating bridge ready, over which his command marched with scarcely a halt when they arrived.

In battle Forrest was the very genius of war. Habitually riding a large gray horse, "King Philip," of great spirit, his towering form was seen everywhere on the field. At the investment of Murfreesboro, in December, 1864, it was the writer's fortune to witness one of those characteristic but unconscious displays of martial heroism by Gen. Forrest of surpassing grandeur. He had posted a division of infantry to meet a daring sortie of the Federal garrison, and, taking a cavalry brigade, had sought the enemy's rear. Learning that the infantry had given way, he came bounding back on his grand horse, and, pausing a moment, rose in his stirrups to survey the scene. Then, throwing off his military cape, his saber flashed in the air, and, seizing a flag, he plunged, with blazing eyes, into the mass of fleeing men, right under the awful fire of the enemy's guns, staying the stampede by sheer force of will power, and rider and horse presenting a picture in the terrible tragedy it were worth all the perils of the battle to have witnessed.

In war he was always aggressive, never waiting to receive an attack, but, after a rapid personal reconnaissance, invariably hurling his whole command on the enemy. He seemed at all times imbued with

> That fierce fever of the steel,
> The guilty madness warriors feel,

even to the point of unreasoning rashness. But there was method in his madness, and no charge was ever made by Forrest that was not justified by the outcome.

It is stated that he was one hundred and seventy-nine times personally under fire in his four years of service, and it was rare that he suffered a check, never a defeat. His constant successes against almost incredible odds inspired his men with unbounded confidence in him, and he was thus enabled to hurl his unquestioning brigades like thunderbolts upon his less active enemy, and always with disastrous results to the latter. Nor was this all. Without training, but by instinct a very master of the art of war, he was quick to see an enemy's vulnerable point, and concentrating with marvelous rapidity would strike the deadly blow before his opponent could correct the mistake. Brice's Cross Roads, or Guntown, was a type of one of his battles. Having but three thousand and two hundred cavalry, and his enemy, [U.S. Gen.] Sturgis, moving on the rich stores of grain about Tupelo with eight thousand and three hundred men, of which five thousand were infantry, Forrest, who was watching on the flank, observed that Sturgis' Army was marching in a straggling column of eight or ten miles in length along a narrow, muddy road, and impeded with enormous wagon trains. Quickly conceiving his plan of action, Forrest galloped his command to the head of the Federal column, and, concentrating in front of the enemy's first brigade, a cavalry force about fifteen hundred strong, by a common impulsion threw his whole command upon it and crushed it before help arrived. Attacking in turn the succeeding brigades of cavalry and infantry as they arrived and took position—the latter so exhausted by a double-quick march for miles in the mud under a hot June sun that they could not at once begin the fight—they were successively crushed, and by 3 p.m., after five hours' fighting, the whole mighty host of Sturgis was a defeated and flying rabble, run down and captured by hundreds as they scattered. So great was the terror inspired by the furious energy of their pursuer that the Federal commanders report that the flying fragment of infantry covered the entire distance to Collierville, Tenn., ninety miles, in a little over forty hours, leaving all their trains and artillery and more than one-third of their force dead, wounded, or captured, in Forrest's hands. No such annihilating overthrow overtook any other command of either army during the war.

But it is not my purpose to describe Forrest's battles in detail, and I will present only a brief synopsis of his military career. Gen. Forrest joined the Confederate army June 14, 1861, at Memphis, as a private soldier in Capt. Josiah White's Tennessee Mounted Rifles, afterwards Company D, 7th Tennessee Cavalry. His career as a private soldier was uneventful for about a month, but was rendered notable among his comrades by his constant and lucid criticism of the current military movements of the great armies. Having been authorized, in July, 1861, by Gov. Harris, of Tennessee, to raise a command, he at once went to work, and by October had, with characteristic energy, raised a battalion, and soon after a regiment, of which he was elected colonel.

With this regiment of dare-devils he soon became famous, and at Fort Donelson, Shiloh, and Murfreesboro, where he earned his promotion, he gained a distinction never before enjoyed by an American cavalry commander. As a brigadier-general, he rose rapidly in public esteem, gaining great distinction at Chickamauga, and, during the Streight raid, capturing that daring Federal commander and eighteen hundred men with less than three hundred of his own troopers.

But it was in his characteristic operations in Tennessee, on the enemy's lines of communication—destroying railroads, capturing blockhouses and garrisons, with thousands of prisoners and hundreds of wagons, teams, etc.—that he became the terror of the Federal generals. "If I could only match him," wrote [U.S.] Gen. Sherman, "with a man of equal energy and sagacity, all my troubles would end."

"WITH FATE AGAINST THEM."

However, it was only when Forrest was given a cavalry department with the rank of major-general, his district embracing North Mississippi and West Tennessee, that he attained the utmost splendor of his renown. Here he was made guardian of the granary of the Confederacy, the rich prairie lands of Eastern Mississippi and Central Alabama. Having a domain without troops, he rode straightway with a small force through the enveloping Federal lines into West Tennessee, and, collecting several thousand hardy young volunteers, mostly well-grown boys, he mustered them in a few weeks into that famous band which, with some veteran troops collected together, is now known to history as Forrest's Cavalry.

The Federal commander at Memphis, Hurlbut, who had thousands of men guarding the railroad from Memphis to Corinth, was superseded by [U.S.] Gen. Washburn because of his failure to prevent Forrest's movement into and return from West Tennessee with his recruits and supplies. In February [U.S.] Gen. Washburn sent Gen. William Sooey Smith, with a powerful force of seven thousand men, to find Forrest and punish him for his impertinence, and, incidentally, to destroy the great grain stores about Okolona. Forrest fell upon him with his new recruits, about three thousand strong, at Okolona and Prairie Mound, and utterly routed his great host, driving it back to Memphis. In return Gen. Forrest rode again into West Tennessee, penetrating to the Ohio River and capturing Fort Pillow, Union City, and other points, with their garrisons.

After his return, in June, Gen. Sturgis, with eighty-five hundred men, marched against the grain fields in Eastern Mississippi, and at Brice's Cross Roads, or Guntown, was fallen upon by Forrest and annihilated, losing more than one-third of his force with all his artillery and equipage.

Sturgis was followed in turn by [U.S.] Gen. A. J. Smith, with fourteen thousand men, who, after a terrible battle with Forrest at Harrisburg, near Tupelo, July 14, returned hastily to Memphis. Enraged by his defeat, Gen. Smith reorganized at Memphis and started again, in August, by way of Oxford, with a powerful army. Forrest, with his exhausted command, was unable to check this army by force, and resorted to strategy. Leaving half his force under [C.S.] Gen. Chalmers in front of Smith at Oxford, he rode with the remainder, less than two thousand men, by way of Panola—one hundred miles, in less than sixty hours—to Memphis, capturing the city, and almost capturing Gen. Washburn, getting his uniform, hat, boots, and papers in the residence. This caused [U.S.] Gen. Hurlbut to remark, as related by Gen. Chalmers: "There it goes again. They removed me because I could not keep Forrest out of West Tennessee, while Washburn can't keep him out of his bedroom."

The movement, however, as Gen. Forrest anticipated, resulted in the rapid retreat of Gen. Smith again to Memphis. Then for a period Forrest, gathering his forces, roamed at will over Middle Tennessee, destroying the Federal railroad lines and trains and capturing garrisons; and, though finally enveloped by thousands of the enemy, escaping across the Tennessee River with rich spoil. Then, riding leisurely down the west brink of that stream to Johnsonville, more than one hundred miles, he destroyed the enemy's great depot of supplies there, with more than six million dollars' worth of property and their gunboat fleet—"a feat of arms," wrote Gen. Sherman, "which I must confess excited my admiration."

Next followed perhaps the grandest achievement of Forrest's military career. [C.S.] Gen. Hood had moved on Nashville, fighting his way to the Tennessee capital, with Forrest in advance, and had rashly risked a battle with a foe outnumbering him two and one-half to one, and been defeated. His army, for the first time in its history was routed and disorganized. Halting at Columbia, he sent for Gen. Forrest and appointed him commander of his little, hastily formed rear guard. There were two thousand infantry, picked men, and fifteen hundred cavalry, but every man was a hero. With these Forrest calmly undertook to hold in check the victorious Federal army of nearly seventy thousand men, and so he did. Backward, step by step, from Columbia to the Tennessee River, for eight days and nights, did Forrest and his Spartan band hold back the eager enemy, while Hood's routed columns gathered at and crossed over the river.

In vain did the great blue masses essay to break over this slender barrier and get at Hood, by crushing whom they could speedily end the war in the West. Forrest's mailed hand was everywhere, and struck sturdy, deadly blows, which paralyzed every effort of their advance guard to break through his lines. The weather was bitter cold and the sleet came down, while the roads were streams of freezing water; but the ragged, barefoot heroes and their grand leader never faltered. The enemy were delayed until Hood's last men and wagons were across the river, and finally the little rear guard, cut and slashed and weather-beaten, crossed at midnight with their indomitable leader, to rest in safety beyond. This masterly achievement has only its parallel in the heroic Ney, who covered Napoleon's beaten columns in the retreat from Russia.

Such was the great leader whom Memphis gave to the Confederate army.

And now one word about duty. Out in beautiful Elmwood, with only a plain circlet of marble to mark the spot, sleep the remains of this great soldier. No marble shaft there points to heaven, with scroll or tablet to tell the passer-by: "Here rests a hero." Only a sprig of oak carved on the circle tells of his fame. Thoughtless thousands, in whose interest and for whose benefit his mighty deeds were done, pass daily to and fro about this city without giving a thought to his history or a tribute to his fame. O shame upon our people! If we cannot, like the appreciative Roman populace, bring his [proposed] statue to stand in our beautiful square, I urge that at least in the great Battle Abbey about to be erected Memphis build into the wall a tablet that will rescue from oblivion the name and fame of the greatest cavalry leader perhaps that the world has ever seen.[175]

THE YANKEE BULLET

☞ Bill Calhoun always finds some compensation for an injury inflicted upon him by the Yankees in a joke on a Confederate. Some weeks ago a bullet buried itself in the fleshy part of his thigh, and, after gouging it out with his fingers, he limped back to the rear. There encountering a surgeon new in the business of attending to gunshot wounds—in fact, a gentleman whose practise at home had ceased to be lucrative enough to support him, and who had recently decided to take pay from the Confederate Government for the exercise of his limited abilities—Bill thought it prudent to have the wound examined. The surgeon probed here and cut a little there, until patience, fortitude, and silence ceased to be virtues. "What the are you carving me up so for, doctor?" inquired the victim.

"I am searching for the ball," explained the doctor.

"Searching for the ball?" exclaimed Bill with inimitably sarcastic inflection of voice, as, diving with one hand into a pocket, he produced a battered piece of lead and held it out. "Here it is, if that's all you want."[176]

HUNDREDS OF YANKEES DESERTED EACH NIGHT

☛ For the first week or ten days after we took over the defense of this part of General Lee's line the enemy pickets conducted themselves very gentlemanly. They were very anxious to have some intercourse with us and often invited us to come over and exchange commodities with them; but that was a very dangerous business and depended entirely upon the humor of the officer in command of the pickets whether a visitor from our side ever came back. One night shortly after I was put on this duty the enemy in front of me asked me to come over and have a talk, giving their word and honor as Irishmen that they would let me return. But I could not accept, as I knew that if I did I should be violating my instructions and if detained would be considered a deserter. Between the picket lines was a low place in which there were a few scrubby willows. A slight depression extended up from this to my pit. One dark night as I sat there peering out into the darkness, with my gun ready for use, I thought I heard a faint voice saying, "Don't shoot, don't shoot; I'm coming in," and then the footfalls of a man approaching I heard distinctly. He continued to repeat as he came. "Don't shoot; I'm coming in," and a big Yank, with his gun in hand and fully equipped, rolled over in on me, at the same time telling me to pass the word to the next man on the left not to shoot, as others were coming in. I called out to my little comrade, Perkins, and told him I had a deserter and not to shoot, as others were coming in. In a very short time seven men, well armed and equipped, fell over into Perkins's pit. He hallooed to me in a very excited tone: "There are seven of them. What shall I do with them?" I told him to send them to the rear. This class of men was not to be feared. They were what the Yankees called "bounty jumpers," men who enlisted only to get the thousand-dollar bounty which Lincoln was giving at the time. They deserted the first opportunity and were allowed to pass through the lines, where they changed their names and no doubt reenlisted. Our thin line at this time extended thirty-five miles, and sometimes hundreds came in during a night.[177]

"ENGLISH HISTORY"

☛ A Bostonian was showing a British visitor the sights of the Hub. They were driving past Bunker Hill Monument. Not wishing to make any pointed reference to the fact that at one time we had been fighting with our cousins, the Boston gentleman merely indicated the monument with his thumb and said: "Bunker Hill."

The Englishman looked at the hill intently and asked: "Who was Mr. Bunker, and what did he do to the hill?"

"You don't understand," said the Bostonian. "This is where [famed American patriot and Revolutionary War hero Gen. Joseph] Warren fell."

The Englishman screwed his monocle into his eye, leaned back, and, looking at the top of the towering shaft, remarked inquiringly: "Killed him, of course?"[178]

FROM A SPEECH BY CONFEDERATE GEN. DANIEL H. HILL

☛ [Circa 1867] I will tell you, young people, of the South which has passed away, that you may admire and imitate whatever was grand and noble in its history, and reject whatever was wrong and defective. The scandals that have brought shame upon the American name occurred when the old South was out of power. No official from the old South was ever charged with roguery; no great statesman of that period ever corruptly made money out of office.

. . . I love to hear the philanthropists praise Mr. Lincoln, and call him the second Washington, for I remember that he was born in Kentucky, and was from first to last, as the *Atlantic Monthly* truly said, "a Southern man in all his characteristics." I love to hear them say that [U.S. Gen.] George H. Thomas was the stoutest fighter in the Union army, for I remember that he was born in Virginia. I love to hear of the wonderful deeds of [U.S. Generals] McClellan, Grant, Meade, and Hancock, for if they were such great warriors for crushing with their massive columns the thin lines of the ragged Rebels, what must be said of [C.S. Generals] Lee, the two Johnstons, Beauregard, and Jackson, who held millions at bay for four years with their fragments of shadowy armies? Pile up huge pedestals and surmount them with bronze horses and riders in bronze. All the Union monuments are eloquent of the prowess of the Rebels and their leaders.[179]

AT GETTYSBURG

☛ I left the "Bower" and rode to Martinsburg, where I was to join my command as it marched through. I stayed all night with my aunt, Mrs. Dr. Pendleton, had a good wash, and "fixed up" nicely, clean linen

collar, etc., so that when I went up to the main street the next morning
to wait for the battalion my appearance attracted the usual attention.
Hood's Texas "boys" were marching swiftly along, dirty and dusty, and,
after several comments had been made, one of them called out: "O
jiminy, don't he look nice? John (to his comrade), throw a louse or two
on him." I joined heartily in the laugh that followed. It seemed that the
very privations of our service added to the gaieties. The fun and jokes
always rose superior to cold, hunger, and fatigue, and seemed to mitigate
their severity. It was certainly a happy diversion in the terrible hardships
that we had to endure, and a visitor to a camp or an onlooker at a march
might think us the happiest of men.[180]

THE SPIRIT OF CONFEDERATE WOMEN
☞ The generation that has grown up since the war cannot possibly
understand the privations and hardships undergone and the heroism
displayed by the women of the South during the war. While their
fathers, husbands; brothers, and sons were at the front fighting the
battles of their country, they were at home taking such care as they could
of their Lares and Penates, nursing the sick and wounded, feeding the
hungry stragglers, and in a hundred ways helping along the cause as best
they might. They cheerfully, though tearfully, spared their loved ones to
serve their country. No sacrifice was too
great for their beloved Southland. At
Appomattox and Greensboro the heroes of
the army succumbed to overwhelming
odds and laid down their arms; but the
women of the South—God bless
them!—have never surrendered yet.
There arc some amusing anecdotes of the
women of the war as well as of the men.

When [U.S.] Gen. Kelly commanded
the Federal troops occupying the country
around Front Royal, Va., he was very
severe in impressing all the live stock he
could find. Among others, he impressed a
cow belonging to an old man, John
Arnold. This was about the last piece of
property that previous depredations had
left the old man, and her milk was almost
the only resource left him and his daughter
for food. The next morning after the loss
of the cow Miss Sue Arnold, the daughter,
went to Gen. Kelly's headquarters and
applied to him for the release of the cow.
Gen. Kelly turned around in his chair,
and, in his most pompous manner, said:

TYPICAL CONFEDERATE SOLDIER.

"Miss Arnold, this rebellion must be crushed!"

Miss Arnold, with eyes flashing and arms akimbo and defiance in her attitude, replied: "Gen. Kelly, if you think you can crush this rebellion by stealing old John Arnold's cow, just steal her and be damned!"

She got the cow.[181]

EVIDENCE OF TRUE COURAGE

☛ As a Georgia regiment was about to enter a battle which threatened to be sharp and bloody, the colonel, very pale, rode along the line, and as he passed, one of his captains looked up and remarked: "Colonel, you are as pale as death. I believe you are afraid."

"Yes," said the colonel. "I am afraid; and if you were half as much afraid as I am, you would run."

An army made up of such stuff as this colonel, who was brave from a sense of duty and of patriotism, may be crushed by numbers, as ours was, but when all else is lost it can say in the words of the celebrated French general: "All is lost save honor."[182]

STONEWALL & YANKEES IN HELL

☛ During one of the long and rapid marches which so often fell to the lot of Stonewall Jackson's "foot cavalry," two of the boys belonging to the old Stonewall Brigade, which always held a warm corner in the heart of its old commander, fell into conversation. One of them remarked to the other: "Bill, I wish all those damned Yankees were in hell."

"I don't," replied Bill.

"Why not?" asked Jim.

"Because, if they were, old Stonewall would order the First Brigade to go after them."[183]

THE YANKEE GEN. WHO LOVED STONEWALL "AS A BROTHER"

☛ Having mentioned the name of Stonewall Jackson, I am loath to leave it. There is a charm in it which brings back vividly the stirring scenes of Confederate times. Who can hear his name mentioned without recalling that marvelous career of the almost unknown professor at the Virginia Military Institute who in three short months fought and defeated five separate armies, each numerically superior to his own ?

A few years after the war the writer met [U.S.] Gen. Shields at Carrollton, Mo., where he resided. On being introduced to him, I said: "Gen. Shields, I have always admired your character and honored your military record, but I am especially glad to have the honor of meeting you after having heard you in a speech during the last campaign refer in glowing terms to my hero of heroes."

"What, sir? Stonewall Jackson?"

"Yes, sir," said I; "Stonewall Jackson."

"Give me your hand again," said the General. "I loved him as a brother. He was the greatest man that ever lived."

He then went on to say that in the same political campaign of which I had spoken he referred, in his speech at a certain town, in the same eulogistic terms to Stonewall Jackson, when a hot-headed fellow in the crowd called out: "Aren't you the Gen. Shields who whipped Stonewall Jackson at Kernstown?"

"No, sir," replied the old general; "the man that whipped Stonewall Jackson never lived; but I have the honor of saying that I gave him a drawn fight at Kernstown; and no other man can make as proud a boast."

MISS BELLE KINNEY'S DESIGN FOR THE SOUTHERN WOMEN'S MONUMENT, 1910.

And yet [dear Southern reader] . . . our histories tell us, and our sons and daughters are taught to believe, that Shields whipped Jackson at Kernstown. Who should know better than Gen. Shields himself?

The General then went on to illustrate the feeling that existed between worthy foemen by saying that on one occasion, a year or two previous to this conversation, he was taking a party of friends to see a circus. As there was a great crowd around the ticket wagon, he concluded that he would try paying at the door of the tent. As they approached the entrance, one of the party happened to address him as "Gen. Shields." A one-armed, military-looking man, who was taking the tickets, looked up quickly and said: "Are you the Gen. Shields who fought in the Valley of Virginia?"

"I am, sir," replied the General.

"Pass in with your party, General; you can't pay a cent here."

"Thank you, my friend." said the General. "I see you have lost an arm. I presume you were one of my soldiers in the Valley."

"Well, no, not exactly, General: I was the next thing to it, though: I was one of Stonewall Jackson's men."[184]

MORE CONFEDERATE IRISH WIT ON THE BATTLEFIELD

☛ No series of anecdotes of the war would be complete without some which display the wit of the Irishman. . . . During [a] . . . battle the firing had become so hot that some of the men concluded they had very urgent business in the rear, and among them was an Irishman. His captain noticed him starting for the rear, and commanded him to come back. Pat paid no attention to this, but kept on. The captain drew his pistol and threatened to fire if he did not stop. The Irishman, without stopping, looked back over his shoulder, and yelled: "Shoot and damn you! What is one bullet to a bucketful?"[185]

CONFEDERATE GENERAL CHEATHAM & THE IRISH SOLDIER
☛ Every one agrees that discipline is absolutely essential in an army, but in the Confederate army some of our soldiers had a queer idea of discipline. While the private soldier would obey his officer's commands with the utmost exactness, he never for a moment acknowledged the superiority of the officer socially. He would fight like a hero and work like a stevedore, but he never gave up or forgot his manhood. On one occasion Gen. ["Old Frank"] Cheatham found one of his men, an Irishman, committing some act of which he did not approve. He reprimanded him in the most forcible manner, and, in fact, it is said that the language used was so forcible that the air turned a beautiful cerulean hue. When he stopped to get his breath, the Irishman said: "Bedad, Gineral Cheatham! if you wasn't a gineral, you wouldn't talk to me that way."

Gen. Cheatham was like the hero of [Arthur] Conan Doyle's novel, *The White Company*: he was always willing and anxious to accommodate any gentleman who was looking for trouble. He pulled off his coat and threw it on the ground, saying: "There lies Gen. Cheatham, and here is Old Frank. Now pitch in."

The Irishman did pitch in, and it is related that for once in his life Old Frank didn't get the best of a fight.[186]

IMPERSONATING AN OFFICER TO GET HOG MEAT
☛ [Circa 1898?] [Tennessee] Senator Turley said that we remember the humor and the good times better than we do the privations through those four memorable years. In illustration, he stated that a man with gray beard called at his room in the hotel and asked if he was [the former Confederate soldier] Tom Turley. He replied to the cordial visitor that he was, but in response to a hearty greeting he had to admit that he had no recollection of having seen him before. The name John Jones being given, he instantly recalled a night on the Hood advance into Tennessee when the army camped on hills surrounding a well-appointed farm. Some enterprising soldiers on the opposite side of the farm were prompt to silence some fat hogs near the farm-house that "might be vicious." John Jones took in the situation promptly. He went to his captain and asked his uniform coat and sword, and by the time he had donned them a group of comrades had their guns, and in quick time they were on the way to that hog-pen. Nearing it, one of the number ran ahead, pretending to be a friend of the boys who were skinning the fat hogs, and in a husky whisper warned them: "Provost-guard!" The skinned hogs were taken to the opposite hill.[187]

CHAPTER SIX

A YANKEE DUTCHMAN & LEE'S CANNON

☛ When Gen. Lee made his great march into the enemy's territory, and was on the way to Gettysburg, of course it created consternation among many of the "Pennsylvania Dutch" who had remained at home, and were non-combatants, though perhaps they were in sympathy with the Union sentiment. A portion of the Confederate army had passed across a certain little stream. Some of the heavy artillery came on, and in the stream one of the heavy guns bogged up to the axle in the soft mud bottom. It took some time to get it out. While the men were struggling in the stream to help out the battery the teamsters were "cussin'" and kicking at the mules to pull it out, and the poor brutes were pulling with all their might and main. On the roadside was a fine field of waving wheat, owned by a fat Dutchman. It was his joy, his pride—that field of wheat. The Dutchman came to the ford to see the struggle at the gun. While the mules and men were tugging at the gun in the stream others came up on the road. Finding the crossing obstructed so, they soon began to tear down the fence and march across the field of grain by an oblique movement to a crossing at a ford higher up the creek. Of course that excited the Dutchman, and he became angry. Finding that he was unable by remonstrance to check the tide of invasion on his fine grain, he began to jump straight up and down and to exclaim in a loud voice: "Mine Gott! mine Gott in himmel! If dot is der vay dis var is ter pe carried on, I vants it shtopped righd now."[188]

THE C.S. SOLDIER WHO SHOULD HAVE BEEN AN ACTOR

☛ In our old marching days the privations we endured seemed to stimulate the imagination, and the story of our sufferings lost nothing of pathos as the sufferer told it. We had a deep sense of our sacrifices, and often used them to stir the soul of pity in some good woman, so as to add to our rough and scanty rations. Very seldom was a prosperous farmhouse visited by a soldier who had eaten anything in three days, and the look of gaunt, hollow-eyed hunger he could assume would melt the heart of a graven image, and has brought forth many a good dinner from the unsophisticated, who had not learned to distrust the pitiful plea.

One case comes to mind where the tale was so touching that it moved even the soldier himself to tears over his own sad case—at least that was what some of the boys who saw it all reported afterward in the regiment.

After a hard day's march, we went into our camp a little before sundown, and three days' rations of corn bread and bacon were issued to us and stowed away in our haversacks. Near our camp there flowed a beautiful stream, and on its banks were fine farms that seemed to have an abundance of things good to eat. The instinct and the appetite of the men at once told them that it was a good place to replenish rations, and so a number of them, with or without permission, started out to forage, not waiting to lay aside or empty their haversacks.

Pretty soon they came to a farmhouse in which the family were just sitting down to supper. They sent in one of their number to see what could be gotten. This one was very skillful in gaining the good will of any one that sympathized with the "poor soldier." As he walked into the dining-room he saw a great dish of broiled ham, plates of hot biscuits, pitchers of milk, jars of honey, and he also detected the fragrance of "sure-enough" coffee. There were dainties to make his mouth water.

He found the family to consist of a mother, evidently a woman of refinement, and three or four children, while there were plenty of servants. At once he put on his best manner, for he was a gentleman "to the manner born," and in a moment he was invited to supper. He proceeded to make himself agreeable, for he was a delightful converser, and he found that the family were intensely Southern, the father being with Lee, in Virginia. As the farm was rather out of the line of the armies, it had not been visited before by hungry soldiers, and they were glad to see a Confederate. After an extraordinary meal—for our boy was long and "hollow to his heels"—he told the lady that this was his first meal in three days, and asked if she would have three dozen biscuits made for him, with a slice of broiled ham in each. He wanted them for himself and his two messmates, and would pay well for them. She, good and guileless woman, told him that she would gladly do what she could for a Southern soldier, and would not think of taking pay—which was well, as he had "forgotten" his purse. The cook was ordered to prepare the biscuits and ham.

Meanwhile he laid himself out to entertain the lady with the story of our privations. With touching pathos he described the pangs of hunger, and emphasized his own sufferings in contrast with the abundance he had left at home. He painted the weary march and the long and lonely vigil of the sentinel, almost exhausted by his lack of food. So moving was the story that the lady wept and the children sobbed in sympathy. At last the soldier himself was so carried by the pity of it that he shed tears freely over the mournful memory.

Right in the midst of the sad scene the cook came in, bringing the great dish of ham and biscuits, and set it down before the sorrowing soldier. He at once began to take care of it, and, picking up his haversack from his side, he took out pone after pone of corn bread, and then a big "hunk" of bacon, laying them on the table, while their place in his haversack was taken by the more toothsome viands. All the while he went on with the tale of his sufferings.

Directly he noticed that the sobbing had ceased and there was a strange stillness with his weeping auditors. Looking up, he saw the lady gazing at him with an expression of wonder and amusement, while the tears still glistened on her cheeks, and it flashed on him that he had forgotten to empty his haversack before he came in, had forgotten in his anguish of spirit how this fat haversack would discredit his story. His imagination was so vivid that it neglected the facts entirely, and he really believed his own story. He had simply allowed the embellishments to hide the facts, until the facts asserted themselves.

Of course there was no explanation possible. The soldier was too fine an artist to offer one. The lady, fortunately, was gifted with humor, and saw the comedy of the situation. As he waited for her reproaches she broke into the merriest laugh, in which he could only join, a self-revealed fraud. She said he was welcome to the rations, for she had not enjoyed so good a

AT THE TOMB OF THE UNKNOWN SOLDIER, ARLINGTON, VIRGINIA. TRIBUTE BY THE U.D.C. IN CONVENTION, NOVEMBER 1923.

cry in a long time; it was such a relief to her. But she begged that in the future he should not give way to his grief, but try to bear up under his sufferings, and no doubt, when he was again nearly starved, a kind Providence would come to his relief, as in this case. Then she bundled up his bacon and corn bread for him to take with him, for she knew such an appetite would need all it could get.[189]

THE ELITE

☞ Lieutenant Card was born in Atlanta and was mighty proud of that fact. Never did he miss an opportunity to impress upon the world at large the fact that an Atlanta man was just a little better than any other sort of human being.

One day a big, burly negro brought in his service record for indorsement, and the lieutenant noticed that the man had given his birthplace as Atlanta.

"Ah!" he ejaculated. "So you were born in Atlanta? That's where I came from too."

The negro rolled his eyes. "Well, well!" he exclaimed. "So you and me is from de same town! Kain't be nobody wuff while left down to Atlanta dese days a-tall."[190]

PICKET GAMES

☛ January and February [1862] passed with but two little breaks in the dull monotony of camp-life. One was the desperate but successful [Confederate] resistance made on the Occoquan, quite near the enemy's lines, by a party of Texas scouts to the attack of a regiment of Federals. There were only nine of the Texans, and, although the house in which they sought refuge was surrounded, they held the assailants at bay for several hours, and after killing and wounding quite a number, [they] frightened the survivors away by a stratagem which ought not to have deceived a schoolboy.

I shiver at the mere remembrance of the other incident. Company F was sent on a two days' tour of picket and fatigue duty to Cockpit Point, on the Potomac, where an effort was being made to establish a masked battery to play upon our shipping on the river. Brahan has become acquainted with my inborn and cultivated aversion to handling pick, shovel, and spade—in fact, doing any kind of manual labor—and I shall always believe he arranged with Capt. Cunningham the deceptive scheme to call for volunteers from the company for the picket duty that was to be done. Anyhow, such a call was made as soon as we reached the Point, and, glad of an opportunity to escape hard labor, and beguiled to my undoing by a seemingly friendly wink from Brahan, I was one of the first to step to the front in response. For the first six hours I had no reason to regret my rashness. After three months' camp-life it was positively a recreation to sit and inhale the salt atmosphere of the tide-water, listen to its music, as, stirred by gentle breezes, it broke in little waves upon the shore, gaze up, down, and across the broad Potomac, and enjoy the life apparent everywhere. Then, suddenly and most calamitously, a stray norther [storm] came sweeping down from the Arctic regions, the hitherto bright sun hid himself behind threatening clouds, and rain, sleet, and snow, in turn, began to beat upon my face and drip unceasingly down the front and rear of my cap. Under these distressing circumstances I awoke to the error of my ways, the foolishness of my choice, and as cheerfully as King Richard would have bartered his kingdom for a horse I would have given a horse for a man to take my place and let me sneak back to the huge fires which my comrades—who, on account of the rain, had been relieved from their task—had built, and were enjoying in a sheltered place hundreds of yards from the river-bank. Convinced that the Yankees would never choose such weather for an attack, I found solace in the fancy that the pickets would also be relieved, but that straw of comfort was too fragile to lean upon.

When dreary night had wrapped its impenetrable mantle over all things mundane the captain came trudging through the snow to my post, and, with a disgustingly obvious pretense of compassion, informed me that until daylight the safety of the Confederate army would be entrusted wholly to the vigilance of Charley Brown, Herman Gabbert, and myself; and that, as it would be very inconvenient for an officer to tramp from the fire to the post every two hours to relieve us in regular military style, we were expected to sleep near enough to the post to wake each other.

"Bu-bu-but, Gabtain," chattered Gabbert, who is a Dutchman, and was then on post, "how—how—how vill ve know ven der zwei hours ish oop?"

"Oh, you can guess at them, I reckon!" responded the officer, who turned on his heel and made what he thought was a bee-line for camp.

Neither of the shivering monuments of man's inhumanity to man whom he left behind felt in the least inclined to apprise him that he was proceeding in the wrong direction, and he had not gone fifty yards when he stumbled over a hidden log and fell headlong into a muddy branch. Rising to his feet, he sputtered entreatingly: "Say, boys! which way is the camp from here!"

"Oh, you can guess at it, I reckon!" I answered instantly, repeating his own words of a minute before.

But Gabbert, more tender-hearted, shouted: "Go up mit der grick, Gaptain, und yer fin's her purty quick, by tam!"

Then we arranged a program. A bed was made down, to be occupied by the two not on duty, while the third kept watch for an hour, as nearly as he could calculate the time—Brown to wake me, I to wake Gabbert, and Gabbert, in his turn, to wake Brown. Fair and equitable as the plan appeared, there was too much guesswork in it to be wholly satisfactory, and that was the longest, coldest, and most wretched night I ever lived through. Each of us went on duty thirteen times before daylight; but if there was any miscalculation it was by Gabbert, for Brown and I were positive we made a liberal estimate on each hour we were on post. The Dutchman, however, declared stoutly: "Mine Gott in Himmel! boot by tarn! I schust stand oop effer time more as von hour und a half!"[191]

AN OVERLY EXPENSIVE MILITARY OVERCOAT
☞ About the 1st of March a rumor went flying broadcast through the camp that some grand movement of the [C.S.] army was in contemplation, but "old Joe" deemed it wholly unnecessary to inform us that it was to be a retreat until the morning of the 8th and of our department for this place.

There is a member of my company whom I shall dub Jack, lest, by revealing his identity, the tale I relate should cling to him longer and closer than did that of his overcoat. Looking more to his own comfort and sense of the fitness of things than to uniformity of dress and the consequent soldierly appearance for which my friend Brahan is such a stickler, Jack disdainfully rejected the munificent offer of the Confederate States Government to furnish him a gray and strictly military overcoat for $5 on a credit, and expended $25 in the purchase of one of a quality and fashion to commend itself to the most fastidious aristocrat. The first night out from Dumfries the weather was so intensely cold that he decided not to remove any of his garments, and so, wrapping himself in a couple of blankets, he laid down very close to a huge log fire, where, lulled by the genial warmth, he soon fell soundly asleep, and began to snore at his liveliest and merriest gait. About midnight Bob Murray's acutely sensitive olfactory nerves were offended by the scent of burning cloth. He had only to look once to discover that the fire had burned lower and lower, Jack had edged his back nearer and nearer to it, and that at last a stray coal had lighted a flame that was playing sad havoc with his blanket and coat. Aroused by Bob's shouts, Jack did some rapid hustling around, but alas! too late to preserve the anatomy, the pristine symmetrical *tout ensemble*, of the cherished garment, and prevent its transformation from an elegant frock into a nondescript, altogether too open at the back to be comfortable, and with two, tails hanging in front, instead of in the rear—in short, in two sections, whose only bond of union was the velvet collar. Next morning the crestfallen owner sought to repair the damage by sewing the burned edges together, but that heroic remedy, while reducing the tails to one, and that pointing in the right direction, rendered it impossible to button up the front, and kept him so busy during the day answering questions that when night came he was too hoarse to talk.[192]

A COMPLIMENT—SORT OF

☛ "Two men got into a fight in front of the bank to-day," said a man at the family tea table, "and I tell you it looked pretty bad for one of them. The bigger one seized a huge stick and brandished it. I felt that he was going to knock the other's brains out. and I jumped in between them."

The family had listened with rapt attention, and as he paused in his narrative the young heir, whose respect for his father's bravery is immeasurable, proudly remarked: "He couldn't knock any brains out of you, could he father?"[193]

MRS. JEFFERSON DAVIS REPAIRS A DRESS

☛ Miss Frances S. Bell, daughter of Hon. Casper W. Bell, of Salisbury, Mo., who has served in Congress, and was also an officer in the Confederate army, writes of a visit to Mrs. Varina Jefferson Davis, and in her girlish way gives a vivid description of a torn dress, etc. Introductory to the article, an extract is made from a letter of Senator Vest, of Missouri, stating that "she is a young lady of the highest character, refined and accomplished."

The red-letter day of the writer's life is the one on which she received a missive written by one of the grandest and noblest of women, Mrs. V. Jefferson Davis, who stated in this note that at four o'clock the same day, at the Marlborough Hotel, New York, she would "be glad to receive the daughter of an old acquaintance." At the appointed hour, arrayed in a brand-new dress (the newness was its only recommendation), the writer, accompanied by a friend, went to the Marlborough. On entering the hotel passage the brand-new dress caught on and had a hole torn in it by a piece of projecting lumber that the workmen were using in repairing the building. Suddenly sunshine turned to shadow. To make a first appearance before the distinguished lady in such a plight seemed out of the question, but finally it was decided to make the best of the accident and be announced to the hostess at once. The writer was greatly frustrated by the occurrence, and was bemoaning her fate when the elevator stopped.

A lady stood at the landing, whose cordial smile was so reassuring that all embarrassment and thoughts of torn clothes were forgotten. Mrs. Davis—for it was she, though obliged to walk with a cane—had come to the elevator to meet and conduct her visitors to her private apartments. This gracious act worked like a charm. All flutterings and frowns were dispelled, and by the time the drawing-room was reached an onlooker would have thought it was a meeting of old friends.

Attention being called to the torn dress, Mrs. Davis expressed much regret at the accident, and mentioned that she was an expert darner, and if agreeable would mend the torn place. After selecting suitable material from her work-basket, she drew near and began what the writer's superstition would never have permitted any human being except Mrs. Davis to do: mending the dress while she (the writer) was wearing it. Just think! a dress mended by Mrs. Davis! Something to make every Southern girl envious. As the needle, directed by

THE BATTLE OF HAMPTON ROADS, FEATURING THE FIGHT BETWEEN THE CSS *VIRGINIA* AND THE USS *MERRIMAC*, MARCH 8-9, 1862.

the skilled fingers, was weaving in and out, many threads of admiration and love were being woven around a visitor's heart that will last while she lives.

Mrs. Davis is an admirable conversationalist, being conversant with a variety of subjects, but never does she appear to greater advantage and seem more lovable than when engaged in the womanly occupation of sewing. However, more wonderful than her conversational powers is the surprisingly short time it takes her to find out the subjects of which other people can talk. The most taciturn person will say something to Mrs. Davis. She talked of many things—mentioned little incidents that had occurred in her travels, and gave interesting descriptions of several great paintings. She has a fine sense of humor, and tells a funny story charmingly.

That particular portion of the dress has been cut out, and is kept by its possessor as a work of art, as well as a remembrance of the lady who is pointed out to every Southern girl as a model of all the gracious qualities that should belong to a true woman, be her station great or humble. *"Noblesse oblige"* must surely be Mrs. Davis's life motto.[194]

THE HUMOROUS SIDE OF ZEBULON VANCE

☛ In August, 1861, our regiment, the 14th North Carolina Infantry, moved from Suffolk, Va., over to Camp Bee, near Stonehouse Wharf, on James River. [C.S.] Col. Junius Daniel was in command. The company officers of the regiment were drilled daily by one of the field-officers, all of whom were West Pointers. Either Lieut.-Col. Lovejoy or Maj. Faison was drilling them one day, when he gave a catch command to "order arms" from a support. Capt. Vance promptly came down with his gun, amid the laughter of the other officers. The Major said: "No, no, Captain; you can't do that." Vance replied with a merry twinkle in his eye: "Well, Major, I'll be darned if I didn't do it!"[195]

THE SPEEDY RECOVERY

☛ [C.S.] Brig.-Gen. E. W. Pettus, with his Alabama and Georgia troops, arrived on top of Lookout Mountain the day before the battle. We were posted on the right of our line from about sundown until relieved by Gen. Clayton's Brigade at midnight.

While waiting for Gen. Clayton's command to line up, we fell back a few steps in a ravine. Comrade Jess Davis and I were sitting on a log together, when a spent ball struck him on the stomach. He fell over the log, claiming that he was shot through, and declaring it was fatal. I felt for the wound, and found the ball flattened and lodged next to his skin, not having entered the flesh. "Jess, you are not hurt very badly," said I; "here is the ball. You are all right." He revived quickly, and, jumping up, declared that the Yank should lay his gun down, for he had "caught him out."

The bullet passed through his blanket, which was rolled and tied at the ends and worn over the right and under the left shoulder. The bullet made seven holes in the blanket, then passed through his coat and two shirts, and left a black spot about the size of a hand on his abdomen. The lead was mashed to more than an inch in diameter. Jess was all right for duty, and fought all the next day on Missionary Ridge.[196]

HIS BIBLE STOPPED A BULLET

☛ J. W. Allen, first sergeant of Company H, 19th Louisiana Volunteers,

now of Mansfield, La., has a Testament [Bible] with a history. He writes:
This little Testament was presented to me in November, 1861, at Camp Moore, La., by my captain, J. H. Sutherlin. My company, called the Creoles, belonged to Gen. R. L. Gibson's Brigade, and had but one man taken prisoner during the war. I participated in every battle and skirmish in which the regiment was engaged, from the great battle of Shiloh to that at Jonesboro, Ga., August 31, 1864.

In the battle of Chickamauga, September 20, 1863, the first charge in the morning was repulsed. Being a little in advance of the line, I did not know when the order was given to retreat, and on looking around I saw the brigade two or three hundred yards away in full retreat, I only left to hold the line or follow suit, and I followed suit in a turkey trot for twenty or thirty yards, when the music of so much lead caused me to take a tree, but not to climb it, as the boys in blue were looking at me from their line of battle. After resting a few moments I decided to make my escape, even at the risk of my life. On leaving the tree it seemed that they fired a peck of balls at me, only one striking my knapsack on my back, passing through my blanket twenty or thirty times, through two company books, clothing, and entered my Testament, breaking through the back and mashing itself nearly flat. It is in the book now, just where it struck thirty-four years ago. My compliments to the boys in blue, whose aim was so bad.[197]

FITZ LEE WITH "THE BOYS" IN RICHMOND
☛ On the night of April 18 [1898?] the R. E. Lee Camp of Richmond celebrated its 15th anniversary in their splendid quarters. Commander Laughton opened the meeting, and Chaplain Smith led the prayer. The minutes of the first meeting of the camp (April 18, 1883) were read, and were quite edifying.

Maj. Norman Randolph talked of the history of the camp, from which more than eleven hundred camps have sprung. Thirty-eight men organized the camp, and in all the camps one hundred thousand veterans have been enrolled.

Capt. Curtis, who was of the C. S. Navy, emphasized the fact that the first torpedo was made by a Confederate soldier, Capt. Hunter Davidson.

At the conclusion of a rich recital, "The Last Old Gray," by Polk Miller, Maj. Randolph entered the hall with Consul-Gen. Fitzhugh Lee. "It was as if pandemonium had loosened its fastenings. Every old veteran rose to his feet and yelled himself hoarse; and when yells had lost their virtue, Gen. Lee was taken into arms bodily, and for twenty minutes a wild scene reigned, which included every mode of enthusiasm."

This was followed by Polk Miller with his string band. An enthusiast called out: "Go on, Mr. Miller! If the Spaniards heard you, there'd be no war."

Gen. Lee asked Capt. Cunningham, during one of the intermissions, if he was going to war, and if he would sing "Star-Spangled Banner." Capt. Cunningham replied that he was going to the war, but he would carry a Confederate flag in his pocket. He then sang the "Star-Spangled Banner." Polk Miller and his band followed with "Bonnie Blue Flag." Gen. Lee and all the boys joined in both choruses.

. . . Commander Laughton pleasantly called upon Gen. Lee to speak, and to give expression to "guarded" remarks. Gen. Lee smilingly complied. After the cheer had subsided Gen. Lee shouted: "Turn out the guard. I'm going to make some guarded remarks." He then went on to express the comfort he felt when among Confederate soldiers, and stated that he was reminded of the progress the camp had made in its fifteen years. It struck him as funny that these boys should be singing the "Star-Spangled Banner," when they had, in 1861, fought so hard against it. "There never was a band that fought against that flag harder than you boys," he said, "and here you are singing 'Star-Spangled Banner.'" The thought made him feel good, and the tear born of the throbbing of his grandly patriotic heart threatened to spill over. It seemed strange to him that Capt. Cunningham should be singing "Star-Spangled Banner," but he didn't wonder at his not getting the pitch the first time. After paying fine tribute to the "Star-Spangled Banner" and his pride in it while at Havana, he referred to our great war here in the sixties, and said: "We fought for a cause we knew to be right, and we made a magnificent record. I have never read of such a fight as we made."[198]

AMUSEMENT AT THE BATTLE OF GAINES' MILL

☛ All battles have their amusing incidents, ever enjoyed by participants in after days, and I will . . . [now offer] one which occurred at Gaines's Mill while in line of battle before the attack. My position was in the rear rank near the foot of the company. Fred Sollie, now of Luther's Store, Ala., was my front rank man. Just as we got to our feet the Yankees poured a murderous volley into us. One of the Minie balls tore off the first joint of Fred's right forefinger and imbedded itself in the fleshy part of his thigh. He instantly fell on his back, hoisted his feet and hands in the air, and exclaimed: "Boys, for God's sake don't tramp on me!" Fred was always a funny fellow, any way, but the anguish of pain or fright, or whatever it was, as depicted on his face and the manner of his request and the position he was in was most amusing.[199]

YANKS STEAL THE CHILDREN'S HORSE

☛ Mrs. Kate Lee Shaw Nichols, a daughter of one of Forrest's soldiers, gives the following as literally true:

A sultry August noon, with the sun's piercing rays beaming down upon two little figures trudging up a long, dusty lane.

"Somehow it seems awful far to-day, Milly. Maybe, though, it's because I have such a headache."

"Hurry on, Mary; we'll soon be there. Just think how hungry sister must get waiting for her dinner!"

They quickened their footsteps, and soon reached a stone stile leading into a cool, shady yard, in the center of which stood a low, rambling log house, with here and there a room added to suit the fancy of its owner.

When they entered the front room a scene of disorder and confusion confronted them. It was plain that something had happened, for there on the lounge lay Aunt Amelia, sobbing and muttering incoherently. Between her disjointed sentences and outbursts a vague fear seized the children, until they asked in one breath: "Where is George, Aunt Amelia? "

"Those vagabond Yankees took him off to Carthage a little while ago. Oh, dear me! I know that Miss Sallie will be heart-broken when she hears of it."

Mary and Milly exchanged glances. A fixed determination suddenly filled the hearts of both little girls. Seizing their pink sunbonnets and darting out of the door, they called back to the dazed old woman: "Tell sister we've gone for George."

In vain she called after them as they sped out the back gate and through the orchard. On through the meadow into the stubble-field ran the panting children, oblivious of briers or stubble. They knew that the road wound around many a broad acre, and, if their strength did not fail them, they could, by going through, overtake the Federal cavalry before they reached the main Carthage pike. Once they paused when a vicious dog pursued them into a yard, where they sought refuge upon an ash-hopper. The noise of the clattering boards and the shrieking children brought the owner to the door in

PAST COMMANDERS-IN-CHIEF OF THE SONS OF CONFEDERATE VETERANS, BIRMINGHAM, ALABAMA REUNION, 1908.

time to witness a ludicrous scene. Perched upon one corner of the dilapidated hopper was a brave little creature, with one arm clasped tightly around the smaller and younger sister, while with the disengaged hand she hurled clods of hardened ashes at their pursuer, and at intervals wailed: "Oh, do come and take your dog away! for we're in a *dreadful* hurry."

Released from their embarrassing position, they fled without any intelligible explanation. They soon spied blue uniforms mingled with the dust in the distance. Nearer and nearer they drew, until Mary waved her bonnet aloft. The captain drew rein, as did the entire company, and awaited the approach of the flushed little girls. They clambered over the fence, and, walking up to the foremost man, Milly asked timidly: "Are you the captain, sir?"

The surprised officer answered in the affirmative.

"Then, sir, do, oh, please do, give us back George!"

A magnificent bay, bearing a ruddy-faced Dutchman, nickered at the sound of his name and sight of those children.

Not waiting for a reply, the quavering little voice hurried on: "Oh, sir! he was the only horse we had, and we would miss him like he was one of our family."

Mary stole to the horse's side, and, fastening her fingers in his dark mane, she looked up with eyes full of pitiful entreaty. "Oh, Mr. Captain, do let us take him back home, for we do love him ever so good."

In a few polite phrases the young officer tried to explain that all such captures became [U.S.] Gen. Payne's.

"But, oh, sir, just think how your own little girls at home would feel if some big, strange men were to take away their own dear horse!"

The man's face softened as he turned to the glowering Dutchman and said in a low, imperative tone: "Dismount, and give that horse to these children!" Then, alighting himself, he took a blanket from underneath his own saddle, and, placing it on George, proffered to assist the happy children in getting up.

What a glad pair they were returning home![200]

UNCLE JACK & PRESIDENT WILSON

☛ An American Red Cross officer, who served in the Italian campaign with the American army, reached his home in Mississippi last summer while the daylight-saving law was in effect. He found one of the old negroes of the town doing a hacking [taxi] business with an automobile. The major immediately engaged him for a ride every day. To begin with, he took a drive of twenty miles to view the scenes of his boyhood.

"Now, Uncle Jack," he said, "be back here at four o'clock, and we'll go out again. But be sure to be on time."

"Yas, suh, I'll sho be there."

The old darky started off and then stopped his car.

"You remember the hour, don't you?" asked the major.

"Yas, suh, I know you said fo' o'clock. But look here, boss, does you mean fo' o'clock by God's time or President [Woodrow] Wilson's time?"[201]

A CONFEDERATE WOMAN CONFRONTS A YANKEE COLONEL

☛ After Sherman's march from Memphis to the relief of Chattanooga, in the fertile valley of Elk River, his column having subsisted upon the country through which it passed, many families were destitute of provisions. The [U.S.] guards left to protect the bridge over Elk River, on the line of the Nashville and Decatur railroad, depended upon foraging parties to procure their subsistence. These parties had so repeatedly called at Mrs. Dr. Upshaw's, a mile or two south of the bridge, that her supplies were reduced so low as to threaten starvation. She saddled her pony and rode alone to the headquarters of the colonel commanding at the bridge, and told him in a polite and bland manner that it was her wish that he would send a couple of wagons to her house and get the rest of her provisions, as she was tired of the daily visits of his foragers; her husband being away from home, she always felt alarmed when they came there.

UNVEILING THE FLORAL DESIGN AT THE ARLINGTON CONFEDERATE MONUMENT, CIRCA 1916.

The colonel expressed his pleasure at so frank an offer, pronouncing the policy she was pursuing the best that could be adopted by all the Rebel families in the neighborhood. The next day he sent a commissioned officer in charge of a detail of men with two wagons to Mrs. Upshaw's. The lady politely conducted the officer to her smoke-house and corn-crib and through every apartment in her dwelling. Nowhere did he find a pound of meat or a dust of meal or flour. Going to the kitchen, she directed the men to put a single shoulder of bacon and a bushel of corn stored there—all the provisions she had in the world—in their wagons. Turning to the officer, she said: "Now, Captain, you have seen all that is left, and have it in your wagons; please notify the fact to your colonel, and tell him I hold him to his promise not to permit his foraging parties to come here again."

Instead of the colonel being offended, he chivalrously "took in" the lady's condition, and ordered one of the wagons full-laden with provisions to return to Mrs. Upshaw's with his compliments and the assurance that should she at any future time be destitute of provisions, upon notifying him of the fact, she should be supplied. The colonel put a restraint upon indiscriminate foraging, and afterward had little difficulty in procuring supplies for his command from those in the vicinity who had a surplus.

It was after this period that Sherman said that a crow could not find sufficient food in that section.[202]

THE WRONG FOOT-WARMER

☛ On the 21st and 22nd of November, 1861, the 17th Alabama was encamped near the navy-yard, about seven or eight miles below Pensacola, Fla., and about one and one-half miles in rear of Fort Barancas and other Confederate forts and sand batteries, when the celebrated fight took place between Fort Pickens, on Santa Rosa Island, and two navy ships (Federal). The ammunition of the Federals was evidently faulty, because not one-half of the shells thrown from Pickens and the two vessels exploded. Hundreds of the Yankee shells passed over the forts and fell in and near our camp, and did no damage, not exploding. A few days after the fight the 8th Mississippi (I think it was the 8th), [Confederate] Col. Chalmers (afterward general) commanding, was assigned to camps adjoining our regiment. Many of them were suffering from chills. The surgeon made the usual prescription in such cases, and suggested to the messmate of one of the sufferers to heat a rock and place it at the feet of the sufferer about the hour the chill usually came on. The messmate could not find a rock, but he found one of those unexploded, innocent-looking, ten-inch Yankee shells, and rolled it into the fire. After he thought it was hot enough he rolled it into the sick man's tent, raised the blankets, and carefully placed it against his feet, and took his seat near his friend. In a few minutes or seconds a tremendous explosion took place. The whole camp was aroused. Result: A demolished tent, the patient lying about ten feet from where the tent had stood, his blankets on fire, and his friend, trying to stand up, exclaiming: "Have the Yankees opened fire again?" Strange to say, neither of these good Mississippians was much hurt, but it is certain that the sick man had no more chills while the regiment remained in Florida.

A month or so after this this regiment was ordered to join the army either in Virginia or Tennessee, for more active fields of usefulness in the cause we loved.[203]

A BLACK COOK & THE DISAPPEARING CONGREGATION

☛ On the Sabbath after the battle of Chickamauga the men of a certain [Confederate] regiment were gathered just beyond the top of Missionary Ridge for religious service. A good congregation of the soldiers was seated on the ground. In the early part of the service a battery belonging to "our friends the enemy" sent a shell, which exploded some two or three hundred yards below our position. A negro cook, who had his belongings just outside of the place occupied by the congregation, put them over his shoulder with the significant remark: "This nigger is gwine to git out o' here." That caused a ripple of laughter in the congregation, but all sat still. During the long prayer of our service another shell came much nearer. When the prayer was finished and the chaplain's eyes were opened he saw that the congregation, with the exception of five or six, had followed the cook.

It was amusing in the war to see how quickly a body of men could go completely out of sight when a shell, against which they could offer no resistance, came close to them. It seemed sometimes as if the ground had opened and swallowed them. So it was here. The chaplain and the few remaining soldiers had a laugh over the situation, but, like the rest of the congregation, disappeared.[204]

A MULE AS CANNONEER

☛ A small party of Confederate soldiers were left at Fort Smith, Ark., to guard the crossing. The boys found a small cannon, so determined to mount and load it, and give the boys in blue a shot before they vacated. It was suggested that they lash the loaded gun on a big mule, and after the shot take it along with them. All things were ready just about the time the bluecoats appeared in force on the west side of the river. The mule was led to the edge of the water, and the new-made gunner sounded out: "Match her off." The old mule stood quiet until the match was touched to the fuse that had been introduced into the touch-hole, but when it began to sizz and the fire to fall upon his neck and withers his discomfort caused him to turn round and round. The boys, except the one holding the mule's bridle, instantly fell to the ground. The command, "Down, boys!" attracted the captain from slumber in the old storm fort. Seeing the regiment in blue across the river and his men in a scattered condition on the ground, he commanded: "Up and into line, boys!" No one stirred. The command came again and again with deeper earnestness, when Sam Moore replied; "Up and thunder and lightning! We will stay down till that mule shoots." In another instant the gun fired, the mule tumbled down upon his knees, and the shell struck far from its mark on the hillside and exploded. The captain cried out: "Every man take care of himself; they are all around us." The laugh was on the captain, and all retreated in order with mule and gun.[205]

MAGRUDER'S CONFUSION

☛ On the night following the battle of Malvern Hill, [C.S.] General Magruder, known as Prince John, having been unfortunate in the attack made that day, on account of misunderstanding his orders, rode up to General Lee, and, saluting him, said that he had come to ask permission to storm the heights at daybreak with his division. "If you give me permission," continued Magruder, anxious to redeem himself, "I'll promise to carry the heights at the point of the bayonet." "I have no doubt that you would carry them," replied General Lee, "but I have one objection." "Name it," said Magruder, seeing honor and glory before him, and expecting to be able to remove the objection. "I am afraid," said General Lee, with a quiet smile, "that you might hurt my little friend Major Kidder Meade, of the engineering corps, who is over there reconnoitering, the enemy having left about an hour ago."[206]

"WHO THE DEVIL ARE YOU?"

☛ During the war [C.S.] General McLaws (afterward Postmaster at Savannah) was riding down his picket line, and encountered a genuine son of the Old Pine Tree State on duty, who had taken his gun apart with the intention of giving it a thorough cleaning. The general halted in front of him, when the following conversation ensued: "Look here, my man, are you not a sentinel on duty?" "Well, y-a-a-s, a bit of a one!" "Don't you know it is wrong to take your gun apart while on duty?" "Well, now, who the devil are you?" The general saw his chance, and with a sly twinkle of the eye replied: "I'm a bit of a general." "Well, gineral, you must excuse me. You see, thar is so many damned fools ridin' 'round here, a feller can't tell who's gineral and who ain't. If you will jist wait till I git Betsey Jane fixed I will give you a bit of a s'lute." The general smiled and rode on, firmly convinced that that sentinel would prove equal to any emergency.[207]

THE BRAVE SOLDIER WHO LOVED HIS WHISKEY

☛ One of the Alabama regiments was fiercely attacked by a whole brigade in one of the battles around Richmond. The Alabamians, unable to withstand such great odds, were compelled to fall back about thirty or forty yards, losing, to the utter mortification of the officers and men, their flag, which remained in the hands of the enemy. Suddenly a tall Alabamian, a private in the color company, rushed from the ranks across the vacant ground, attacked a squad of Yankees, who had possession of the flag, with his musket, felled several to the ground, snatched the flag from them, and returned safely back to his regiment. The bold fellow was of course immediately surrounded by his jubilant comrades and greatly praised for his gallantry. His captain appointed him to a sergeancy on the spot, but the hero cut every thing short by the reply: "Oh, never mind, captain! Say no more about it. I dropped my whisky flask among the Yankees and fetched that back, and I thought I might just as well bring the flag along."[208]

CHOCK FULL OF PIE

☛ Some years ago a great debate between a Northern printer and a Southern compositor on the subject of the late war was overheard. The Southerner was hot, impetuous and sentimental; the Northern champion calm, cool and even phlegmatic. "Why, didn't we lick you out of your boots at Manassas?" "Granted," said the Northern type-sticker. "Didn't we smash you at Cold Harbor, and wipe up the ground with you in the Wilderness?" "Granted," said the other. "Didn't we tie you all up in knots and make rags of you all through the Peninsular campaign?" "Granted," said the Northerner; "but how was it at Appomattox?" "Yes, how was it at Appomattox?" shouted the Southron, growing sentimental as the mingled beers and whiskies they were consuming rose to his head. "We had 13,000 poor, ragged, footsore, tired, starved veterans, without a single round of ammunition, while you had an army of 300,000 fat, sassy soldiers, provided with every luxury, and ev-every m-m-mother's s-son of 'em," he sobbed, "chock f-full of pie."[209]

SPECIAL PROVIDENCE
☛ An officer, during the battle of Malvern Hill, had occasion to report to General Jackson, and after hunting for some time found him and his staff under one of the heaviest fires he had ever experienced. Soon Jackson directed those about him to dismount and shelter themselves, and Dr. Dabney found a place behind a large and very thick oak gate-post, where he sat bolt upright with his back against the post. Just then there came up Major Hugh Nelson, of [C.S. Gen.] Ewell's staff—a gallant gentleman and a devout churchman, who had heard Dr. Dabney's sermon, and whose theological views did not fully indorse its doctrine—and, taking

MRS. CORDELIA POWELL ODENHEIMER, PRESIDENT GENERAL 23RD ANNUAL CONVENTION U.D.C., DALLAS, TEXAS, NOVEMBER 5-12, 1916.

in the situation at a glance, rode direct for the gate-post of "Stonewall's" chief of staff, and, giving him the military salute, coolly said: "Dr. Dabney, every shot and shell and bullet is directed by the God of battles, and you must pardon me for expressing my surprise that you should want to put a gate-post between you and special Providence." The good doctor at once retorted: "No, major; you misunderstand the doctrine I teach. The truth is that I regard this gate-post as a special Providence under present circumstances."[210]

MARRIED AN ORFANT
☛ In the early days of September, 1864, General Forrest made his celebrated Middle Tennessee raid, smashing things in Sherman's rear and playing havoc generally with the designs of that general of the Federal Army.

Upon Forrest's return to Corinth, Miss., he found that the Federal raider, General B. H. Greason, had raided North Mississippi during his absence, cutting the Mobile & Ohio railroad at several places between Okolona and Corinth, thereby causing a scarcity of rations for a few days, and during that period his troopers were compelled to subsist upon scant half rations.

In the meantime General Forrest came to division headquarters, which were located in the field, to consult General Buford upon some military move, during which interview Bill Ettenworthy planted himself upon a log, some fifty feet from where the generals were confabbing.

Pulling an old letter from his pocket, which he pretended to read, at the same time crying, almost to the top of his voice, exclaiming: "Oh, my poor wife! my poor wife! Just to think that she is up in Kentucky starving, and me here living on the fat of the land!" and, continuing, said: "If I was only permitted to divide with her, my happiness would be unbounded."

At the same time the tears were streaming down his cheeks, as if he were in mortal distress. Finally he attracted the attention of the officers, his prime desire, when General Forrest approached and accosted him as follows: "Hasn't your wife any relatives to whom she could apply for assistance?" "No, General, she haint; I married an orfant; she haint got no kin; she never saw her mother, poor child; her mother died before she was born; she is prothumous."

At this General Forrest turned and walked away, convinced that he was a victim of a joke, but nevertheless satisfied that no nostalgic genius would ever generate where that soldier grazed.[211]

CIVILIAN SUES GENERAL FORREST FOR BATTLE DAMAGE

☛ At one of General Forrest's battles in West Tennessee, in the winter of 1862, a battalion of his cavalry, in forming a line of battle, demolished an ash-hopper belonging to an old lady who chanced to live in that vicinity.

Some fifteen months later, as General Forrest was passing that way accompanied by a division of his cavalry, Bill Ettenworthy, on hearing the old lady bitterly complaining about her losses, persuaded her to upbraid General Forrest, and demand pay for the ash-hopper, which she proceeded to do in genuine rural style. Bill told her he was a lawyer, and that he would, for a small retainer, guarantee the collection of damages, upon the presentation to General Forrest of a bill for the same, which Bill drew, and the old lady at once presented to the General.

The bill read as follows:

> The claimant, Liza Livingston, is entitled to damages in the sum of one thousand dollars in Confederate money for losses sustained at the battle of _____, in the total deprivation of her only ash-hopper, worth the above amount; that one Mr. Forrest and his critter company, through unmitigated carelessness of the former, in forming a "streak of fight" with one of his critter companies in the claimant's back yard, did then and there willfully and wantonly demolish the said ash-hopper, as also her garden fence, and left the premises without reimbursing the said claimant therefor, who, through her attorney "de bonus non," demands the above-mentioned sum of money; otherwise, the claimant will garnish the Confederate States paymaster and have the salary of the aforesaid general paid her, or so much thereof as her attorney may adjudge necessary to compensate the claimant in the full liquidation of said claim, with interest and cost of this action, and that the said attorney "de bonus non" have a lien on said claim for his fee, to the amount of one hundred per centum per annum of said one thousand dollars until paid, and attorney's fees and other expenses in collecting. Should suit be brought, and the said attorney prays that an order may be granted, holding the debris of said ash-hopper in escrow, as additional collateral until the attorney's fee

herein and as above stated is fully paid, and that the said debris be held also as corroborating evidence of the damage sustained by the afore said claimant. Bill Ettenworthy, of Co. Q, Attorney in Fact for Liza Livingston.[212]

GENERAL MCNAIR'S DEFEAT AT THE BALL

☞ We remained in camp near Brandon, Miss., for several weeks. While there the ladies concluded to give a supper and grand ball to the big officers of McNair's Brigade.

The ladies wrote [C.S.] General McNair, inviting him and the commissioned officers of his staff to attend this supper and ball. They were not acquainted with him, but, like a great many other fools, thought that an officer was better than a private soldier, and the people were wonderfully stuck on officers. The ladies, I reckon, were right in this, because it was a sign of awful poor judgment for a woman to fall in love with a private soldier; they were so apt to get killed, you know. But back to the anecdote. We, the private soldiers, were somewhat chagrined at the thought of being snubbed on account of our race, color or previous condition, or perhaps other reasons best known to ladies, so we fell to work advising and devising ways and means to let them know that a private was as good by nature, if not by practice, as officers. We procured an officer's uniform and sword, some of the regimental officers agreeing to help us out in this matter. On the evening of the ball we sent a spy into Brandon to get their plans. He reported that they had one man to act as boss or floor manager, and one as gate guard. The person interested in the ball knew General McNair personally. A private by the name of Charlie Gammon, who was the regimental clown, donned the officer's uniform and sabre, and lit out for the ball. Several of us went up to McNair's headquarters—to see him on urgent business and to keep him away from the ball till late. In the meantime Charley had gone in and introduced himself as General McNair, and was having a gay old time. None of the people at the ball knew the difference except an officer, however, he kept "mum" to see the joke played out.

MRS. HERBERT M. FRANKLIN OF TENNILLE, GEORGIA, PRESIDENT OF THE GEORGIA DIVISION, U.D.C., CIRCA 1916.

Suddenly the floor manager accosts "our" General McNair and tells him there is some one at the gate who claims to be General McNair, but that the guard refuses him admittance, and the floor manager wants to know what to do about it. Everybody was as silent as the tomb for a moment. Finally Charlie broke the silence.

"Well, I declare, it is some of those private soldiers trying to raise a disturbance. Take three or four of your town guards and arrest him. Take him up town and guard him until morning. I will settle with him for this impudence. Go, now; do as I tell you, and pay no attention to anything he may say."

The boss went out with his guards and told the General to consider himself under arrest.

"What in the devil do you mean?" says the General.

"Come, dry up, dry up. We won't have any of your impudence here. Lay hold of him, boys, and take him to the guard house."

"Hold on, you—fools, I am General McNair."

"Lay hold on him, boys, and take him on. General McNair is in the house enjoying himself for some time."

By this time the real General saw that a joke had been played upon him, and commenced to try to reason the matter with them.

"Why, fellows, don't you see that I am General McNair by my uniform?"

"Oh, you are damned liar; come on to the guard-house."

And to the guard-house he went. No amount of coaxing would convince them that he was the true general.

Charley danced all night. Next morning some of the officers went to the guard-house, identified the General and brought him up to camp. He offered $500 reward for the man that looked like him, but never found him.[213]

SOUTHERN ECONOMICS 101 FROM 1920

☞ It has been found that two families out of three who are classed as poor owe their condition to bad habits of spending rather than actual lack of money. It is almost as important, therefore, that we learn how to spend money as well as how to make it. It has been said that even the great World War [I] would have been worth all it cost if it had only taught us as a nation how to be economical. A great educational movement is on foot to teach boys and girls, even in the early grades of the schools, how to spend money intelligently. One of the first steps is to learn to keep a budget of expenses, no matter how small they may seem. With such a foundation a boy begins life with an excellent start in the right direction.[214]

DRESSING IN DIFFICULT TIMES

☞ "One finds it difficult in these times to dress as one ought."

"O, I don't know. I have a suit of clothes for every day in the week."

"Really?"

"Yes, this is it."[215]

THE ONLY TIME STONEWALL JACKSON WAS FLANKED

☛ Stonewall Jackson was my professor four years just preceding the war, and many were the funny things which illustrated his character. When John Brown invaded Virginia the V.M.I. [Virginia Military Institute] cadets were ordered to the county seat, Charlestown, Va., now West Virginia, to guard him, and were the guard of honor taking Brown to the gallows, and Stonewall Jackson, then Major Jackson, was in command.

When we passed through Washington, he being in charge of the artillery detachment, left his guns at the Baltimore depot, and took the detachment down to a little hotel not far therefrom to feed the boys and give them shelter for the night. He slept in the same room with them. Mr. John M. Otey, afterwards Lieutenant-Colonel on Beauregard's staff, was one of these boys. When he was about to go to bed he was placing his purse and his watch under his head. Major Jackson seeing this said, "Mr. Otey, what are you doing?" Said Otey, "I am putting my valuables under my pillow." Said Jackson, "Now, Mr. Otey, do you not know that this is the most unsafe place you could put them; for if a burglar were to come in here the first place he would look for your valuables would be under your head." Said Otey, "That is no doubt true, Major, but it would be likely to awaken one," and, continuing, he said, "Well, Major, where do you put your watch?" "Well," said the Major, "not only is it the place the burglar would have for his objective point, but in the event that there was no burglar you are so much more apt to go away in the morning and leave them." Otey said that there was force in this, and again asked the Major what he did with his valuables. Said Jackson, "Well, I always put mine in my sock, because this is the last place that a burglar will suspect as being the receptacle for valuables, and again it is impossible to forget them, as the first thing you do on getting out of bed is to put on your socks." Otey followed the example of Jackson, and soon all were sound asleep. Early in the morning Jackson got up and went to the depot, leaving the boys asleep, and attended to having the guns put on flat cars for transportation to Harper's Ferry. After awhile the boys got up, ate their breakfast, which Jackson had taken care to order for them, and after they had finished, moved on toward the depot. Otey met Major Jackson returning. "Good morning, Major. Quite early; have you been to breakfast?" said Otey. Jackson replied, "Yes, sir," and nothing more. "Major, can I go back for you?" said Otey. "No, thank you," said Jackson. Otey, rather persistent, said: "Major, can I not do for you what you are going to do for yourself?" said Otey. "No, Mr. Otey; I left my watch, and I know exactly where I left that and my pocketbook both," Jackson rejoined. Otey, with a twinkle in his eye, said: "Major, I thought you always put your watch and purse in your sock because a burglar would not look there for valuables, and also because you could not forget them; so how is it that you came off without them?" Jackson saw that for once in his life he was flanked, and owned up as follows: "Yes, Mr. Otey, I did put them in my sock; but, Mr. Otey, I put on a clean pair of socks this morning, and in my hurry I left the dirty pair with my watch and purse in them under the bed. I'll be back in time for the train. The guns have all been put on the flats."

This was at the beginning of the war, before Sumter fell, and Jackson told us at Charlestown, when we were standing in front of the gallows of John Brown, looking down the plains which stretched from the gallows down for a mile, nearly to the woods, as follows: "If the enemy should approach, they will probably come from that direction, in which event we will give them a round or two from the guns, and then put them to flight at the point of the bayonet."[216]

CONFEDERATE GENERAL BRAXTON BRAGG.

CHAPTER SEVEN

CAPTURED OUR OWN MEN

☛ After the great battle of Cedar Creek, where I was commanding a brigade, there was, as you know, a great stampede in the afternoon. I was run over by the cavalry, as was my brigade, and ordered to the rear. I took to the left, looking to our rear, and got across the river, and on the road leading to Front Royal, some twenty men, besides another officer and myself, got together. Our objective point was Massenutten Mountain. As we went down the road to Strausburg, before crossing the river, however, we were fired into, and hence our oblique movement across the river. The road, after crossing the river, was pretty straight, and ran through pines. We thought we were safe, and were proceeding leisurely down the road, when, all at once, we saw several Yankees, their blue

CONFEDERATE WOMEN'S HOME AT FAYETTEVILLE, NORTH CAROLINA.

coats identifying them, before the picket fire, which was now plainly visible. I was the ranking officer in this crowd of fugitives. All the men had their guns, and I had urged them to keep them. As soon as I saw the pickets I suggested that we could get by them only one way, which was to capture them. So we divided, and the plan was that Captain _____, from Georgia (his name I now forget), would take a detachment of these men and make a circuit through the pines till he passed them, and circle back around in the road, and I, with the others, would conceal ourselves till he appeared in the road on the far side of the Yanks. The sod and pine leaves made the tread one of silence, and no sound was heard. I watched with a great deal of anxiety for the appearance of Captain _____ in the road beyond the Yanks. The signal was that he was to get out in the road beyond them, and I was then to jump suddenly from my hiding place, exhibiting the men with me and demand the surrender of the pickets, numbering about ten men. Finally I saw him, and I jumped out in the road and commanded them to surrender, using the same pleasant sobriquet applied to me by them but a few hours before, when I was run over by the cavalry. To my delight and surprise they held up their hands—at least the one who was standing as if on guard did—followed by the earnest protestations of the others that they surrendered.

With considerable pride I closed in on them to receive this surrender, and, to my greater surprise, they were all old Rebs, clad in the blue overcoats, to which they had fallen heir but a few hours before, as with victorious tread they had cleaned up Sheridan's camp, including his headquarters.

These are facts that I give you. There is nothing humorous about the recital, but the humor is in the preparation made to capture the Yanks, and the zest with which these old Rebs went at it, although then retreating before a victorious army, and the manifest disappointment when our gallant and heroic deed should be so suddenly turned into a joke. The Rebs thought we were Yanks, and hence surrendered; and we thought they were Yanks, hence tried to capture them.[217]

"TELL US WHAT HE LOOKS LIKE"

☛ The following reminiscence of General John Marmaduke, C.S.A., would lose much of its value, were not a personal description of the hero attached. He was tall, thin, and angular. His complexion florid, his eyes dark and sparkling, and his head covered with a wealth of white hair (not gray), that, from infancy, had borne the same hue.

During the war it was deemed advisable to make a change of commanding officers, and General Marmaduke was ordered to the Army of Tennessee. The news of the anticipated arrival of the new commander was the subject of camp-fire discussion, and naturally the soldiers were on the *qui vive* to see the General.

Breathless, one of the soldiers ran to a gathering of his comrades outside the tent, exclaiming: "Boys, I've seen him! I've seen him!" A shout followed: "Tell us what he looks like." "Now, do you listen? He's the image of an albatross." He evidently meant albino, and when the story reached the General's ears, he failed to see anything amusing in it, and is said never to have forgiven its perpetrator.[218]

WHO DARES TO SAY GENERAL WISE RETREATS?

☛ When the Confederate troops stationed on the Roanoke River, West Virginia, under command of General Wise, of Virginia, felt mountain air more healthful than river flats, and were resting at Genley Bridge, the following incident occurred:

On the veranda of the hotel, in the moonlight, the officers, with friends, were discussing the situation of affairs. At one end, concealed amidst a wealth of vines and foliage, sat General Wise. The Captain of a company in his command remarked to a lady: "How sad and unfortunate it is that we have to retreat!" Before the last word had died upon his lips, up sprang General Wise, with the buoyancy of youth, and, fire flashing indignation from his eyes, shouted: "Who is it that dares say General Wise retreats? He has never yet learned the meaning of the word 'Retreat.' He may act, as he now is doing—fall back, for prudential motives; but retreat, never."[219]

COULD NOT KEEP UP WITH THE CAPTAIN

☞ In our regiment we had a runaway-from-home thirteen years old. His name was Maddox, but we called him "Grubbing Hoe," for he was a hard knot. On one occasion the bullets came whizzing terribly by us, and Grubby ran. Captain P., of the regiment, who was especially fond of measuring trees, saw him "flying." After the battle, Captain P. said: "Grubby, you ran like it quarter horse." "Yes," replied Grubby, "but, Captain, I could not keep up with you," a reply too true to make the Captain comfortable.[220]

THE PIG BETWEEN THE LINES

☞ On one of the many times when the writer was in command of the picket line, a fat pig of one hundred pounds measurement was between the lines. Rations were scarce, and the Confederates had an eye to business. Firing from both sides was in genuine picket earnestness, which brought recruits of Yankees and Confederates. The pig was "in status quo," not knowing where to go.

As soon as recruits arrived, I gave orders for "our boys" not to fire at the pig, and to fire only occasionally, for I knew if the Yankees enjoyed the fun the pig would come to our side. Sure enough, the Yankees opened fire very furiously, yelled and enjoyed the fun, and the pig came into our open arms and was captured. It was a grand and fully-appreciated pig treat.

Shells, as if from mortars, commenced to shower about us, the fuses being plainly seen in their revolutions in the air. We had two negroes as cooks (faithful and efficient), Old Trance and Pete, both able in prayer and song, and both equally afraid of shells and the devil. Pete began one of his long, earnest and fervent prayers to the Lord. In his prayer (he and Trance believed the devil was the agent of war), he prayed to the Lord to "curtail the powers of the devil." "Yes, Lord," Trance said, "cut his tail clean off. Cut it off right close to the butt."

When the pig was cooked, in good Confederate fashion, the tail, "close to the butt," was given to Old Trance, who, for once at least, fully recognized and appreciated the full "power of prayer," for never were negroes more famished than Trance and Pete. They believed their prayers were answered.[221]

EATING GREEN PERSIMMONS

☞ I had a half-witted youth in my company, whom we called General Lee, which seemed to please him very much. One day, on the march, he was eating half-ripe persimmons. General Trimble, who was a good man and officer, addressed his men as "my lad," or "my lads." Noticing Lee eating the persimmons, he said: "My lad, why do you eat green persimmons?" Lee replied: "Why, General, to draw up my stomach to suit the size of my rations." This is evidently the origin of the expression quoted.[222]

A THOUSAND SHIRTS

☛ During the memorable campaign from Dalton to Atlanta, in 1864, a few days before reaching the Chattahoochee, General Johnson ordered a Sunday-morning inspection of the whole army, and staff officers were directed to perform the duty and report to their respective chiefs. On Hardee's staff was a dapper little lieutenant, who wore a uniform for which he had just paid $1,100 in Confederate money, and whose previous service was confined to office duty in some city. There was in the command assigned for his inspection an Arkansas regiment more famous for its fighting qualities than for its soldierly appearance on dress parade. The fact of the matter was, clothing of any kind was growing alarmingly scarce at this time in Dixie. However, the aforesaid lieutenant, in the course of his inspection, came upon a soldier of the before-mentioned regiment, whose upper garment consisted only of a coffee-sack, with holes cut for his head and arms. Whereupon he asked the soldier: "Is that all the shirt you have?" to which the soldier naively replied: "Do you expect a fellow to have a thousand shirts?"[223]

MARY & HER LITTLE CUP

☛ During the battles around Petersburg, in the summer of 1864, New Market was used as a hospital by [C.S. Gen.] Hoke's Division, and the square was generally full of helpless soldiers in every state of exhaustion and suffering. Until the shelling of the city caused the removal of the hospital, there came alone every day, at a certain hour, a little girl—perhaps ten or eleven years of age—to the market. She was very neatly and nicely dressed, very quiet and gentle in her manners, and very efficient in her labors. She carried a silver cup, which she filled at a pump close by, and, beginning at one end of the market, she handed water to each soldier as she came to him, refilling the cup as often as he desired. This she did throughout the whole line of soldiers, which was a long one. Then, beginning once more, she went through the lines, pouring water on their wounds, washing away the blood and adjusting the cloths when they were uncomfortable—in fact, doing anything and everything she could to make the situation more agreeable. If talked to, she answered kindly and briefly, and performed her self-imposed task in a quiet and business-like manner, inspiring every one with respect. The soldiers could learn nothing of her, except that her name was Mary. Her daily appearance was hailed with delight. As soon as she was seen one would exclaim: "Yonder comes Mary and her little cup!" and they often wished the friends at home could know of this little girl and her kindness to them. One poor fellow thought she ought to be put in all the little children's reading books.[224]

FIRST TIME UNDER FIRE—EXPERIENCE OF MY BODY SERVANT
☛ By J. M. Pearson, late Second Lieutenant C.S.A., now Brig.-Gen. "United Confederate Veterans."

Henry was an old -time negro belonging to my father, J. M. Pearson, of Dadeville, Alabama. I enlisted as a private in Company E, 30th Alabama Volunteers, and while stationed at Tazewell, Tenn., I wrote to father to send me a servant to cook, and otherwise wait on me. About sundown one evening, in the fall of 1862, father came to Tazewell, bringing Henry, who was then about sixty years old. I told Henry to make a fire and prepare supper. When he started his fire, and had his flour converted into dough, orders came to prepare for marching at once. I said: "Henry put up your frying-pan and dough and get ready to march."

He said: "Mos Matt, how long, fore you gwine to stop for to get supper?"

"I don't know," I replied, "I expect we will march all night."

"Good God!" Henry said, "you gwine to break your res dat way? Hit will jes be de ruination of you."

We started soon, and all night long we marched. About day break we stopped at Powell river, and were preparing to wade through, when Henry came up and said:

"Mos Matt, whar de bridge you gwine to cross on?"

"There is no bridge," I replied, "for us to cross, we have to wade; but you can go down the river one or two hundred yards, where the wagon train is crossing, and you can ride over in a wagon."

" Is dat so, Mos Matt, and can't you git de Kurnel to let you ride over in a wagon, Mos Matt?"

"No," said I.

"Well, if dat don't beat me," said Henry; "seems dat a white gemman ain't got de showin' of a nigger in dis country."

We finished crossing and rested on the north bank of the river, in plain view of Cumberland Gap, which was about five miles off. About nine o'clock Henry came to where we were, and said:

"Mos Matt, whar bouts de Yankees?"

Having been posted at the Gap before that time, I was able to give him a good description of the location. I told him that on the right-hand peak was located a large cannon, and that I was expecting, before long, that the Yankees would open fire on us.

"Good God!" Henry replied, "dey ain't fools enough to waste dey aminition dat way."

In a short time I discovered a white-looking puff of smoke from the right-hand peak, and at once I called Henry's attention to it, and he laughed at "de fools wastin' dey aminition." Before his laugh was over, the dull boom of the cannon was heard, and immediately the shell was whistling through the air; and as Henry said afterwards, the shell was saying "which-way, which-way, which-way, which-way, which-way, which-way, bang!" and exploded across the river.

Henry took up his knapsack and started off, but I stopped him, and told him maybe they would not shoot again. But he stood there with his eyes as big as saucers and watched the mountain summit. Again the puff of smoke came out, and Henry was terribly restless and uneasy, but said nothing about the "Yankees wastin' dey aminition;" and again the dull explosion fell upon our ears, followed by the wild shrieking of the shell, which burst, with a terrible crash, among the trees, about two hundred yards to the rear. The sound was appalling to Henry, who seized his knapsack and said:

"Good-bye, Mos Matt, I must go back yonder whar your baggage is; some dem fool niggers gwine to steal your baggage, sho; an Moster told me to be sho and take keer your baggage; good-bye, Mos Matt, take keer of yosef." And he left, and I never saw him for four days.[225]

CONFEDERATE GENERAL EWELL & THE PRIVATE

☞ At the battle of Port Republic, on the 9th of May, 1862, after the charge of the Louisiana brigade commanded by General Dick Tyler, and the 25th Virginia Regiment, on the celebrated battery of the 1st Ohio, after the battery of six guns was captured and a charge was ordered along the entire line, General Ewell, who was not known by many of Jackson's men, passed by the captured battery, where death and destruction were around—every horse killed or wounded and nine-tenths of its members killed or wounded—and got off his horse, and was leaning over a wheel of one of the guns, looking intently at the terrible work that had been done. A private of Company A, 25th Virginia Regiment, by the name of John Hatterman, who had assisted in its capture, approached General Ewell, who had no insignia of rank on his garments, and remarked to him, not knowing him: "Hello, old conscript; you look like you had captured the battery. Get your gun and come along with us." The regiment passed on. Some one inquired of Hatterman if he knew he was talking to General Ewell. He said: "No; and he did not give a damn." General Ewell looked at the boy and smiled, but said nothing.[226]

MISS LOTTYE WEBB, MAYFIELD, KENTUCKY, MAID OF HONOR FOR FORREST CAVALRY CORPS.

DON'T THINK YOU DID, CAPTAIN

☞ 'Twas in the month of March; 'twas night—one of those weird, mysterious-looking nights, which recalled forcibly to our minds the encounter of "Tam O'Shanter" with the witches in the old ruined kirk. The veiled moon peeped from a cloud and hung above the ivy-mantled church. We watched the mortars spangling the heavens. The grate was polished, guiltless of fire or warmth, save a fagot of lightwood (in default of other light), which shed its flickering rays over the gay occupants of the room. Each soldier had some anecdote to tell—each officer some incident of his experience to relate. [This one is] . . . remembered at this time: [C.S.] Generals Gordon and Pegram were being pressed rapidly back. At last they broke and retreated before overwhelming numbers. Mahone came in on a double-quick. We flung ourselves down to allow Gordon to pass over. Gordon and Pegram quickly reformed and gallantly supported us. In ten minutes we were driving the enemy helter-skelter before us. Later in the day, as we were walking over the ground, a courier rode up to a staff officer and asked: "How went the day, Captain?" "Fine, fine! We drove them at the point of the bayonet." He rubbed his hands with great glee. A soldier, helping himself to a comfortable overcoat, looked up and replied: "Don't think you did, Captain; but I think we fellows what carries the muskets did." The two remembered that they were wanted at headquarters, and rode away.[227]

A FISHING PARTY

☞ Parties were all the rage in Petersburg, during the siege starvation parties. There were as many officers and soldiers in the social circles of the city as in camp, and many were the schemes and plans resorted to to come to town. [C.S.] Colonel Lester, of Thomas' Brigade, had made arrangements for a party on Thurs day night, and the officers and soldiers composing this club had made engagements, and the ladies had accepted their escort. The day arrived; the club met at the Colonel's tent to talk over the expected pleasure of the evening; but the "schemes of men and mice gang aft agley." Orders came down from General Thomas, about 2 o'clock, that neither officers nor men were to leave camp, except on special permits, until further orders. In a moment all was changed—no mirth, no singing, all were sullenly silent. Hours passed, and no scheme presented itself. The Colonel was going to the Masonic lodge, and would tender the regrets of his comrades to the ladies. This was the best to be done. The sun was down, and the Colonel cantering down the road to the city, followed by the earnest ejaculation: "I wish I was a Mason!" Suddenly Lieutenant Lane and Captain Perry exclaimed: "Boys, we've got it! We've got it! Be ready, now; quick!" Taking some poles in their hands, they repaired to the General's quarters and modestly asked permission to be allowed to go to Ellerslie Pond to catch some fish. "Certainly," said the General, and they withdrew. Two hours later they assembled in a parlor, took up the thread of the last flirtation, and "chased the flying hours with flying feet." When the Colonel, at 10 o'clock, came to apologize for Thomas' Brigade of Georgians, knowing Mahone's Brigade of Virginians would supply the deficiency, judge of his surprise at seeing the entire club. He was greeted with a loud laugh, and informed that they started for the fish-pond, at Ellerslie, but the night was so dark they missed the road and found themselves in the city. They could not be blamed for getting lost in the dark. The joke soon got out, and wherever they went they heard the inquiry throughout their division: "What do you ask for your fish?" "Been fishing lately?" "Dealers in fish? Fresh or salt?" and when the division failed to come in (though they were under arms, waiting for Pickett's Division) on the 25th of March, the soldiers said the division must have gone fishing and got lost.[228]

THE OLD MAN & THE PRIVATE

☛ In the early part of the war I was a private soldier, under Stonewall Jackson, in Virginia. At that time I was a mere boy, and my gun was almost as big and heavy as I was. You can imagine how tired and hungry I was after I had marched two days without any food. A driving rainstorm came on, and I could hardly drag my feet along the muddy road.

A tent by the roadside attracted my attention, and I saw a gray-bearded face peeping out at the marching troops.

"Hello, old man!" I shouted; "got anything to eat in there?"

"Yes; what's the matter?" the man in the tent replied.

I told him that I was hungry and had been marching two days without a scrap of food.

"Come right in," said the old fellow, pleasantly.

Into the tent I plunged in a hurry, throwing down my gun and smacking my lips in anticipation of a square meal.

The stranger opened a camp chest and invited me to help my self. You should have seen the way I sailed into the rations. I ate ravenously, without saying a word, and for the time forgot all about my kind host.

Finally, he asked me if I would have a drink of water, and handed me a gourd from a bucket in one corner of the tent. I took a big drink and got ready to depart.

"You have been very kind to me," I said to my new friend, "and I would like to know your name."

"My name is Lee," was the answer.

"Lee—what Lee?" I asked him—"not General Lee?"

"That is my name," was his quiet response.

Well, I was taken aback, of course; but I was young and cheeky, and I made the best of it. Soldiers had no handkerchiefs, so I wiped my hands on my breeches and gave the General's paw a cordial shake.

He asked me my name, and told me to take care of myself as I left. A few days later my command was on the march, and had just reached a bridge, when it was ordered to open ranks to let General Lee pass.

I was standing at the head of the line, and when the General dashed up, followed by a negro servant riding on another horse, I could not keep still.

"Howdy, General!" I shouted.

"Why, Smith, my boy!" he replied, as he pulled up his horse. "Here, Smith, get on this horse and follow me."

The negro turned over his horse to me and I mounted him.

I rode off with my commander, feeling mighty good, I can tell you; but those rascals at the bridge were bound to have their fun, and about a thousand of them set up a yell. "Take him along, General," they howled. "He ain't no good—never was on a horse before in his life—can't do nothing but eat—take him along and keep him!"

That was the send-off my comrades gave me; but the General understood the humorous side of camp life, and he merely smiled and kept straight ahead.

I accompanied him a short distance, and returned to my company in the course of an hour or two, after the General's staff had joined him.

That is the story of my meeting with Bob Lee. Do you wonder that we boys all took a fancy to him? He was just as clever to Private Smith as he would have been to a General, and I could see that it was a pleasure to him to share his rations with me.

But the boys guyed me about it a long time. They told the story with lots of fanciful flourishes, and three years later, when I went to the West, as an officer on General Forrest's staff, I found that the tale had preceded me and had made me well known in army circles.

Ah, those were great days; full of great men and great deeds. Even now, after the lapse of a generation, my heart thrills with pride when I recall my two meetings with the Confederacy's grandest chieftain—the idol of the people, the father of his soldiers—royal old Bob Lee![229]

NOTHING TO EAT
☛ Said a hungry Confederate to the lady who met him at the door, when out foraging one day, "Madam, will you please give me something to eat? I haven't had a mouthful for three days, to-day, to-morrow and next day."[230]

SHOOT 'EM IN THE LINE
☛ A straggling Yankee soldier was in a squad that was captured and passed before [C.S.] General Paul Jones Semmes. One of the men remarked that this prisoner was hungry. "Feed him," said General Semmes. "Shoot 'em in the line, but feed 'em on this side of it."[231]

NAMED AFTER U.S. "GENERAL BURNSIDE"
☛ When the 18th Virginia Regiment was encamped at Centerville, one of the privates, while sleeping, caught afire, and all of his clothes on one side were burned off. He was ever after called "General Burnside" by his comrades.[232]

RATHER SEE HER AFTER IT IS OVER

☛ Just before the battle of the Wilderness, Sergeant Billy Bass received a letter from his wife. She said she heard that there was to be a big battle, and she did so wish to see him before it was fought! When Billy read it, he said he would like also to see her before the battle, but he would a great sight rather see her after it was over.[233]

WHY THEY WERE THE BEST TROOPS

☛ Captain M., of the Louisiana Brigade, Army of Northern Virginia, says that, in his opinion, the North Carolina infantry were the best troops in that army; they would follow their leaders anywhere. A North Carolina man, if lucky enough to get it, could eat a side of bacon without its making him any heavier. When dead his body never decomposed: he simply turned as yellow as a saddle, then dried up and blew away. A field full of dead Tar Heels would cause no stench.[234]

THE STONEWALL JACKSON INSTITUTE, ABINGDON, VIRGINIA: A COLLEGE FOR GIRLS AND YOUNG WOMEN.

SOLDIER TALK

☛ A company of Confederate soldiers, bound for Chattanooga, on the cars, were indulging in some Munchausen stories of the war. One had seen a man shot through the head, and he lived; another had seen a soldier whose arms and legs had been carried away, and he lived; a third had known a man to be shot in the side and through the head, and he lived; and the fourth had seen a man shot clean through the body by a ten-pound cannon ball, and—"He lived?" asked his listening comrades. "No," quietly responded the narrator, "he died."[235]

DOING HIS FULL DUTY

☛ Corporal G., of the 6th Kentucky Infantry, was fortunate enough to have some cider in his canteen at the battle of Murfreesboro, and was unfortunate enough to have a minie-ball pass through that canteen just as the command started on a charge. The corporal hesitated but a minute; but, in that minute, he had thrown down his gun, placed a finger on each side of the hole made by the bullet, and, at one huge swig, drunk the precious fluid, and regained his company, conscious of having done his full duty to himself in saving the cider.[236]

ON THE VERGE OF EMANCIPATION
☛ Billy is an "Old Virginy" negro, proud of his state and prouder of his manners. His silver locks show that he has reached, if not passed, the allotted term of three-score-and-ten; but his form is still erect, and he tries hard to keep up his end of the log. "Well, Billy," said a gentleman the other day, "you'll soon have to root with the hogs at the dump-pile for a living." "Nary time," said he, straightening up, with indignation, "I come of too good a stock for that. My old master was a gentleman, born and bred, and I can't go back on my raising."[237]

GENERAL LEE CURES A FURLOUGH-SEEKER
☛ On one occasion a man from Georgia had been persistent in personal application to General Lee for a furlough. One morning the General asked his tormentor if he understood the position of a soldier. The latter said he did. He was ordered to assume it. General Lee then gave the command, "Right about face; forward, march." As he never gave the command to "halt" the Georgian kept on marching until he got tired; but this little hint cured him, and his next application was through the usual channels.[238]

THEY WENT SILENT IN A HURRY
☛ During the retreat of the Confederates through South Carolina, at the time of Sherman's advance, Sergeant McD_____, of Western North Carolina, was sent on detail to the town of M_____, where a regiment of home guards was stationed. These valorous heroes, seeing a soldier from the front, gathered around him, eagerly inquiring the news. "News?" says Mac, solemnly, "I believe there is none. Yes, there is a little, too, but it's not of much importance. Old Hardee burned up a regiment of home guards at Florence, the other day, to keep them from falling into the enemy's hands." No more questions were asked.[239]

GENERAL JACKSON'S "PSYCHIC" SERVANT
☛ General Stonewall Jackson's body servant was a negro boy, who seemed to have a prescience of any forward movement; his camp utensils and his master's baggage were always ready, packed in anticipation of the order to advance. This peculiarity excited remark amongst the General's staff, and one day several young officers called the black boy up and asked him how he guessed so accurately the intentions of the General. "Well, gemmen, whenever I sees Massa Stonewall get up in the night and go to kneeling and saying his prayers, I know there's a fight on hand, sure, and I makes preparations accordin'."[240]

THE STARVING CONFEDERATE INFANTRY
☛ A column of infantry was one day marching along a dusty road, under a broiling sun. Close by, under some trees, were discovered a cluster of sleek commissaries seated at dinner. A tall, rawboned and dust-begrimed

North Carolinian went up to the fence, and, putting his chin upon it, stared long and earnestly at the tempting table. At last, bursting with envy, he yelled out: "I say, misters, did any of ye ever hearn tell of the battle of Chancellorsville?"[241]

NO RESPECT FOR THE WRITINGS OF GENERAL HARDEE
☞ General Hardee once came across a straggler, and asked him "why he did not travel faster and keep up with his command?" The soldier wished to know "what in the deuce he had to do with it?" "Only that I am General Hardee, the commander of this department," was the reply. "Oh, you wrote a book on tactics, did you?" "I did," said the General. "Well," said the private, "I have been taught, according to your rules, how to double column at half distance. Now, I wish you would tell me how to double distance on half rations." General Hardee struck spurs to his horse and traveled on.[242]

DIAMOND CUTTING DIAMOND
☞ In the old First Virginia, in 1861, two of the boys, whom we will call A and B, had left sweethearts in Richmond. One of them soon forgot the soldier boy who had left her behind, and married a gentleman named Point. At this time B was much pleased, and joked A terribly. All day long he would ask him "If he could see the Point?" etc. Soon after this B's sweetheart, whose name was Hurt, forgot the vows she had made, and got married also. This was A's sweet revenge, and he gave B no peace by constantly asking him "What Hurt him?" "Where he was Hurt?" etc. It was a case of diamond cut diamond.[243]

"CAN'T CROW OVER GEORGIA"
☞ In the winter of 1863-64 there was great rivalry between an Alabama and a Georgia regiment attached to the same brigade. No matter what one did, the colonel of the other tried to excel it. It was during the great Madison Run revivals. One Sunday the Georgia colonel noticed a great commotion in the Alabama Regiment. He sent over and found out that thirteen of the Alabamians, the fruit of the meetings, were to be baptized. He sent for his adjutant, and then thundered out: "Captain _____ go to work at once and detail fifteen men, and have them baptized without delay. These damned Alabamians can't crow over Georgia."[244]

"DON'T MIND THEM BOYS, MISTER"
☞ A certain officer of Company C, 9th Virginia Cavalry, was noted for his neatness, and, consequently, was chaffed by the boys a great deal. He had occasion, in the fall of '63, to pass through the camp of [C.S.] General Barringer's North Carolina Brigade. He sat as straight as an arrow, and, with great dignity, rode along amidst such bantering as "Good morning, General," "Come out of that hat," and "Where did you

get those boots?" On arriving near the General's tent, he was stopped by the Tar Heel guard, who observed to him, with great sympathy: "Don't you mind them boys, mister. They are always hollering at some fool going along by here."[245]

ONE WAY TO GET MEAT

☞ A soldier, being on picket reserve, went to a farm house, as he said, to borrow a frying-pan, but for what none could imagine, as there was nothing to fry. However, he went to the house and knocked at the door, which was opened by a lady, who asked what he wished. "Madam, could you lend me a frying pan? I belong to the picket down here." "Yes, sir;" and forthwith came the pan. He took it, looked in it, turned it over again, and looked into it very hard, as if not certain it was clean. "Well, sir," said the lady, "can I do anything more for you?" "Could—could—could you lend me a piece of meat to fry in it, ma'am?" and he laughed, in spite of himself. He got it.[246]

THE RAILROAD MEN OF THE STONEWALL BRIGADE

☞ One of the best companies of the Stonewall Brigade was composed of railroad men from Martinsburg, West Virginia. In a charge at Manassas, the story goes, the captain offered a barrel of whisky to the man who first reached the guns. When the captain got there one of his men, already astraddle of a cannon, cried out: "Don't forget that barrel, captain!" The next day an admirer of the hero asked him how war compared with railroading. "Well," said he, " the life of a soldier is pretty rough, but it has one advantage over railroading." "What is that?" was asked. "'Tain't near so dangerous," said the man of the rail.[247]

CONFEDERATE MUTUAL ADMIRATION SOCIETIES

☞ A few days before the battle of Seven Pines, [C.S. Gen.] Kershaw's South Carolina Brigade was moving to take position on the right of [C.S. Gen.] Semmes' Georgia Brigade. As the South Carolinians came in front of our brigade, they gave three cheers for the gallant Semmes, of Georgia. Not to be outdone in courtesy, we gave lustily back, "Three cheers for the chivalrous Kershaw, of South Carolina." The last lingering notes had hardly faded on the breeze, when a voice from far down our line was faintly but distinctly heard, "Three cheers for me, boys, and I am damned drunk at that." This was but a step from the sublime to the ridiculous. The South Carolinians were soon out of sight, but not out of hearing of the laughter following the burlesque upon the scene between the mutual admiration societies.[248]

THE INDESTRUCTIBLE IRISHMAN

☞ Private Cushman, of the 5th Alabama Battalion, a gallant son of Erin, was known as one of the best soldiers in the command. He never missed a battle in which his company was engaged, never straggled, never missed duty on account of sickness, never asked for a furlough, and was, in every way, a faultless soldier, except that he would, occasionally, "get a brick in his hat." He was offered the first furlough of indulgence for meritorious services. He answered: "What do I want with a furlough? Jist let me go away for a day or two for me health; I have a bit of a weakness in me stomach, and a wee drop would be afther doing me good." He went to Richmond, invested all his Confederate "promises to pay" in the stimulant he loved so well, and came back, when his funds were all exhausted, with blackened eyes, a swelled nose, a mashed-up face, and the general appearance of a used-up Rebel. "I'm hearty as a buck now, me honey; all the wakeness is gone out of me stomach, and I'm ready for another turn at the bloody Yanks." He served to the close of the war most gallantly, without ever having been sick or wounded.[249]

HE DIVIDED THE SOAP

☛ Bob J. was, in most respects, an exemplary Christian soldier, and kept the Decalogue holy, except in one particular—he believed that "cleanliness was next to godliness," and would steal soap. The army of General Early was nearing Washington city, and Bob saw a bucket of soft soap, which he confiscated and took to camp. It was the work of but a few minutes to find a creek, divest himself of his dusty clothes, and, after a generous smear of the saponifier, to plunge into the grateful water. A disappointed look overspread his features as he emerged from the water, but this was quickly concealed behind a contented smile thrown out to a group of soldiers who were appealing to him for a "divide" of the soap. Bob hesitated for a long time, but finally told them not to use it all, and then hied himself to camp, where he startled his messmates by screams of maniacal laughter, which, of course, they did not understand until Bob "double-quicked" from camp, closely followed by a crowd of half-dressed

CONFEDERATE MONUMENT, ROCKVILLE, MARYLAND.

soldiers, on whose exposed shoulders great drops of greasy water stood out like beads. Bob had stolen a bucket of wagon-grease instead of soap, and the obliged bathers wanted to find the "feller who didn't want them to use all the soap."[250]

NOBLE ACT OF GENERAL MAHONE

☛ Early one morning in August, 1870, a Sister of Charity, while returning from church in Richmond, Va., saw ahead of her a lady, whom she [had] supposed to be in New Orleans, as the whole family belonged there. Hearing her gentle call, the lady turned to find a former friend in the humble sister's garb. Learning that the lady in question was in very straitened circumstances, and anxious to return to her people, the good sister studied how to proceed, gladly donating some small change of her own private funds to the purpose, but she found it insufficient. She then determined she would call on General Mahone at his hotel. Doing so, she related the facts that the lady had had several brothers who were valiant soldiers in the cause, and that it would be a truly worthy deed to aid the lady in reaching her people. Listening, with all the attention of a soldier and a gentleman, to the case, he drew from his pocket a crisp five-dollar bill, modestly folded up so that its amount could not easily be seen, and then added his authority for a pass on the railroad, as far as his power extended, with a recommendation to the connecting road to continue the good service. All this was the work of a moment and so charmingly done that no one could have given more merit to the noble act than the graceful, gracious and polished General Mahone.[251]

THE REPRIMAND
☞ A certain captain of the 4th Florida Infantry, feeling it his duty to reprimand the members of his company for straggling from the line of march, did that needed work to his own satisfaction and to the apparent contrition of the offenders. The good results of the lecture were evident until an apple orchard was spied and its bright, red fruit seemed to invite the plucking. At once, by a common impulse, the newly-disciplined boys broke for the orchard, while the captain completed his work of reform by shouting: "Boys, if you will go, bring your captain a few."[252]

CAN'T FOOL A CONFEDERATE DOCTOR
☞ A tall, fine-looking fellow [that is, a Confederate soldier], the picture of health, went to the doctor for an excuse for the day. When his turn came the surgeon looked at him, in surprise, and said: "Well, sir, what's the matter with you?" "Well, Doctor," said he, putting on a most woebegone look and rubbing his eyes, "my eyes are sore, and it hurts me to dress to the right!" He didn't get his excuse that day.[253]

REBEL GRIT
☞ [Confederate Lieut.] Beverly Kennon, who was in command of the [CSS] *Governor Moore*, one of the gunboats opposed to the Federal fleet in the battle on the Mississippi, below New Orleans, was a thoroughly brave and gallant man. When his craft was actually sinking, riddled like a sieve by the ordnance of the [USS] *Oneida* and other [Yankee] vessels, [U.S. Captain Samuel P.] Lee, who was in command of the *Oneida*, shouted out to him, pointing, as he did so, to the Stars and Bars, which were still streaming over her deck: "I say, there! haul down that damned rag, will you?" "I'm damned if I do!" yelled Beverly Kennon in return;

"I'll see you in hell first!"[254]

HOW STONEWALL GOT TO HEAVEN

☛ Two Confederate captives in a Yankee prison heard of Stonewall's death. "Bill," said one, "do you know how Stonewall got to heaven?" "No; how was it?" "Well, when the news of his being killed got to heaven, two angels were sent to escort him up. They went to our army, looked all around the field of battle and about headquarters, but couldn't find him. They went over to the 'Feds' and hunted for him there; and still they couldn't find him. So, after searching all day, they gave it up and went back to heaven, where they found he had flanked them and got there without their knowing about it."[255]

ABOVE, IN THE SPIRIT OF GREAT BRITAIN'S MULTINATIONAL FLAG, THE CONFEDERATE VETERANS' PROPOSED "NEW" U.S. FLAG DESIGN, COMBINING THE CONFEDERATE STATES BATTLE FLAG AND THE UNITED STATES NATIONAL FLAG, 1913. (THE PROPOSAL WAS, OF COURSE, REJECTED BY THE U.S. GOVERNMENT.)

HOW TO UPSET GENERAL EARLY

☛ When Jackson's corps was on the march from the valley to Fredericksburg, we passed through a certain village, where lived one of the intensest "original secessionists" in the state. General J. A. Early (who had been one of the leaders of the "Union" party in the Virginia convention, who had been firm to the last in trying to avert the war, but when it came, drew his sword for his native state and "threw away the scabbard") rode up to a group of citizens and inquired: "Where is Mr. _____?" Being informed that the gentleman was absent, the grim old soldier replied: "I am very sorry; I should like very much to see him. He is the gentleman who used to denounce me as a submissionist, and say that he did not want a peaceable settlement; that he wanted to show the

Yankees what Southern valor would accomplish, and that he meant to wade through seas of blood, and all that sort of stuff. I am anxious to see him. I want to see how much blood he has on his breeches. I understand that he holds high office in the grand army of spectators, who have been fighting us in the rear, while we have been at the front trying to protect his precious carcass."[256]

THE BORING HOME GUARD
☛ A "home guard" once bored General Stonewall Jackson on the Virginia Central Railroad. Elated at being treated with that gentlemanly courtesy, as little expected as little deserved, but which General Jackson invariably extended to all, he pressed the conversation, and finally clinched it thus: "Well, General, where do you intend to make your next strike?" "Are you a good hand to keep secrets?" asked General Jackson, earnestly. "Oh, yes!" breathlessly gasped the fellow, inching close up to the General to catch the mighty secret. "Well, so am I!" the General half whispered in his ear. Home guard mysteriously vanished, and has never been heard of since.[257]

FASTEST METHOD OF CURING THE CHILLS
☛ There was a cadaverous soldier belonging to the hospital at Greensboro, Ga., who often contrived to get a stout draw of real old apple or peach (none of your commissary stuff), by feigning to be suddenly seized with chills. He would stroll to some gentleman's door, shake all over violently, and beg to get a warm drink, lest his chill should terminate fatally. He had such a sickly, unhealthy look, that no one suspected the trick, and so he went on from day to day, getting his hot toddies, and abundance of sympathy from kindhearted ladies. He was about to become that most hopeless and incorrigible of all nuisances—"a hospital rat,"—when his pleasant style of living was broken in upon by an unexpected incident. He had taken his seat, on this occasion, on the door-step of a very shrewd, or a very benevolent, old lady, I do not know which, and there began to shake as though every bone would come out of his body. The tender-hearted lady coming to the door seemed but to aggravate the violence of the attack; he stammered out, "'Most froze to death, can you give me some liquor?" The compassionate eyes of the old lady took in the situation, and her orders were given with military precision, "You, Jim, here's a poor soger a shakin with the ager, you tote him in that thar room and put him in the feather-bed. Lizy Ann, you run and get some hot bricks fer his feet; and you, Betsy Jane, make him some real strong red-pepper tea, hot as pisin." The orders were literally obeyed, poor Tom was smothered in a feather-bed in June, roasted with hot bricks, and drenched with fiery pepper-tea. But the prescription was admirable; he had no more chills, all the unhealthy humors in his body were effectually sweated out of him.[258]

"YOU SWEET DARLING CONFEDERATES"

☛ One day during the war a detachment of [C.S.] General Basil Duke's troops was moving through the northern part of Kentucky. Dick Wintersmith's son was in the band and its leader. The guerrillas were worn out and hunted down. Their horses were nearly foundered. The men were dirty and ragged. They halted for a rest near a seminary for young ladies, all sympathizers with the Confederacy. Out came the ladies when they saw the gray coats. They brought out food, drink, and armfuls of flowers. They hung flowers around the necks of the hunted men, and sang out in a musical chorus, "Oh, you darling Confederates." A straggling Confederate, fat, greasy and ragged, came pounding up at this, flogging a jaded hack along, swearing because he could not keep up with his better mounted associates. He was just in time to hear the invocation of the young ladies. He yelled out, "Oh, you sweet, darling Confederates, the Yanks are coming." There was a bolt at this. The laggard pounded on behind, swearing, "Oh, you damned sweet darlings, I hope the Yanks will get you." The Federals were right at his heels. The flying Confederates wheeled in their saddles, laughing at the certain capture of the slow rider. Suddenly the tired horse stumbled, fell, and threw the fat rider over into the ditch, where he escaped notice, while a detachment of Federal troops headed off the main band and captured every one but one man, who was saved by having the poorest horse. The prisoners never heard the last of "Oh, you sweet, darling Confederates."[259]

A BLACK CONFEDERATE SOLDIER WITH A SENSE OF HUMOR

☛ Early in the war John Williams, a full negro, fired with Southern zeal, besought his master, a Georgian, and obtained permission to accompany a regiment from that state, which was soon placed under the command of General Floyd. The history of that campaign is well known. On the retreat John became homesick, and was allowed to depart. He had become well known to General Floyd and all his command. On his departure he went to take leave of the General, when the following dialogue was had: "Well, John, you are going to leave us, eh?" "Yes, Mars Floyd; it 'pears like I could do more good at home now dan bein' here; so I thought I'd go home and 'courage up our people to hold on." "That's right, John. But are you going to tell 'em that you left us when running from the Yankees?" "No, sir; no, Mars Floyd, dat I ain't. You may 'pend upon my not tellin' nothin' to 'moralize dem people." "But how will you get around telling them, John?" "Easy 'nough, Mars Floyd. It won't do to 'moralize dem people. I'm goin' to tell 'em dat when I lef' de army it was in firs' rate sperrits, and dat, owin' to de situation of de country, and de way de lan' lay, we was a-advancin' back'ards, and de Yankees was a-retreatin' for'ards."[260]

LOCHLAINN SEABROOK ∽ 171

THE HORSE THAT OUTSMARTED FORREST

☛ Early in the War, while Forrest was still a colonel, he and his men were camped at Hopkinsville, Kentucky.

One morning it was discovered that a horse had slipped its halter and was happily munching away on one of the great piles of horse corn that was stacked in the center of the camp. The owner, a young private, was brought before Forrest and given a lecture on carelessness.

"But," the boy protested vigorously, "my hoss is the smartest hoss around. I swear that there ain't no gear that kin restrain 'im!"

At this, Forrest gave him detailed instructions on how to tie off a halter, and the lad, rolling his eyes, went away lamely promising to follow them to the letter.

The next morning the offending horse was found at the center of camp once again, calmly chewing away at the huge mound of corn. And once again the boy was brought to Forrest for a thorough scolding. This time Forrest threatened to have him arrested for refusal to obey orders.

"But I done jes' as you told me to Colonel," the boy replied innocently enough, "tied 'im up nice and neat. Like I said, that thar hoss cain't be haltered!"

Forrest said that he himself would make sure the horse was tied up properly that night, that way there would be no more problems with the animal.

THE BONNIE BLUE FLAG.

OPENING LINES OF THE POPULAR SOUTHERN TUNE "THE BONNIE BLUE FLAG," BY IRISHMAN HARRY MCCARTHY.

When dawn broke the next day, however, there was the empty halter hanging from its pole again, and there was the horse back at the corn pile, oblivious to the furor it was creating around camp.

A flustered Forrest brought the boy back into his tent one last time. "I shore didn't mean to embarrass you sir," the young private pled in his defense, "but thar it is. Thar simply ain't no man that kin keep my hoss from gittin' loose if'n he has a mind to."

Still mystified, Forrest crinkled his brow, studied the animal for a moment, then said gravely: "I reckon any horse that hardheaded deserves an extra heapin' of corn now and agin." This was the only time Forrest was ever known to surrender to an adversary.[261]

THE "EXPLODING" BAND

☞ Almost every one is familiar with the tremendous crash made by a brass band at the commencement of certain pieces of music. I once saw it have quite an amusing effect upon a Confederate soldier in Virginia. When the Washington Artillery, of New Orleans, was removed from the 2nd South Carolina Brigade, in 1861, the band of our regiment, the 5th South Carolina, decided to give them a serenade on the night previous to their departure. Accordingly, the band, accompanied by a considerable crowd of the 5th, went over to the artillery camp. It was a calm, clear night, all the noise of the camp had died away, and with the exception of one or two, here and there, the whole section was fast asleep. The musicians took their stand between one of the caissons and a large spreading oak, at the root of which, stretched out upon his blanket, lay one of the artillerymen, quietly taking his repose, and utterly unconscious of anything that was going on around him. At last the entire band, with drums, cymbals, horns and all, struck up some lively air, with a crash equal to the discharge of a twenty-four pounder—away they went, blowing most furiously and entirely ignorant of the immense excitement they had created in the mind of the poor fellow lying under them, who, at the first sound of their instruments, bounced into the air like an India rubber ball, and apparently without moving a single muscle—it seemed as if the sound of the horns had tossed him up, without changing the horizontal position of his body. He lit on his feet, however, and, still half asleep, with the most ludicrous expression of horror on his face, exclaimed, or rather gasped out "Great Heavens; has the whole damned battery blown up?" He was agreeably surprised when informed that only the horns, and not the battery, had been blown up.[262]

OVERLY ENTHUSIASTIC DRILLING

☞ Immediately after the ordinances of secession had been passed, and it became apparent that there would be war, the attention of the Southern youth was directed almost exclusively to [the popular military instruction book] "Hardee's Tactics," and especially the Drill of the Company. Military organizations sprang up thick as hops all over the country, and the rivalry between them, as well as the interest elicited from their civilian friends and admirers, was immense. There was one very fine company organized at Memphis which acquired a wide reputation for excellence in all the evolutions. It was commanded by a Mexican veteran who was a master of tactics and martinet in drill. Every afternoon a throng of people would resort to the large vacant lot whereon this company was receiving instruction, to witness and applaud its performance. On one occasion, when an unusually large and appreciative crowd was collected and many ladies present, the Captain became so enthused that, after exhausting every recognized movement, he began to extemporize, and shouted out the command: "Company, right and left oblique; march!" The men gallantly essayed to obey the order, and, diverging from either flank, scattered widely. The Captain racked his brain for a proper command to bring them together again, but the tactics provided no formula for such a dilemma. At length, when the boys had become strung out like a flock of wild pigeons, and seemed about to separate forever, he yelled, in desperation: "Huddle! Gol darn ye!"[263]

STREET SCENE, HOUSTON, TEXAS, OF THE 1920 "GREAT REUNION" OF THE UNITED CONFEDERATE VETERANS.

CHAPTER EIGHT

THEM POKEY YANKS

☞ City Point, on the James River, was the landing for transports with soldiers released from Northern prisons on parole. One day, a most woebegone and emaciated "Johnny" sat swinging his shoeless feet from a barrel, awaiting his turn, when a pompous Federal major remarked to no one in particular: "It isn't far to Richmond?" "Reck'n et's near onto three thousin' mile," drawled Johnny, weakly. "Nonsense! you must be crazy!" replied the officer, staring. "Wal, I ent a-reknin' edzact," was the slow reply. "Jest thought so, kinder." "Oh, you did! And why, pray?" "'Cause it took youens nigh onto foore years to git thar from Washington," was the settling retort.[264]

WHY GENERAL HARDEE THRASHED A TRAIN CONDUCTOR

☞ No officer was more beloved by the [Confederate] soldiers than General Hardee, yet, he was, at times, austere and given to sudden bursts of uncontrollable anger. Upon one occasion he was riding aboard a train, when the conductor fell into an altercation with a sick soldier. The latter had no ticket, but offered Confederate money in pay for his fare. The conductor refused to take it, and started to put the soldier off the train. General Hardee at once interfered, and gave the conductor a terrible mauling, saying, at the conclusion of his efforts, "I have beaten you for two reasons: first, for mistreating a sick soldier; second, for refusing to take Confederate money."[265]

A BLACK CONFEDERATE SOLDIER REMINISCES

☞ "Sam," said a Confederate the other day to a negro in his employment, "were you in the army during the war?" "Yes, sir; a little longer than I keered to be." "Were you ever in a fight?" "Lots of 'em." "Which side whipped in your fights?" "Well," said he, resting on his spade and looking away off, "I kin hardly tell. My rigiment was mostly overpowered when we fit." "What was the cause of that?" "Dunno. The Rebs seemed to cover the yearth, and when they yelled it was awful." "Were you ever wounded?" "No, sir; and I never intended to be. Wounded? No, indeed, sir. I'd rather been killed stone dead than had them sturgeons cuttin' and slashin' at me!"[266]

YOUNG LADIES & BESOTTED CONFEDERATES

☞ A party of four Confederates paid a visit to some young ladies staying at a farmhouse about six miles from camp. The night was dark and cold and the road was horrid. They were, however, amply rewarded by the warm welcome they received. Three were in love, and soon there were just three pairs of the most absorbed young people to be seen anywhere. The remaining soldier was obliged to talk to the elderly mistress of the house and witness in agony the happiness of his comrades. By twelve o'clock the two had exhausted the war as a topic, and still it was impossible to catch the eyes of any of the other wretches, so fascinated were they by their fair companions. By three o'clock A.M. they had confided to each other all they knew of earthly things, and sat scowling in gloomy silence. The fire, though often replenished, at last went black out. The candle flickered in the socket. The lady of the house, in despair, left the room. "Gentlemen," said Captain G., arising when the candle was on the point of leaving them in darkness, "the fire has gone out, the lady of the house has gone out, and the candle is about to follow suit. I, at least, am going home." It is needless to say that the visit terminated suddenly, and they failed to get back to camp by morning roll call.[267]

TOO DRUNK TO KNOW

☞ After the battle of Kernstown, when Jackson, with his broken columns, was slowly retreating up the Shenandoah Valley, there was a great deal of miscellaneous fighting between small detachments of the opposing armies. Robert Smith, a Confederate, was quite active on the

CONFEDERATE GENERAL WILLIAM MAHONE.

advanced lines of reconnaissance. Robert, we regret to say, was unduly fond of firewater, and many were the bold efforts he made to get it, on doubtful ground. Upon one occasion he captured a Yankee straggler and led him triumphantly off toward the Confederate lines. Passing a spring, the two stopped to take a cooling draught and sat down to rest. The prisoner pulled out a concealed flask and hospitably offered Smith a drink. The courtesy was highly appreciated, and very soon, while swapping yarns, the bottom of the flask was reached. "Come," said Smith, "it is time we were going. I must take you to headquarters." "That's cool," said the Yankee "from a prisoner, too!" Both were fuddled, but Smith particularly. "Didn't I capture you?" said the Confederate. "Not by a damned sight!" said Mr. Yankee. "I captured you!" "How is

that?" said Smith; and down they sat and argued the question. Just as Smith was about to yield to the overpowering logic of his prisoner, another Confederate arrived and settled the question.[268]

YANKS CHECKING FOR BULLET HOLES

☛ Not long after the first battle of Manassas I was hunting in the neighborhood of Centreville, Va., through which the bulk of the Federal army fled. All of a sudden, upon emerging from a piece of woods, I came upon an old woman doing up her week's washing by a spring. After taking a deep draught I sat down on a log and entered into conversation with her. "Did any of the Yankees run back this way?" said I. "Plenty of 'em," she said, stopping the rubbing process and straightening up, holding a dripping garment in one hand. "Did they give any reason for their running away?" said I. "Oh, yes. I hyearn 'em say that masked batteries riz up out ov the groun', and that thar was a hull division chargin' on black hosses." "Pretty badly scared they were, I suppose?" said I. "Well, I should say so," she replied, as she laid the wet rag down. "Two of 'em come through my yard and didn't seem to notice me. They didn't have no arms [weapons] and mighty little clothes on. One of 'em was bareheaded and barefooted. Sez he, turnin' roun' an 'roun', 'Bill, take a good look. Do you see any holes in me?' Bill said no, he couldn't. 'Well,' sez he, 'thank heaven, I am alive!'"[269]

THE CONFEDERATE WHO SURRENDERED TO A HOG

☛ Tom Black was a tall, cadaverous-looking cavalryman from the knobs. His [massive] gun carried an ounce ball, and the boys called it the "mountain howitzer." Wonderful were the stories he told of killing "varmints sich as painters an' the like" at a quarter of a mile range. There was a great curiosity to catch sight of the Yankees just to see Tom slay them at long taw. "Oh, you better believe old Bet never flickers! Just show me one!" Pretty soon Tom was put on picket. The place was lonely enough in the daytime, but at midnight, when it was so still you could almost hear the stars in their courses, and when under the cover of darkness savage beasts come from their lairs and assassins crouch and watch for their victims, the loneliness was awful. The Yankees were said to be five miles off, but it was not long before Tom was convinced they were sneaking upon him. The fall of every leaf was but like the catlike step of a murderous foe. Presently there was a rustling sound of human feet among the leaves. It was a hungry hog searching for acorns. The sound grew louder and the enemy was plainly no longer trying to conceal his presence. Tom's "each particular hair" began to rise. At last the hog, discovering the sentinel, suddenly wheeled. "Don't shoot!" cried Tom. "I surrender!"[270]

AN IMPOSSIBLE TACTIC—THAT SUCCEEDED

☛ In January 1863 Forrest and his men found themselves near Clifton,

Tennessee, surrounded on at least two sides by advancing Yanks. One of Forrest's subordinates, Colonel Charles Carroll, came running up to his imposing commander in a great state of panic.

As bullets whistled by on every side the terrified officer yelled out: "Sir, we are between two lines of battle. What shall we do?"

Not one to waste time or words, Forrest immediately screamed: "Charge 'em both ways!"

The daring tactic worked and Forrest and his men escaped to fight another day.[271]

BUILDING A BRIDGE "IN GREAT HASTE"
☛ During "Stonewall's" brilliant campaign in the Shenandoah Valley it became necessary that a bridge over a small creek should be built in great haste. One evening Jackson sent for his old pioneer captain, Myers by name, and, put to him the urgency of the occasion, saying that he would send him the plan of his Colonel of Engineers as soon as it was done. Next morning Jackson rode down to Captain Myers' quarters, and saluting the veteran, said: "Captain, did you get the plan of the bridge from Colonel _____?" "Well," said the Captain, "the bridge, General, is built, but I don't know whether the picture [plan] is done or not!"[272]

A BLACK CONFEDERATE SOLDIER GETS THEM LAUGHING
☛ One dark and rainy winter's night the writer was ordered to carry food to the men in the trenches. A team was hitched up, and with a loaded wagon and driver we started out. Every challenge was made with the least noise, as the enemy was only a few rods in front. "Halt, dismount, and give the countersign!" came at every thirty paces. It was rough on my [black] teamster [Jehu], who was rheumatic and cold. However, we made the trip, and halted at a cavalry post. Major _____, a very paladin for courage and strength, had rolled in my blanket for a snooze; he had driven the enemy with slaughter that day. My Jehu began to recite his annoyances thus: "Cuss the durned infantry, they made me halt, dismount, and give the countersign till I was weary and tarrify wid their foolishness." A roar [laugh] followed from the couriers. At this moment a trim staff officer of a general, who had lost an arm, put in his say-so: "I say, hold that noise; the

WHITE HOUSE OF THE CONFEDERACY: PRESIDENT DAVIS' WAR RESIDENCE AT RICHMOND, VIRGINIA.

General wants to rest; don't let me hear any more of it." Staff had hardly gone into darkness before Jehu began his old story. It was folly to try to keep back the laugh. A second outburst, and a second entry of staff. "Darn it! did I not order you to stop this noise? Who is it? I'll have him arrested!" Just then, by some strange accident, a donkey put his demure snout in at our fire, and flapping his ears, began his unmistakable bray. Jehu jumped to his feet, and shaking his fist at the donkey, said: "One at a time, if you please!" Staff left amid a burst of laughter, as Major _____ (the prince of soldiers) rolled over and over with my blanket, trying to restrain a big laugh.[273]

THE YANK & THE SECESH CALF

☛ One day a Federal soldier, a member of an Illinois regiment, while lounging on the banquette in front of Mrs. R.'s house at Bolivar, Tenn., was assaulted by a belligerent calf; in turning around to defend himself, and looking askance at Bully, he exclaimed: "Are you a Secesh too?" and rapidly decamped from a neighborhood where opposition to Yankee invasion was so strikingly developed.[274]

ADVENTURES OF A REBEL IN NEW YORK CITY

☛ A young Scotchman, named Black, whose parents lived down in Dixie, happened to be in New York City at the breaking out of the war. The lines were at once closed, and Black was snugly caught. Seeing no other way to get back home, he joined the Northern army with the intention of deserting at the earliest opportunity. The command to which he attached himself was immediately ordered to Edwards' Ferry, near Leesburg. One day, while on picket duty at the river, he pretended to be bathing, and being an expert swimmer, he dexterously struck out for the Virginia shore. When about midway the river, the daring little rogue turned and shouted: "Good-bye, boys! I'm bound for Dixie." "Come back, come back, or we'll shoot," answered the guard. "Shoot and be damned to you," shouted Black, and, in the midst of a shower of minie balls, he reached his destination. He immediately entered the Confederate ranks (joining my company), and very soon proved himself a gallant soldier and a good fighter. In the battle of Leesburg (Ball's Bluff) he performed many acts of daring, and when approaching night was closing the scene for the day, he was one of a corporal's guard that escorted a full company of Yankees off the hotly-contested ground. As Black was laughing and joking the prisoners, the Federal Captain remarked to him: "I ought to know that voice." "Well, I guess you ought, for I dare say we have met before." "Why, hello, is that you, Charlie Black?" "This is me," jocosely replied the renegade Scotchman. "I couldn't stay with you, Captain, but 'twas not because I was scared to fight; it was just because I did not like the side you were on." Singularly enough, brave Charlie (as he was called afterwards) was escorting his old company, officers and all, to a "Confederate guard house."[275]

THE COLONEL WHO COULDN'T WHISTLE

☛ While on outpost duty one night, a peculiar whistle was given for the countersign, and any one giving that in reply to the challenge was to be considered "a good man and true." I was lying down, outside the bivouac or lice-eum, as I termed it, when one of the sentries sang out a challenge, which not being properly answered, the sergeant of the guard was called for. I was but a few steps away, and though rather dark, I could see somebody on horseback a short distance off. The sentry whispered to me that it was the Colonel of our own regiment, and his answer to my challenge convinced me of the fact, but I let on I didn't know him from Queen Victoria, and ordered him to dismount and approach. I met him half way, when we could both see, and recognize each other and he exclaimed: "O, Sergeant, is that you?" "It's me, Colonel" [I replied]. "It's a whistle, I know, two short ones and a long one, but I can't whistle, I never could" [said he]. He seemed so distressed about it, and being quite an old man, his distress seemed the more pitiable, though rather comical, and knowing nothing in the Articles of War to make a man whistle if he couldn't, any more than the girl could whistle though she was promised a cow, and being quite satisfied he was all right, I let the old man proceed. He made some further remark about having no whistle, but not doubting but what I had, he gave me a little sumthin' to wet it. "Pass, friend, and all's well."[276]

TWO BLACK CONFEDERATES RATE THEIR GENERALS

☛ During the late war there were two darkies, servants, attached to Gordon's Brigade, Cheatham's Division, of the Confederate army, who, like some of the soldiers of that army, were divided in their opinion as to the relative merits of [C.S.] Generals Braxton Bragg and Joseph E. Johnston as commanders. Their names were Marsh and Bill. One day they were in a tent by themselves, when a controversy on the subject arose and was overheard by Colonel Horace Rice, who was in an adjoining tent. Marsh was the champion of General Bragg, and after his making a long, incoherent and senseless harangue in support of his favorite, Bill replied as follows: "You arganize and you arganize, but you never locates. You talks and you talks, but you never ascertains no subject." It is needless to say that this was an extinguisher from which Marsh never rallied.[277]

THE CONFEDERATE THIEF

☛ A poor fellow, moved and instigated by the father of all mischief, had taken some property not belonging to himself. He was brought before a court-martial, and having failed to establish an alibi, he next resorted to the expedient, so often practiced, of proving "previous good character." Jerry O'Flynn was called upon to prove the integrity of the Confederate purloiner. Now, it so happened that Jerry did not know anything particularly good about the accused, and his conscience was too tender to permit him to swear to an untruth to save an afflicted friend, though his kindness of heart prompted him to say all that he could, consistently with the obligation of his oath. He stood, therefore, scratching his head, with a perplexed air, when the prisoner proposed the point-blank question: "From your previous knowledge of my character, don't you believe me to be an honest man?" Truth and conscience were on one side, friendship and good feeling were on the other. Jerry was sorely puzzled. At length, a bright thought seemed to strike him, and with a happy smile and relieved expression, he exclaimed, "Faith, an' you would be an honest mon, Jock, ef there was nothing to stale!"[278]

A GEORGIA BELLE & HER DRESS
☛ There were crowds of sick and wounded soldiers in Augusta, and going up Green and Broad Streets any pleasant day you would see the side-walks thronged with them, getting the fresh air and enjoying the sunshine, many looking pale and haggard, but cheerful and bright, and if there was any fun to be had, they were always ready to enjoy it.

There was a noted belle, of Augusta, that could be seen frequently on the streets. She had a magnificent form and graceful carriage, and as she came with her stately walk she always attracted attention. A friend told me that he was standing on the pavement one day as she passed, and he noticed a pale, cadaverous, ragged soldier looking eagerly at her, and saw a merry twinkle in his eye. The lady had on a dress with a very long train to it, and as she turned the corner she looked back, and gave her skirt a slight pull. The soldier, still looking intently at her or the train, now said: "Go on, marm, it's a comin'. It's jest turnin' the corner." She blushed and hurried on.

Of course there was a hearty laugh, in which my friend joined. He said it was ludicrous in the extreme. They were so full of fun that an occasion like that was irresistible.[279]

FORREST HAS HIS HEAD EXAMINED
☛ In 1854, several years prior to Lincoln's illegal War on the South, Forrest attended a free lecture at a hall in Memphis. The speaker was New York phrenologist Dr. Orson G. Fowler. When the physician finished his talk he asked the audience to select someone for one of his famous phrenological examinations. The first name called out was "Forrest," at which the lanky frontiersman strode quickly up to the stage.

After admiringly inspecting Forrest's head with his fingers Dr. Fowler noted the Tennessean's most predominant traits, saying:

> Here is a man who would have been a Caesar, a Hannibal, or Napoleon if he had had the opportunity. He has all the qualities of a great military genius. If he could not go over the Alps he would go through them.

The audience applauded thunderously as Forrest walked back to his seat. Little could he have dreamed that in just seven short years the exact characteristics Fowler discovered in the bumps on his cranium would make him a household name.[280]

A MOTHER'S DESCRIPTION OF WAR'S END
☛ [As refugees during the War, after Lee's surrender my family and I were anxious to return to our home in Tennessee's capital city, which we did by rail.] We finally reached Nashville, and I went to my sister's and stayed until we could get possession of our house. Then I learned of the many changes that had taken place in the four years. Many were in deep mourning for dear ones killed in the numerous battles fought. Many of the old citizens had passed away, while others had spent months in the prisons for not taking the oath, and large sums of money had been extorted from the citizens to support idle negroes and poor white people who had followed the Federals here.

COMPANY A, UNIFORMED RANK UNITED CONFEDERATE VETERANS, CIRCA 1895.

I had received very few letters, and those unsatisfactory, while away, as all had to be submitted to the military authorities for inspection. I learned that the old [Nashville Female] Academy, my dear Alma Mater, had been stripped of everything, and my mind reverted to my childhood and to the eight happy years that I had spent there; to the cabinet of curiosities, containing shells from all parts of the world, and many rare specimens of art; to the immense library, and the numbers of pianos. All these accumulations of years were packed up and sent North to enrich some Yankee officers' families. The old empty house was left standing as a monument of one of the largest and most successful female schools in the South, and Dr. C. D. Elliot, as Principal, was much beloved, and was considered a prince of educators.

A friend moved into our house and kept it from being turned into a Federal hospital. We had to pay a large sum of money before we got our house released from the [corrupt U.S.] Freedman's Bureau, and thanks to our old servants, found most of our furniture scattered around among different friends, where they had placed it for safe-keeping before going to Washington.

After we had been home several days, a number of the girls' friends came to see them. They were upstairs having a jolly time, all talking at once, when the doorbell rang. I went to open it, and there stood eight or ten Federal soldiers on the porch. I began to tremble, and was greatly startled, and thought: "What have I said that could have been reported to them, and maybe cause my arrest?" For from the time of my arrival I had tried to be very prudent in expressing myself, and felt all the time that I was almost in purgatory. Down South we had had full scope [freedom of speech], and now that we were almost too full for utterance we had to bridle our tongues, and it was a great deprivation. We were advised that if we did talk, to close our doors and watch the keyholes. Well, there I was, confronting all those soldiers. I at last ventured to ask what they wanted. They were so engaged looking up at the pretty girls (for by this time every window was filled with heads, eager to see what was the matter) that they scarcely noticed me. I waved my hand to the young folks, and they immediately left, and then I got the soldiers' attention and asked them again what they would have. They all seemed in great glee, and said that they had been in the army a great while and had been paid off to go home, but hated to go back without seeing something of the ladies of the South, and they wanted me to board them for two or three weeks, and said that they would pay me well. You can imagine my disgust, in the frame of mind that I was in then, but I had to present a smiling face and tell them that it was impossible, as I had a very large family, and that all of my rooms were full; but they still insisted. I told them that there were many hotels and boarding houses, but they seemed determined [in typical Yankee style] to force themselves on us. While they talked I scanned them closely, and saw that they were dressed very conspicuously and had on a good deal of "pinch back" jewelry. They were very anxious to make an impression, and I wanted so badly to tell them my [honest] opinion of them, and I was really afraid that they would force themselves on us anyway; but they finally left, though they seemed greatly disappointed, and not in a good humor.

. . . Many long months passed, fraught with bitterness and uneasiness. The people of the South felt that they were overcome but not conquered, and many a bitter pill they had to swallow, submitting to the inevitable.

. . . We are now old and gray-headed, and we sit by the fire and tell our children and grandchildren of the deeds of daring heroism and bravery of our dear [Confederate] soldiers who sleep on many a hilltop and valley. They died defending a cause [Conservatism] that they felt to be just. I teach the children to hate war and all its horrors, and to love peace; but to always love and reverence the memory of our brave soldiers, and when all prejudices and animosities shall have been buried our heroes' stars will blazen forth in the galaxy of fame with a brightness and effulgence that may have been equaled, but never surpassed in the world's history.[281]

ABSURD TALES INVENTED TO DISPARAGE GENERAL FORREST
☛ Terrible [and false] stories were told after the raid into Memphis of
how Forrest and his men acted. A number of people anxious to appear
as heroes told ridiculous tales of what they passed through. One of the
best stories told was by a negro soldier, who claimed to have seen
General Forrest as he rode up to the front of the Gayoso Hotel. He
described to his companions how Forrest looked and the size of his
horse. Said he: "I was er stanning right in dis alley when I seed him came
up. He rid his hoss right up to de hotel, and I'm telling you the Gord's
truf, he hitched his hoss right to the second story bannisters. I seed him.
I seed him."
     And there are to-day old negroes in Memphis who show you where
he hitched his horse. The negro's idea was that he was as big as "Colossus
of Rhodes."[282]

MISCHIEVOUS SOLDIERS, A DOG, & A TIN CAN
☛ [At this point, U.S.] General Burnside re-crossed the river and
resumed his position. The Little Confederate [a 17 year old Confederate
soldier] remembered the stories his father had told him about hardships
he endured when a boy. He told of how he had to sleep in the covered
wagons when he was going to Charleston, South Carolina, with his
mother's cotton. The snow would blow in on his blankets, and
sometimes cover them while he slept. They seemed great hardships, and
his father would say: "I hope you will never be called on to endure the
like." But at seventeen years of age, the little fellow could tell his father
stories of hardships, dangers, sufferings and trials, he had never dreamed
of. He wrote home after each battle, and recited the distressful news of
the death of his friends. He was getting terribly tired of the business, but
never a murmur escaped him. The first battle of Fredricksburg was
fought December 12 and 13, 1862.
     Notwithstanding this terrible and bloody battle, scarcely two weeks
passed before the army had settled down to a normal condition. One
would not suppose that in so short a time after they had fought with such
desperation, and seen so many of their friends killed and wounded by
their sides, men could be cheerful and hopeful. But this was a remarkable
characteristic of the Confederate soldier. He could throw off trouble, or
face dangers, as occasion demanded. Merry laughter and jests could be
heard at every mess fire. The men sang and danced at night, and talked
of home and lounged about during the day. It was impossible to break or
even check their spirits. They attended divine service on Sunday and
prayer meeting every other night—that is, they were supposed to do so.
The chaplain of the regiment, Rev. A. E. Hackett, was in every sense a
good man. He always went into battle with the regiment, and used a gun
with telling effect. When the fight was over, he was found among the
wounded, giving them every assistance within human power. He was
dearly beloved by every man in the 18th regiment. Many of us would go

to hear his beautiful and touching prayers, because of his great earnestness. Occasionally the men would go to church in the city. One night, soon after the battle, Billy Blake, John Willis, Lieutenant Wm. McKie, Winter Shipp and the Little Confederate went into town to attend church. Arriving there, they found the pews all filled, more than half of the congregation being soldiers. Lieutenant McKie and Winter Shipp went in and found seats, but Billy Blake, John Willis and the Little Confederate remained outside, near the entrance. They amused themselves in many ways, as best they could, while they waited for their friends to join them after the service was over. Finally a little dog came up and looked in the church door. He seemed to be hunting for his master. Willis tried to drive him away, but he was spunky and would not go. Billy Blake, who was always bubbling over with mischief, caught the dog and addressing the Little Confederate, said: "Little Horse, hold him until I can come back." He was off and back in a few minutes, with an old, battered tin bucket [i.e., a tin can]. He mashed the top together after putting a few pebbles in it, and with a string torn from his shirt, tied it to the dog's tail. The dog did not realize what was going on, but evidently thought he was being caressed. After it was all ready, Billy picked the dog up, carried him off some twenty yards, and put him down, supposing he would run down the street. They looked for great fun, but when he hit the ground he knew something was wrong, and instead of going home, he broke for the church. Down the aisle he ran with all his speed, the bucket striking the floor, making as much noise as a wagon train. He barked at every jump. It threw the congregation into great confusion. Men stood on their seats, and ladies screamed. The dog reached the pulpit. He had not found his master; not even a friendly hand. He rushed into the pulpit. It was all done in a second. The church was poorly lighted with tallow candles, one resting on each side of the Bible. As the dog reached the pulpit, the preacher jumped up on the desk, knocking off the candles and extinguishing them. The dog started down the other aisle, and by this time the greatest excitement prevailed. Men jumped out of the windows, others rushed through the doors. The occasion was so unusual and so unexpected, the best soldiers were knocked completely out. The three boys saw the dog go up in the pulpit, saw the lights go out, and witnessed the confusion, then broke for camp. They ran as rapidly as they could, for nearly a mile before they halted or said a word. When they pulled up, Billy Blake, in the most solemn manner said: "Little Horse, what did you start that derned dog toward the church for?" and then fell down and rolled over in the road. They laughed and talked about it until they heard others approaching, when they put out again. They reached camp, and lay down in front of the fire on the bare ground, and pretended to be asleep. Directly the church goers began to arrive, and the balance of our crowd with them. Lieutenant McKie knew, as soon as he saw them all hugged up together before the fire, who tied the can to the dog, but he never accused the boys. The occurrence was the talk of the camp, as well as of the good citizens of Fredericksburg. Next day [C.S.] General Barksdale instructed each colonel to investigate the matter fully, and if it was found to have been done by a man of his brigade, he wanted the scamp well punished. The boys were the only persons who seemed entirely ignorant of the trouble.

. . . The boys were very quiet and good for a few days, but were soon out roving over the country for something to eat during the day, and making life a burden to their friends at night.[283]

MAKING A NEW WOMAN OUT OF HER

☞ Broken-Down Patient: "Have I a chance in the world to recover my health, Doctor?"

Physician: "Well, I'd say that if you give up all intoxicating beverages, stop smoking so many cigarettes, cut out the late hours, lay off the bright lights, and try eating some good home-cooked foods, I can make a new woman out of you."[284]

HOW GENERAL FORREST HANDLED SHIRKERS

☞ Soon after [C.S.] General Chalmers' command had well settled in camp, General Forrest reached us with his force, including the men he recruited in West Tennessee. He organized what proved to be the most remarkable command in the army. At that time, January 4, 1864, [C.S.] General Polk was assigned to the command of the department. General Forrest was given command of all the cavalry in Mississippi and North Alabama. Two brigades composed General Chalmers' division. One brigade, commanded by Colonel Robert McCulloch, consisted of the Second Missouri, Lieutenant-Colonel McCulloch; Willis' Texas Battalion, Lieutenant-Colonel Theo. Willis; Falkner's Kentucky Regiment, Colonel W. W. Falkner; 18th Mississippi Regiment, Colonel A. H. Chalmers; and Keiser's Mississippi Battalion.

The second brigade, commanded by Colonel Jeffrey Forrest [one of the General's many brothers], was: McDonald's Battalion, Colonel Kelly; 7th Tennessee, Colonel Duckworth; 3rd Mississippi, Colonel McGuirk; 5th Mississippi, Lieutenant-Colonel Barksdale; and the 19th Mississippi, Colonel Duff.

A brigade commanded by Colonel Richardson, and another by Colonel Barteau, were also organized. Within a few days, General Forrest left us for Meridian, to consult with General Polk. General Chalmers was left in command.

We moved to the south bank of the Tallahatchie, and on the morning of January 8, 1864, Henderson's scouts reported that a large [U.S.] force would leave Memphis about the 11th, in three columns, one via Hernando, one via Holly Springs, and the third in the direction of Okolona. Also, that [U.S. Gen.] Sherman, with a large force, would leave Vicksburg at the same time, to co-operate with the force moving from Memphis; the purpose being to destroy all the supplies in the rich prairie section of Mississippi and Alabama. The weather was intensely cold, and our men were scantily clad. Great numbers of them suffered severely from frost-bite. General Chalmers notified General Forrest of the situation, at the same time disposed of the command to meet the advancing Federals. McCulloch was left at Panola, Bell sent to Belmont, Richardson to Wyatt, and McQuirk to Abbeville. The balance of the command was sent to Oxford, where General Chalmers made his headquarters, and at which place General Forrest rejoined us. While we remained at Oxford, quite a number of the new men whom General Forrest had recruited in West Tennessee decided they could not endure the cold and suffering, and therefore determined to leave the service and return home. This was a serious matter, and required severe and heroic action to check it. As soon as the fact was reported, General Forrest sent men to capture and bring them back. Fifteen or twenty were caught, and carried before General Forrest, who ordered them to be shot the next day. He had coffins made for each, and a long grave dug. The crowd sentenced consisted of ten boys and seven men. Intense excitement prevailed in the neighborhood and among the troops. Delegations of ladies and ministers appealed to General Forrest to spare the men, but he was obdurate. He said he would have no such worthless thrash disgrace his command. The hour arrived, and the deserters riding on their coffins moved to the spot selected for the execution. Two companies guarded the procession. They arrived at the grave, and each man, with his hands tied behind

MRS. KATE CABELL CURRIE, PRESIDENT OF THE UNITED DAUGHTERS OF THE CONFEDERACY, TEXAS.

him, sat on the small end of his coffin waiting for the word fire. The occasion was one of the most serious as well as the most solemn ever witnessed by those present. Several hundred soldiers stood around to see what the end would be, and large numbers of citizens and little children were there. The two companies moved to position and loaded their guns. Everything was in readiness awaiting the command. Who can realize the thoughts that crossed the minds of those men and boys, as they sat on the crumbling brink of eternity, and looked into the interminable abyss? It was awful! People waited for the command "fire." The officer seemed to hesitate, but every one knew it must be done.

Those brave, tried and true men, who stood in line with their guns at a ready were suffering almost as much as the deserters. Their faces were pale, but stern. It was the greatest trial of their lives, but they were steady. There was not the slightest quiver. The officer passed in front of the soldiers, and took his position on the right, and faced to the left. The time was short now. Only a moment left for those human beings who had disgraced themselves and the cause. They were doomed. "Here comes General Forrest," some one said, and he rode hurriedly up in front of the condemned. He said: "Captain, untie those men and turn them loose," then turning to the deserters said: "Now, boys, you go to your commands, and see if you can't make good soldiers." General Forrest rode rapidly back to town, and the men who had marched in that solemn procession for execution were free. The town was wild. The terrible gloom which hung over the place gave way to cheers. Men and children went running from house to house telling the news. An hour before both soldiers and citizens were in the depths, now they moved about and laughed. What a wonderful thing is the human mind!

General Forrest was overrun by people expressing appreciation for his pardon of the men. It was a master stroke. There were no more desertions, and the men learned that General Forrest was not cruel, nor unnecessarily severe, but they also learned that he would not be trifled with. The effect was marvelous. The old soldiers who had served under him laughed and said: "We knew he would do it," and the recruits said: "me too."

This circumstance was talked about throughout the South, and hundreds of people heard that the boys were shot. They censured General Forrest greatly, and there are to-day men and women who believe that the men were killed. They have never forgiven General Forrest. But the writer was with General Forrest nearly two years, and closely associated with his campaigns. The statement, as detailed above, is true in every particular. Forrest seemed to know by instinct what was necessary to do. He was pleasant and companionable when he was not disturbed, but no occasion ever arose which he was not master of. He fought to kill, but he treated his prisoners with all the consideration in his power. So he did his own men. But he wanted the latter for service, and not merely to count. I state it with confidence, that any man who followed Forrest was a good one. He could not stay unless he was. A man who can show that he was with Forrest the last year and a half of the war is no ordinary man, you can depend on that.[285]

A REAL BARGAIN
☛ A young matron, in whom the shopping instinct was strong, asked a German butcher the price of hamburger steak.

"Twenty-five cents a pound," he replied.

"But," said she, "the price at the corner store is only 12 cents."

"Vell," asked Otto, "vy don't you puy it down there?"

"They haven't any," she replied.

"Ya, ya," said the butcher; "ven I don't have it, I sell it for 10 cents only."[286]

GENERAL FORREST & GENERAL STURGIS

☛ Toward the latter part of May, 1864, [C.S.] General Chalmers was ordered to move to Monte Vallo, Alabama, to defend the iron works, on the North and South Alabama Railroad, against a raid supposed to be contemplated for their destruction. We remained in that section for a few days, and about the 10th of June, received orders to move back to Columbus with all possible dispatch. Every thing was gotten ready, and we began the march the following morning. [U.S.] General Sturgis, in the meantime, with a finely-equipped army of nine thousand cavalry and infantry, twenty-five pieces of artillery, and several hundred wagons, left Memphis to clean up Forrest, and destroy our bread supply, a feat which several Federal generals had started out to accomplish, but none had succeeded in performing. General Sturgis stated to a lady, at whose house near Salem he remained all night on his down trip, that he was after Forrest this time, and if he would stand up and give a chance, and not run away, he would destroy his command and bring Forrest back a prisoner. The lady replied: "Look out, he may send you back running." But the [Yankee] general laughed, and said: "No danger, and do not be surprised if I stop on my return with Forrest a prisoner." The proud and confident general moved his army forward in military order, with every thing in proper trim. There was not a suspicion of doubt on his mind. He knew he had three times as many men as Forrest, and he also had a splendid artillery battalion. He therefore went forth full of confidence. It will be remembered that General Chalmers, with McCulloch's brigade, was away in Alabama, so that Forrest only had Buford's division and Rucker's brigade, some three thousand all told, to meet that picked army, and its haughty and boastful commander. The forces met at what is called Brice's Cross Roads, where the Ripley and Guntown roads intersect, four miles west of Baldwin, a station on the Mobile and Ohio Railroad. In General Sturgis' command were two regiments of negroes, who had taken an oath on their knees before leaving Memphis, in the presence of [U.S.] General Hurlbut, that they would avenge Fort Pillow. That they would take no prisoners. They wore badges on their breasts, *"Remember Fort Pillow. Death to Forrest and his men."* Our men were not aware of this, however, until during the fight, they saw running negroes tearing their badges off as they ran.

General Forrest struck Sturgis unawares. He rushed at his column and whipped him before he could gather his forces. Our old ragged boys were feeling good that summer morning. If the story of each individual could be told, the acts of bravery and daring would fill a book. Better soldiers never faced an enemy than those who met Sturgis at Brice's Cross Roads. There was no hesitation, but when the order was given to charge, each man went to work as if the result depended on his individual efforts. They charged in front and on the flank. The advance guard of Sturgis was thrown back in great confusion on his main column. His cavalry trampled down his infantry, followed by the invincible band, of Forrest, which rode them to death or capture. Wagons were capsized, the horses cut loose and used to escape on. The artillery was tumbled against trees or left in the road. There was never such a panic and such a rout before. Most of the cavalry escaped, but the infantry were either killed, wounded, or captured. The [Yankee] negroes, such as were not killed, took to the woods and ran for their lives. They tore their badges off and threw them away. The oath they took before leaving Memphis must have been taken with a reservation. Our loss was serious, about one hundred and thirty killed and some five hundred wounded. We lost some grand and glorious men, whose names should be written on the lintels of the eternal city. The enemy's loss was terrible. One thousand nine hundred and seventy killed, besides the loss of over two thousand prisoners, including the wounded, fully one thousand more than Forrest's entire force. We also captured twenty pieces of artillery, twenty-one caissons, and two hundred and thirty wagons, besides all his ambulances.

There was a gallant boy who yielded up his life on that day who deserves a page in history. He was bright and handsome, brave and generous, loved by his comrades, and worshiped by a devoted mother and sister. He carried happiness into every circle he entered, and won the confidence of all he met. He was as pure as the rose-bud glistening with the dews of the morning. He gave his life for a cause which did not succeed, but his name will be remembered, and his memory will be cherished. He was killed in the discharge of duty while he rode at the head of his regiment. This hero was "Billy Pope," adjutant of the 7th Tennessee. Billy and the writer were warm friends. We often talked of home and mothers. Farewell, Billy, may we "Meet beyond the river, where the surges cease to roll."

The pursuit was kept up as long as human endurance permitted. The news of the defeat reached Salem before General Sturgis did, and the lady was standing at the gate to see if he had General Forrest. When he left her his uniform was bright and new, but when he returned he was covered with

THE WORLD'S MOST BEAUTIFUL NATIONAL FLAG, TORN AND TATTERED DURING WHAT GEN. LEE CORRECTLY CALLED "THE WAR OF THE CONSTITUTION."

mud. His horse was exhausted, and both presented the appearance of defeat and disaster. The lady asked: "General, did you find General Forrest?" "No," General

Sturgis replied, "but he found me!"

The battle of Brice's Cross Roads was one of the most brilliant feats in the annals of war. There will probably never again occur such a victory. The future may develop great generals, but none will approach Forrest as a brave, dashing soldier. In the humble opinion of the writer, he was the greatest military man who ever lived, and the future will hardly see his like. The South will enjoy the distinction of having developed two remarkable characters. The first was Forrest, the only commander of an army in the world's history who never suffered defeat. The second was General Joseph E. Johnson, the only commander of an army known in history who never won a victory.[287]

"IS THIS THE ROAD TO ST. IVES?"

☛ A motorist who was lost [in the English countryside] asked a native, "Is this the road to St. Ives?" and received the reply, "I dunno."

Motorist: "Well, can you tell me which is the road to Cottenham?"

"I dunno."

Motorist (exasperated): "Well, you don't seem to know much."

"Maybe I don't, but I'm not lost."[288]

THE CONFEDERATE HORSE WHO DETESTED YANKEES

☛ After the war, General Forrest, with his wife and son, Captain Billy Forrest, went to live on his farm in Coahoma county, Mississippi. It was the middle of May, and too late to plant cotton, but they raised an enormous crop of corn. At that time, the "Mississippi Delta" was known as the "Bottom," and was invariably referred to as such. The country was sparsely settled, and in many cases farm-houses were five and six miles apart, and the general's place was no exception. Less than ten per cent of the country had been cleared; therefore the timber and cane made it a wilderness. There was no occasion for Federal troops in that country, because the population was too small to require watching, and there had been none there until about the first of August. The affairs at the Forrest home were quiet and undisturbed. Both the general and Captain Billy were busily engaged restoring the fences and repairing and rebuilding the houses. The general had erected a saw-mill, to which he gave his personal attention. In fact, he performed the work of what was styled "a full hand," besides managing and looking after the laborers, his old slaves [whom he freed *before* Lincoln's War], to whom he was then paying wages. They were devoted to "Mars. Bedford." Captain Billy was detailed to drive the ox team, which was used to haul logs to the mill. There was a luxuriant Bermuda grass lot in front of the house, where the horses grazed during the day. General Forrest had given instructions that [his magnificent horse] King Philip should never be saddled again. Like the negroes, he was set free. The general appreciated his great services during the war, and decided to emancipate him. Jerry, the general's body servant, and Pat, an Irishman who served him as orderly while in the service, were employed about the house and lot. Fields of beautiful corn surrounded the house, and the rustling of the blades of fodder, together with the graceful bending of the tassels as they yielded to the soft summer breezes, gave the place an air of quiet and domestic life, very different from that which the owner and his family and servants and horses had been accustomed to for several years past.

It was a warm August morning, about ten o'clock. King Philip and the other horses were grazing in the lot, when a company of Federal cavalry rode up to the "big gate" and halted. They were searching for government cotton, and hearing that the rebel General Forrest lived there, desired to take advantage of the opportunity and see him. King Philip was the same character of horse that Forrest was man, and seemed to have been made for just such service as he had seen the past two years. His education had been well attended to during that time. He had never come in view of a company of Federals without having to rush at them with all his speed and energy. No doubt it was with him instinctively a thing which he had no power to resist, and, perhaps, no disposition to avoid. The Federal captain and his company, ignorant of the character of King Philip, and therefore of impending danger, and confident of their ability to defend themselves, opened the gate and rode in. King Philip had by that time, doubtless, forgotten the horrors of war, as he nipped the fresh young grass, and did not discover the presence of the blue coats until they had entered the lot. He heard the tramp of the horses and looked up, and the old passion, born of education and hard experience, took possession of him. With head and tail in the air, he rushed at the company with his old-time energy, nor did he halt until every man and horse had been driven from the lot. He kicked and fought like a tiger. After the gate had been closed, he galloped along the fence-row, neighing and shaking his head defiantly. Jerry, hearing the noise and seeing the commotion, ran down to the gate and heard dreadful threats against Philip. One of the men, who was severely hurt by a kick, swore he would kill him; but Jerry grasped a fence-rail, and announced that he would defend Philip with his life; and that was the situation when General Forrest and Captain Billy returned home for dinner.

The officer explained the occurrence to the general, who, after King Philip had been put in the stable, invited the whole company in for dinner and rest. Jerry said: "Twus not King Philip's fault; dem Yankees opened the gate and rid in bedout sayin nuthin to nobody." After all had been seated on the gallery and had laughed over the affair, the Federal captain said: "General, I can now account for your success; your negroes fight for you and your horses fight for you."[289]

TRICKING A BLIND YANKEE

☞ Here is all that need be said of [U.S. soldier] "Joe Parsons, of Baltimore," as told by a newspaper correspondent: Joe enlisted in the First Maryland regiment, and was plainly a "rough" originally. As we passed along the hall we first saw him crouched near an open window, lustily singing, "I'm a bold soldier boy," and observing the broad bandage over his eyes, I said,

"What's your name, my good fellow?"

"Joe, sir," he answered, "Joe Parsons."

"And what is the matter with you?"

"Blind, sir—blind as a bat."

"In battle?"

"Yes—at Antietam. Both eyes shot out at one clip."

"I was hit" he said, "and it knocked me down. I lay there all night, and next day the fight was renewed. I could stand the pain yer see, but the balls was flyin' all round, and I wanted to get away. I couldn't see nothin' though. So I waited and listened; and at last I heard a feller groan' beyond me. 'Hello,' says I. 'Hello yourself,' says he. 'Who be yer,' said I, 'a rebel?' 'You're a Yankee,' said he. 'So I am,' says I, 'what's the matter with you?' 'My leg's smashed,' says he. 'Can't yer walk?' 'No.' 'Can yer see?' 'Yes.' 'Well,' says I, 'you're a damned rebel, but will you do me a little favor?' 'I will,' says he, 'ef I ken.' Then, I says, 'Well, ole butternut, I can't see nothin'; my eyes is knocked out; but I ken walk. Come over yere. Let's git out o' this. You p'int the way, an' I'll tote yer off the field, on my back.' 'Bully for you!' says he. And so we managed to get together. We shook hands on it. I took a wink outen his canteen, and he got onto my shoulders. I did the walkin' for both, an' he did the navigatin'. An' ef he didn't make me carry him straight into a rebel Colonel's tent, a mile away, I'm a liar!"[290]

ESCAPADES WITH GENERAL FORREST IN NEW YORK CITY

☛ Not long after the war, General Forrest and his son, Captain Billy, went to New York. It was the first time either of them ever saw the great city. At that time, the "St. Nicholas" was the popular hotel for Southern people, and it was at that hostelry they stopped. They arrived about night, and after an early breakfast the following morning, concluded to go out and see the city. The rotunda of the St. Nicholas was on a level with the street. They walked to the front and stopped to get their bearings. There was a great crowd of people in front of the hotel, which rapidly grew larger after they halted. The general wore a grey suit and a broad brimmed light colored felt hat. He was at all times a conspicuous figure, but his friends at home were accustomed to him, therefore did not appreciate his distinguished appearance as strangers did. The papers announced that he was in the city, and there was wide-spread curiosity to see him. He was ignorant of the cause that drew the crowd together, and, having heard that Broadway was a great thoroughfare, supposed it was a natural condition. Finally, he heard a person say, "That's him. That's the rebel, General Forrest," and he made his way out, and, with Captain Billy, walked up the street. The crowd followed, and was augmented at every corner. Those in front were pressed by those following, until finally hundreds of them were blocking up the street and sidewalk looking at the big rebel. The general grew restless and worried over the situation, but, as was invariably the case, he was equal to the occasion. He lifted his big white hat high above his head, and cried out with a voice that had never failed to produce consternation: "Get out of my way, goddamned you." The effect was instantaneous. Those in the rear were knocked down and run over by those in front, and the stampede lasted for several minutes during which time the general and Captain Billy went into a cross street and escaped further intrusion.

The afternoon papers mentioned the circumstances, and the morning papers were full of it. Forrest was discussed by every tongue. The following morning he sat on the side of his bed, had just pulled on his boots, and was coursing his fingers through his hair, a very common habit with him. (The writer has often seen him when his long, iron- gray hair stood up, "like quills upon the fretful porcupine.") He had not yet removed his night-shirt, when some one knocked at his door. Captain Billy occupied an adjoining room with a door opening into the general's, and went to the outer door to answer the knock. He was astonished to find a lady there. She was a typical New England old maid; tall, angular, and thin; her hair was dark and pasted tightly over her high forehead; thin lips, compressed mouth, and a well distinguished jaw. She carried a Bible in one hand, and an umbrella in the other. She pushed Captain Billy aside, and advancing, addressing the General, asked: "Are you the Rebel General Forrest? And is it true that you murdered those dear colored people at Fort Pillow? Tell me, I want no evasive answer!"

The writer does not think that slang is good taste, or good sense, but he feels that, in this instance, a slang phrase conveys the ideal plainly: "She got it in the neck."

The general rose up from his bed to his full height, his hair standing on end, and said: "Yes, madam; I killed the men and women, and ate the babies for breakfast."

The old maid ran screaming down the hall-way and into the street.[291]

A BLACK SOUTHERN SERVANT'S OPINION OF YANKS
☞ "Dat [new] Yankee school-teacher! Whar he come f'om?" asked [our black servant] Aunt Dice . . . [one day], after he was duly installed at Riverside as a permanent boarder.

"From Vermont," answered Sam, shortly.

"Whar's dat?"

"Away up north."

"Furriner?"

"Oh no, Aunt Dice; he's an American."

"He talk cur'ous," she said, musingly, "an' he make too free wid de niggers. Got any niggers?" she asked quickly.

"Yankees don't believe in niggers; or rather, they don't believe in slavery," stumbled Sam, with a southerner's reluctance for the word.

"They hold for equality."

"Huh! fine ekals [equals] niggers be—fur gen'l'mun an' ladies. Who waits on 'em?"

"The Yankees? They wait on themselves commonly, or hire white hands."

"Humph! I mistrus' him," she said, emphatically.[292]

SOME YANKEES LOSE THEIR SHIRTS

☛ A company of some thirty or forty Union men were trying to make their escape to Kentucky, to join the Northern army. They came to a creek which they were compelled to wade. Not wishing to get their clothes wet, they shelled off all to their shirts, and while in this condition they were surprised by a company of Jeff's cavalry boys, who were in hot pursuit of them. Being somewhat frightened, they fled in double-quick, making a "straight shirt sail" up hill and down hill, leaving their clothing in the possession of our boys, who, of course, took possession and appropriated the same. What became of the tories we are unable to say, but rather suppose they are in a poor condition for the cold weather.[293]

REASONS TO BE EXEMPT FROM MILITARY SERVICE

☛ Among the excuses offered for exemptions, some are extremely ludicrous. In Smyth County, Va., we learn, one man on enrolling himself wrote opposite his name, "one leg too short." The next man that came in, noticing the excuse, and deeming it pretty good, thought he would make his better, and wrote opposite his name, "both legs too short"![294]

CONFEDERATE COLONEL JOHN S. MOSBY (SEATED CENTER WITH RIGHT LEG CROSSED) AND 16 OF THE MEN WHO ELECTED TO REMAIN WITH HIM UNTIL HIS DEATH.

CHAPTER NINE

BATTLE OF THE SNOWBALLS

☛ On the morning of the 2nd December I received by a courier information from [C.S. Gen.] Stuart that he had been unexpectedly detained at Port Royal, together with orders that I should join him there at once; so that I started a second time with my portly friend the doctor on our journey. It was a disagreeable ride enough. The cold was intense, the road rough, and the distance long. We had ridden already more than twenty miles, the icicles hanging from our beards and our horses' nostrils, when we met General Stuart returning to Fredericksburg. He laughed heartily at us for our former unsuccessful ride, and ordered us to turn back with him.

The fighting was over at Port Royal, and Pelham, with his horse-artillery had met with his usual good fortune, inflicting much damage upon the enemy, and driving off the gunboats, which, from the narrowness of the stream and the height of the cliffs where our guns were posted, had scarcely been able to respond at all to the destructive fire which was pouring down upon them at so near a range. The return to camp was even more distressing than our ride of the morning, as a heavy snow-storm set in, which continued throughout the night; and we reached our headquarters, men and horses wet and chilled, and almost wearied out by a journey of more than forty miles.

The following morning we were enlivened by snowball fights, which commenced as skirmishes near our headquarters, but extended over the neighbouring camps, and assumed the aspect of general engagements. In front of our headquarters, beyond an open field of about half a mile square, Hood's division lay encamped in a piece of wood; in our immediate rear stretched the tents and huts of

GENERAL LEE AT GETTYSBURG.

a part of M'Laws's division. Between these two bodies of troops animated little skirmishes had frequently occurred whenever there was snow enough on the ground to furnish the ammunition; but on the morning of the 4th, an extensive expedition having been undertaken by several hundred of M'Laws's men against Hood's encampments, and the occupants of these finding themselves considerably disturbed thereby, suddenly the whole of the division advanced in line of battle, with flying colours, the officers leading the men, as if in real action, to avenge the insult. The assailants fell back rapidly before this overwhelming host, but only to secure a strong position, from which, with reinforcements, they might resume the offensive. The alarm of their first repulse having been borne with the swiftness of the wind to their comrades, sharpshooters in large numbers were posted behind the cedar bushes that skirt the Telegraph Road, and hundreds of hands were actively employed in erecting a long and high snow-wall in front of their extended lines. The struggle had now the appearance of a regular battle, with its charges and counter-charges—the wild enthusiasm of the men and the noble emulation of the officers finding expression in loud commands and yet louder cheering, while the air was darkened with the snowballs as the current of the fight moved to and fro over the well-contested field. Nearer and nearer it came towards our headquarters, and it was soon evident to us that the hottest part of the engagement would take place on our neutral territory. Fruitless were the efforts of Stuart and myself to assert and maintain the neutrality of our camp, utterly idle the hoisting of a white flag; the advancing columns pressed forward in complete disregard of our signs and our outspoken remonstrances, clouds of snow balls passed across the face of the sun, and ere long the overwhelming wave of the conflict rolled pitilessly over us. Yielding to the unavoidable necessity which forbade our keeping aloof from the contest, Stuart and I had taken position, in order to obtain a view over the field of battle, on a big box, containing ordnance stores, in front of the General's tent, where we soon became so much interested in the result, and so carried away by the excitement of the moment, that we found ourselves calling out to the men to hold their ground, and urging them again and again to the attack, while many a stray snowball, and many a well-directed one, took effect upon our exposed persons. But all the gallant resistance of M'Laws's men was unavailing. Hood's lines pressed resistlessly forward, carrying everything before them, taking the formidable fortifications, and driving M'Laws's division out of their encampments. Suddenly, at this juncture, we heard loud shouting on the right, where two of Anderson's brigades had come up as reinforcements. The men of M'Laws's division, acquiring new confidence from this support, rallied, and in turn drove, by a united charge, the victorious foe in headlong flight back to their own camps and woods. Thus ended the battle for the day, unhappily with serious results to some of the combatants, for one of Hood's men had his leg broken, one of M'Laws's men lost an eye, and there were other chance-wounds on both sides. This sham-fight gave ample proof of the excellent spirits of our troops, who, in the wet, wintry weather, many of them without blankets, some with out shoes, regardless of their exposure and of the scarcity of provisions, still maintained their good humour, and were ever ready for any sort of sport or fun that offered itself to them.[295]

AN "ATTACKING FORCE" OF WOMEN

☛ Middleburg [Va.] is a pleasant little place, of some 1500 inhabitants, which, by reason of its proximity to the Federal lines, had often been visited by raiding and scouting parties of the enemy, and had suffered specially in the shameless barbarities committed by those Yankee robbers [that is, war criminals: U.S. Generals] Milroy and Geary. The citizens had awaited the result of our late combat with the greatest anxiety, and manifested their satisfaction at our success in loud expressions of rejoicing. Riding up the main street of the village, I was brought to a halt by a group of very pretty young girls, who were carrying refreshments to the soldiers, and invited me to partake of them, an offer which I was not strong enough to decline. In the conversation which followed, my fair entertainers expressed the greatest desire to see [C.S.] General Stuart, and were delighted beyond measure to hear that the bold cavalry leader was my personal friend, and that I should probably have little difficulty in persuading him to devote a quarter of an hour to their charming company. This spread like wildfire through the village, so that half an hour later, when Stuart galloped up to me, I was attended by a staff of fifty or sixty ladies, of various ages, from blooming girlhood to matronly maturity. The General very willingly consented to remain for a while that every one might have an opportunity of seeing him, and was immediately surrounded by the ladies, all eager to catch the words that fell from his lips, and many with tears in their eyes kissing the skirt of his uniform coat or the glove upon his hand. This was too much for the gallantry of our leader, who smilingly said to his gentle admirers, "Ladies, your kisses would be more acceptable to me if given upon the cheek." Thereupon the attacking force wavered and hesitated for a moment; but an elderly lady, breaking through the ranks, advanced boldly, and, throwing her arms around Stuart's neck, gave him a hearty smack, which served as the signal for a general charge. The kisses now popped in rapid succession like musketry, and at last became volleys, until our General was placed under as hot a fire as I had ever seen him sustain on the field of battle. When all was over, and we had mounted our horses, Stuart, who was more or less exhausted, said to me, "Von, this is a pretty little trick you have played me, but in future I shall detail you for this sort of service." I answered that I would enter upon it with infinite pleasure, provided he would permit me to reverse his mode of procedure, and commence with the young ladies. The General and Staff bivouacked with the cavalry near Middleburg, while for me was reserved the agreeable duty of riding on special business to Upperville, where, beneath the hospitable roof of Dr. Eliason, I passed some pleasant hours with the family circle, to whom I had to recite fully the events and adventures of the day.[296]

SOME CURIOSITIES

☛ A match has a head, but no face.
A watch has a face, but no head.
A rooster has a comb, but no hair.
A river has a mouth, no tongue.
A wagon has a tongue, but no mouth.
An umbrella has ribs, no trunk.
A tree has a trunk, but no ribs.
A clock has hands, but no arms.
The sea has arms, but no hands.[297]

JOLLITY AMID HOWLING YANKEE CANNONBALLS

☛ It was about five o'clock when [C.S.] General Stuart returned with us to his cavalry, which had been, and were still, suffering severely from the fire of a [U.S.] battery that had been boldly pressed forward to a favourable position, and kept thundering down on our much exposed horsemen with rapid and terrible discharges. Just as we were galloping along the line, the enemy opened upon us with grape and canister, and our men began to waver a little, the ranks getting into some confusion. At this moment General Stuart, who had to ride a few hundred yards farther to meet Colonel Fitz Lee, turned round to me, saying, "Captain, I wish you to remain here with my Staff and escort until I come back, to give a good example to the men." So we had to stand for many minutes in this diabolical fire of canister, which came rattling along the hard dry ground, or howled over us right and left—a pretty severe trial. It requires but little courage to attack the enemy, or even to ride about composedly under fire, in comparison with what is demanded to sit quietly in face of several batteries, from which, with every momentary puff of smoke from the mouths of the guns, one may reasonably expect the messenger of death. A shell which exploded directly over our heads tore nearly to pieces the captain of the squadron nearest to me, with whom I had just been talking, and killed or wounded several of the men. But our example had a telling effect; the ranks closed up and remained in good order until the command was given, and the long line of horsemen, soon in rapid trot, disappeared behind a range of friendly hills.

General Stuart and Staff now galloped forward again to our artillery, which in the mean time had lost many men and horses, but was still answering with the greatest energy the galling fire of the numerous batteries of the enemy. Just at this time a little incident occurred, which, in the very carnival of death, provoked our hearty laughter. One of our

CONFEDERATE PRESIDENT JEFFERSON DAVIS IN 1889, THE YEAR HE CROSSED THE RIVER.

Staff-officers, Captain _____, whom we had often joked about the nimble and successful manner in which he dodged the shells of the enemy, and who had this day again made the politest obeisance to their missiles, annoyed at our raillery, had declared that he would never again bow at their approach, and was sitting with the utmost gravity bolt-upright in the saddle, when a 12-pounder solid shot screamed through the air only a few feet over his head. Down went the head not merely to the saddle, but, with the body to which it was still securely attached, to the earth, amidst the convulsive shouts of his comrades and the cannoneers. Another incident which we witnessed about the same time, produced no less merriment amid the fury of the battle. A wounded man was borne along by two of his comrades, his limbs hanging down motionless and his head dangling about as if life was nearly extinct. The fire of the enemy was still murderous, and one of the carriers, struck by a musket-ball, fell to the ground, dropping his charge, who, seeing himself in great danger, suddenly revived, and, jumping up, took to his heels with the most surprising agility. The explosive laughter which followed him in his rapid flight all along our lines absolutely drowned for a few moments the tumult and hurly-burly of the engagement.[298]

THE DANGERS OF "WINDAGE"
☛ About six o'clock in the evening I was sent by General Stuart to order to the front two squadrons of our Georgia regiment to attack one of the Federal batteries which, without proper support, had been making a very bold advance. The enemy had brought up to the distant heights twenty pieces of rifled ordnance, which, by undue elevation, firing too high for the effect they desired, were playing upon an open space of ground over which I had to ride. The fire was so terrific that I found one of our reserve batteries, not actively engaged at the moment, entirely deserted by its gunners, who had sought protection with the horses in a deep ravine, and who cried out to me to dismount and join them, or certain death must be my fate. I pushed on, and reached my destination in safety; but galloping back I felt a stunning blow across the spine, and at the same moment my horse rolled over with me. I was confident the animal had been struck by a cannon-ball; but, to my great surprise, I was not able to discover any wound. As I was myself unhurt, I remounted my brave animal, and continued my way. A solid shot had passed close to my horse's back, and the current of air set in motion by its passage had

knocked over both horse and rider. Afterwards, during the war, I witnessed many similar cases of prostration of men and animals by "windage."[299]

CONFEDERATE CHARGE ON A CHERRY TREE

☛ At daybreak next morning we received orders to move as rapidly as we might eight miles higher up the river, to ford it in the neighbourhood of Bottom's Bridge, and, falling upon the flank of the Federal army, to intercept its hasty retreat; but upon reaching this point we received counter orders, as the Federal army had already passed, and we rode point. Here we found that the enemy, anticipating our movement, had posted artillery and sharpshooters in advantageous position on the river-bank, and we were accordingly received with a very determined resistance. Soon, however, Pelham came up with his horse-artillery, and, by a well-directed fire, opened a passage for us. The enemy retreated in precipitation, leaving their dead and wounded all along the course of their flight, and we were able to make but a very few prisoners. The sun was now pouring down with intense fervour, and as our horses were well-nigh exhausted with our rapid marching and counter-marching, we were compelled to take a few hours' rest on the roadside. We lay down in a corner of the fence beneath the shade of some cherry-trees hanging full of their delicious fruit, the bunches unfortunately just a little too high to serve our parched mouths with grateful refreshment. [Gen.] Stuart and I were standing on the highest rail of the fence, trying with difficulty to pluck some of the cherries, when he laughingly said to me, "Captain, you charge the Yankees so well, why do you not attack this cherry-tree and bring it down?" Without hesitation I jumped from my elevated position, grasping the higher part of the trunk, and breaking down the tree, amid the loud cheers and laughter of the Staff and the soldiers around, who finished the spoil, now so easily to be gathered, in an incredibly short time.[300]

A LITTLE PRISON HUMOR

☛ Some visitors to the prison had as an escort one of the inmates, who aroused their interest.

"Excuse me," said one of them to the convict, "are you in for life?"
"Me? No," was the answer, "just ninety-nine years."[301]

THE MEANING OF "MATRIMONY"

☛ Teacher: "What is the meaning of the word 'matrimony,' Robert?"
Bobby: "Pa says it isn't a word; it's a sentence."[302]

CONFEDERATE CAPTURES CONFEDERATE

☛ During the night which followed the battle of Malvern Hill [on July 1, 1862], we encamped in the orchard of a small farmhouse near the field, but our repose was made exceedingly uncomfortable by heavy showers of rain following one another in rapid succession until the dawn. Profiting by the darkness of the night and the disturbance created by the storm, a spy, who had been captured by some of our men, and who had been condemned to be hanged the next morning, contrived to make his escape. I was rather glad of it. He was an old man of more than sixty, and I had seen him riding along with us all the day on a miserable mule, his hands tied behind him, with such a terrified expression upon his ashy features, that I regarded the poor sinner as sufficiently punished by the agony he had already undergone. The morning opened heavily with rain, and I rose shivering from the damp ground to attend on General Stuart, from whom I received orders to ride at once into Richmond for the purpose of executing some important duties there. As my old grey was very nearly broken down by hard riding, and I might hope to exchange him in Richmond, my captured horse having been lost in the rapidity of our recent movements—and as, in all probability, fighting was not to be renewed—I started gladly upon this expedition. My ride took me over the battle-field and along a portion of the line of the enemy's former retreat. I looked with astonishment at the effect of the heavy artillery-fire of the enemy upon some portions of the forest. Hundreds of the largest trees were riven and shattered, and lay in fragments around, as if all the thunderbolts of heaven had been hurled against them; and in many places the fallen trunks and branches barricaded the road so that it was difficult to get along at all. For miles the ground was thickly strewn with muskets, knapsacks, blankets, and other equipments that had been thrown away in their flight by the soldiers of the retreating Federal army. It was nearly night when I reached Richmond. Wet, cold, and weary, I rode immediately to the hotel and sought my bed—a luxury which no one can thoroughly appreciate until he has long been deprived of it, and compelled as I had been for several nights to sleep in his clothes on the hard ground.

The Spotswood Hotel at this time was crowded with guests, among whom, a neighbour of my own, was no less distinguished a person than a Federal General, M'Call [George A. McCall], who had been taken prisoner in one of the recent battles. As might naturally have been expected, the joy of the people of Richmond was very great at the deliverance of their city from the hands of the enemy; but they took their good fortune with a very becoming composure, and spoke and acted just as if, in their judgment, with such an army as that of General Lee, under such commanders, between them and the invading force, the struggle for the Confederate capital could have had no other result. No powder was wasted in salutes over the victory, no bonfires blazed, no windows were illuminated, and the general appearance of Richmond was in all respects unchanged from what it had been a month before.

My business in Richmond was speedily transacted, and the following day, having procured an excellent horse, I set out with fresh courage and spirits to rejoin my General. Our army in the mean time had been pushed forward towards the James river, being close upon the enemy's formidable positions at Westover; and as I rode along, I heard from time to time the heavy ordnance of the gunboats, which threw their tremendous projectiles wherever the grey uniforms came in sight. Generals R. E. Lee, Longstreet, and Stuart had established their headquarters together in the extensive farmyard of a Mr. Phillips, which spot I reached late in the evening, after a long and dusty ride. Here for a few days we enjoyed rest and comparative quiet. Our generals were often in council of war, undecided whether or not to attack the enemy. On the morning of the 6th, General Stuart removed his headquarters about two miles lower down the river to the plantation of a Mr C., old friends of ours, where we were received, especially by the ladies, with great kindness and enthusiasm.

About dusk on the 6th the General started with two of our regiments, the 4th and the 9th, and six pieces of our horse-artillery, to lay an ambush for the Federal gunboats, which every night came steaming up the river with fresh troops and supplies for their army. Having been detained by some duty at headquarters, I left about an hour later than the column, quite alone, and had on my ride a little adventure which gave rise to a great deal of merriment at my expense. I had been informed by one of our patrols that detachments of the enemy's cavalry had been seen in the neighbourhood, and I had therefore moved on with no little vigilance and circumspection. It was a beautiful night, the air was full of the fragrance of the wild-flowers and forest-blossoms, and myriads of fire-flies glittered in the surrounding darkness. Suddenly, through the profound stillness of the night, there struck upon my quick ear the sound of hoofs upon my right hand, and out of a small dark bridle path on the side of the road there emerged a horse man, who wore, as well as I could distinguish, the Federal uniform. "Halt!" said I. The stranger halted. "What is your regiment?" "Eighth Illinois" (hostile cavalry). The answer had no sooner been given than, putting spurs to my horse, I rushed upon my antagonist, who, seeing my revolver levelled with uncomfortably accurate aim at his breast, surrendered himself without the least hesitation as my prisoner. As I was conducting my capture to the spot where the 9th Virginia Cavalry was stationed, I perceived that he was riding an admirable horse, which I regarded with infinite satisfaction as already my property. He entertained me on the way with many stories about the Yankee army, how long he had served in it, etc., etc. When we had reached our regiment, however, he came out suddenly in the new character of a member of the [Confederate] corps, a private in the ranks, who had replaced his own tattered Confederate uniform with the uniform and cap of a captured Federal soldier, and who had taken me, from my foreign accent, for a Federal officer. As he made this recital, not without a certain latent satire at my prowess in making a prisoner of a private of the 9th Virginia Cavalry, I confess that, recalling his extreme terror at the moment of his surrender, I lost all patience with him, and again levelling my pistol at him, I gave him to understand that I would make short work of him at any future repetition of his jests. But I did not get my fine horse; for upon turning over my prisoner, whom I still supposed to be a Yankee, to Colonel Fitzhugh Lee, he recognised in him at once a man of his own command, who had most imprudently assumed one of the captured Federal uniforms. This substitution of dress was unfortunately very often done by our men, and many a poor fellow has been killed by his own friends because he could not resist the temptation of discarding his dirty rags for a new blue coat and trousers. In addition to the loss of my captured horse, I was very much teased for my mistake, and General Stuart often laughingly asked me, "How many prisoners of the 9th Virginia have you taken lately?"[303]

AN IRISH WAIL
☞ A witty and eloquent Irish speaker was once dumbfounded when the whole glamor of his glowing peroration upon patriotism and a soldier's duty was shattered by a wail from the gallery, "Och, what's the world to a man if his wife's a widow?"[304]

THE RATTLESNAKE & THE CONFEDERATE CAVALRY OFFICER
☞ On the 4th of August the trumpet sounded again for the march, as a reconnaissance in force was to be undertaken in the direction of Port Royal and Fredericksburg. With four regiments and one battery we pushed on all day until we reached the village of Bowling Green, about twenty miles distant, where we made a bivouac for the night. On the 5th, the hottest day of the whole summer, we continued our march, and arrived at Port Royal at eleven o'clock in the morning, just after a squadron of the enemy's cavalry, already apprised of our approach, had retreated lower down the Rappahannock. The joy of the inhabitants at our coming was touching to witness. The ladies, many of them with their cheeks wet with tears, carried refreshments around among our soldiers, and manifested, with the deepest emotion, their delight in seeing the grey uniforms, and their gratitude at their deliverance from the oppressor. At one P.M. we resumed our march, halting only for a few minutes at the charming cottage of a lady, where, at a later period, I was to spend some pleasant days, which had just then been left by a band of Yankee marauders, one of whom had robbed

THOMAS J. "STONEWALL" JACKSON AS A U.S. SECOND LIEUTENANT DURING THE MEXICAN WAR (1846-1848).

an old negro servant of the family of his silver watch. The negro, who recognised Captain Blackford as an old friend of the household, complained to him most piteously of this treatment, and implored him to enforce restitution of his property. About three o'clock we overtook these marauders, whom our advance-guard had made prisoners, and upon one of the skulking fellows we at once discovered the watch, which, to the satisfaction of us all, and to the grinning delight of its rightful owner, Captain Blackford restored to him.

At sunset we reached Round Oak Church, only twelve miles distant from Fredericksburg, where we bivouacked, taking the precaution to form a long cordon of pickets and vedettes, who took care that the enemy should not be informed of our movements from any of our followers, by allowing no one to pass outside their line. At the same time we sent forward some of our Texan scouts, who, soon returning, reported the enemy encamped in large numbers about five miles from Fredericksburg. One of the scouts, a man famous in his profession, had been shot by one of the Yankee sentinels, and brought back with him an arm badly shattered.

In our bivouac I met with a little adventure that turned out fortunately enough, but might have cost me my life. Fatigued by the long ride, and exhausted by the intense heat of the day, I had spread my blanket, soon after my arrival, near an old log, which in former days had been used as a step by the ladies in mounting and dismounting on their rides to church, but which I now proposed, in its decay, should serve me as a pillow. Resting my head upon it I fell at once into a deep sleep, from which I was presently awakened by something crawling over my hand. I quickly shook off the object, which gave out a sharp, clear, rattling sound, and which I perceived in the bright light of the moon to be a snake more than four feet in length that raised itself at me in an attitude that meant mischief. Sleeping, as I always did, with my arms by my side, it was the work of a moment to draw my keen Damascus blade [a large double-edged sword] and sever the reptile in twain. Excited, however, by this unfamiliar hostile attack, and finding that the dissevered parts of the body continued to manifest vitality in wriggling about on the grass, I dealt yet several heavy blows at my enemy, and the noise of the encounter aroused the General with the whole of his Staff. Arms in their hands, they hastened to the scene of action, believing that not fewer than a hundred Yankees had fallen upon me. A roar of laughter burst from them at the nature of my midnight combat; but the affair seemed less ridiculous when they discovered that I had killed one of the largest specimens of the American rattlesnake, a reptile as venomous as the East Indian cobra, whose bite is certain and speedy death—a fate which I had very narrowly escaped. I could obtain little sleep during the remainder of the night; and was ready to move before sunrise when the command was given to mount.[305]

CONFEDERATE GENERAL J.E.B. STUART TAKES A BOW

☛ General Stuart now collected his whole force, except a single squadron left on picket at Massaponax Church, and pressed with all possible haste upon the main body of the enemy, who in the outset were totally surprised, and fled in disorderly rout before us for several miles. As soon as they discovered, however, that they had only cavalry and a few pieces of artillery against them, they made a stand, and became in turn the assailants. Numerous batteries opened fire upon us; and their long lines of tirailleurs advanced in beautiful order. On this occasion I had a good laugh at General Stuart. Among other novelties in offensive warfare, the enemy employed against us in the fight one-pounder cannons, the balls of which being curiously shaped made a peculiar sound in their passage through the air. Just as the General and I had been placing two of our pieces in favourable position, and were riding nearer to the front, one of these exasperating little balls passed directly between us; and my brave General, whom many a time I had seen, amid the heaviest artillery fire, perfectly indifferent to shot and shell hissing around him, now, as the new projectile whizzed past us with its unfamiliar music, made it the politest bow imaginable.[306]

THEY NEARLY ATTACKED FELLOW CONFEDERATES

☛ About two o'clock in the afternoon there was a heavy cannonade and continuous musketry-fire heard in the direction of [C.S. Gen.] Jackson's position, announcing that the enemy had commenced their attack; but, at the same time, we heard a cannonade in the direction of Haymarket, and believing [C.S. Gen.] Stuart to be there at work, I regarded it as my duty to continue my march. Very soon, however, we heard firing all around us, and I was convinced that we had been misled by the sound, and the great number of narrow unfrequented bridle-paths in the woods. As it was impossible to decide where we should find friend or foe, our situation became a very critical one. About dusk we discovered in a small opening before us a negro on horseback, who had no sooner seen us than he galloped off in hurried flight, but was overtaken after a short chase by one of our couriers. It was difficult to make him believe that we were not Yankees, and his delight was indescribable when at last he recognised us as friends. He told me that a squad of Federal cavalry was at that moment engaged in pillaging his master's house, which he pointed out to us not more than three-quarters of a mile distant—that he had saved himself on one of the horses in the stable—that the enemy were all around us—and that Haymarket was occupied by them in strong force. Of Stuart and his cavalry the faithful negro had not seen or heard anything. Being perfectly at a loss, and nearly cut off from our army on all sides, I resolved to attempt returning by the same route we had come, and, protected by the darkness of the fast coming night, to endeavour to rejoin Jackson's men. Silently we rode along the narrow lane for several hours, each one of us fully conscious of the danger of our situation, when suddenly the tramp of a body of horsemen sounded right in front of us—a scouting party, as we could scarcely doubt, of the Federal cavalry. I explained to my companions that there was no choice left but to cut our way through. Our plan hastily formed was this. The two couriers were to ride on either side of Dabney and myself, and to fire right and left with their revolvers, leaving us to open the way in the centre with our sabres. The advancing party having now arrived within twenty-five steps from us, I gave the customary order, "Halt! one man forward!" and, this being disregarded, the loud command, "Charge!" Just at this moment several voices cried out, "That is [C.S.] Major von Borcke! halt, halt; we are friends!" which at once checked our furious onset, and we found, to our great surprise and delight, and amid hearty laughter on all sides, that we had been on the eve of attacking the remaining part of General Stuart's Staff and escort, who had also been separated from the General, and, like ourselves, were in search of him. We heard now that the way to Jackson, who had repulsed the enemy after a sanguinary conflict, was perfectly unobstructed, and that one of our cavalry regiments, the 1st Virginia, was encamped a couple of miles farther to the rear. Thither we at once determined to ride, that we might refresh our weary horses, and seek rest for ourselves for the few remaining hours of the night.[307]

A CONFEDERATE HORSE OF A DIFFERENT COLOR

☞ We joined [C.S.] General Stuart early on the morning of the 29th at Sudley's Mill, where [Stonewall] Jackson had established his headquarters in a building which was used, at the same time, as a hospital for several hundred of the wounded of the previous day's battle. . . . At seven o'clock on the morning of the 29th the attack was renewed by [U.S.] General Pope, who tried his best to crush Jackson before Longstreet, who was rapidly approaching with his strong corps, could arrive. As old Stonewall had already gone to the front at the time of my arrival, I was sent to him by General Stuart to get orders for the disposition of the cavalry; and to my question at starting, "Where shall I find General Jackson?" my chief replied, with a smile, "Where the fight is hottest." So I galloped forward over the battle-field, still strewn with the dead of yesterday's conflict, towards a point where twenty pieces of our artillery, concentrated into one battery, were hotly engaged with an equal number of Federal guns. Here I felt sure of finding Jackson himself. The Yankee batteries were firing much too high, throwing their shot and shell in rapid succession upon a piece of soft swampy ground about a quarter of a mile beyond our position, over which I must ride if I did not choose to make a long circuit around it. My horse had already been sinking several times a little in the bog, when suddenly the ground beneath him, which was covered with a treacherous surface of verdure, gave way entirely, and my brave bay sank till half his body was buried in the morass. I leaped from his back just in time to gain a secure footing myself, but every effort to extricate the animal was in vain. Meanwhile

YOUNG LADIES SELECTED TO RIDE IN THE PROCESSIONS WHEN JEFFERSON DAVIS' BODY WAS RECEIVED AT RALEIGH, NORTH CAROLINA.

shells were plunging and bursting nearer and nearer to me, throwing upon myself and horse a heavy shower of mud and dirt, excited by which, and not a little insulted, the noble beast made renewed exertions to get free, each time sinking deeper and deeper in the mire. I had already decided to abandon my steed and execute my orders on foot, when a body of our infantry marching by came very readily to my assistance, and, by dint of spades, ropes, and poles, managed to liberate the animal, which emerged from the bog perfectly black, and trembling in every limb, as I jumped again into the saddle. Without further accident I reached General Jackson, who, looking at me with astonishment, said, with his quiet smile, "Major, where do you get your dye? I could never have believed that a bay horse might be changed so quickly into a coal-black one." Then, upon my explaining my mission, he gave me orders for Stuart, who was to operate with his cavalry on the right flank, and hold the enemy in check until Longstreet could take his place.[308]

LEGS & THE BOY
☛ As the cup was handed over into the youth's hands, there went up cries of "Speech! Speech!" and the hubbub broke out anew. Meanwhile the lad was able to collect his thoughts and, of course, to catch his breath. Then he stepped up on a bench. There came an abrupt and eager hush. "Gentlemen," he said, "I have won this cup by the use of my legs. I trust I may never lose the use of my legs by the use of this cup."[309]

A CONFEDERATE OFFICER VISITS THE ENEMY
☛ The following day there came some important documents and letters from General R. E. Lee to be transmitted to [U.S.] General M'Clellan, and I had the honour to be selected by our commander-in-chief as the bearer of them into the Federal lines. To make a favourable impression upon "our friends the enemy," I fitted myself out as handsomely as the very seedy condition of my wardrobe would allow; and as all my own horses were, more or less, broken down, I borrowed a high-stepping, fine-limbed chestnut from one of my comrades of the Staff for the occasion. General Stuart took advantage of the opportunity to send under my charge a batch of prisoners for exchange, and, intrusting me with some private messages to M'Clellan, bade me proceed as far as possible into the enemy's lines, and employ all my diplomacy to obtain

a large insight into his positions—to as great an extent, at least, as was consistent with the proprieties of my mission. About ten o'clock in the morning, my fifty or sixty Yankee prisoners were turned over to me by [C.S.] Colonel W. H. F. Lee at his camp, and at noon I reached the Potomac near Shepherdstown, escorted by a cavalcade of our officers, who were interested in accompanying me as far as the river with my flag of truce. This imposing ensign consisted of a white pocket handkerchief on a long pole, and was borne most loftily by one of our couriers, a handsome martial looking fellow, who crossed the river with it, and soon brought me the permission to come to the opposite shore. I was greatly amused, during our passage of the ford, by the bitter complaints of the Yankee prisoners, that they were forced to wade through the cold waters of the Potomac, which wet them from head to foot. I answered them, that I was not myself unmoved by the cruel compulsion, and that I should be yet more deeply affected by it, had not all the boats along the river been seized and burned by their army. On the Maryland shore I was received by a major, who was in command of the outposts at this part of the Federal lines, who handed me his proper written acknowledgment for the prisoners, and said, that as for the papers and documents I might deliver them to him, and he would forward them at once. This, of course, I politely declined, giving him to understand that despatches of such importance I could only deliver to General M'Clellan, or, should this be impossible, to some other general of his army; and adding, that as I supposed [U.S.] General Pleasanton to be supreme in command of this portion of the lines, I should be glad to be conducted to him. The Major here betrayed some embarrassment, and spoke of impossibilities, etc., but at last concluded to send off a mounted officer for further instructions.

Meanwhile all the Yankee soldiers who were not on duty came running towards me, impelled by curiosity to see the "great big rebel officer," in such numbers that the Major was compelled to establish a cordon of sentries around me to keep them at a respectful distance. The only camp-stool that could be produced having been politely offered me for a seat, I soon found myself engaged in a lively and pleasant conversation with a group of Federal officers. Upon one matter only that was brought into the discourse we were unable to agree. They claimed the battle of Sharpsburg as a brilliant victory for their arms. I could not see it in that light.

At length, after a weary time of waiting, came the answer to the Major's message that I might proceed; and a good-looking young cavalry officer was reported to me as guide and protector. Eager to anticipate a disagreeable and awkward formality, I now asked to be blindfolded, but this was politely waived. Starting from the ford, I took a tall and singularly shaped pine-tree, which reared itself far above the tops of its neighbours, as a landmark, and with this constantly in sight, it was not difficult for me to discover that I was purposely carried about in a circle, up hill and down dale, through dense woods and vast encampments of troops. The Federal army at this time certainly appeared to the greatest advantage in its camps. Everywhere was observable the most beautiful order. The soldiers were well dressed, and had the look of being well fed; their arms were in excellent condition; and the whole of their cantonments spoke of a high degree of military discipline, the absence of which I had so often regretted in our own bivouacs.

My companion proved to be a very pleasant young gentleman but inexperienced officer, who, during a ride of eight miles, which brought us to somebody's headquarters, voluntarily gave me much information that he should have kept to himself. Here I saw at a glance a considerable display of the pomp and circumstance of war. What a contrast it presented to the headquarters of our general officers, especially to the simple encampment of our great commander-in-chief [Gen. Lee], who, with his Staff and escort, occupied only a few small tents, scarcely to be distinguished from the tent of a lieutenant! Here a little town of canvass surrounded the magnificent marquee of the [U.S.] General, from which floated the stars and stripes in a reckless extravagance of bunting; numerous sentries were pacing their beats; mounted officers, resplendent with bullion, galloped to and fro; and two regiments of Zouaves in their gaudy uniforms were drawn up for parade.

I had already found out that this was [U.S.] General Fitzjohn Porter's headquarters, and it was evident enough that some very great personage was expected there. Adjoining the General's marquee there had been erected a beautiful pavilion, under which was stretched out a long table laden with luxuries of every description, bottles of champagne in silver ice coolers, a profusion of delicious fruit, and immense bouquets of flowers. A [large gas-filled U.S. army] balloon (I have mentioned before that this means of observation was much in use with the Federal army) was rising every few minutes to the height of several hundred feet, the car, secured by ropes, filled with officers, who, with all kinds of glasses, were looking out narrowly in the direction of Harper's Ferry. I was not mistaken in my conjectures. As I afterwards learned, no less a dignitary than President Lincoln was momentarily looked for. Escorted by General M'Clellan, the President had already inspected a great portion of the Federal army of the Potomac; and as this was to be kept a secret, my visit was necessarily to be a short one.

During the time my young companion was announcing my presence to General Porter, I directed my eye towards the river, and there stood my pine tree, not more than three miles distant in a straight line, plainly in view.

From General Porter's tent I could now hear the sound of voices in excited conversation; indeed, I caught several very angry expressions before my guide returned with a flushed face, in which one could read plainly the reprimand that had been given him, and desired me to enter. General Porter, as he rose to receive me, I found to be a man of rather above the middle height, with a frank and agreeable face, the lower part of which was covered with a luxuriant black beard, and in his whole bearing and appearance the soldier. The floor of his ample tent was carpeted, easy-chairs and a couch offered their accommodations, and his headquarters had all the comfort of a well-furnished drawing-room. After a brief interchange of salutations, ensued the following colloquy.

Federal General.—"You will allow me to express my regret that you have been brought here, and to say that a grave fault has been committed in your coming."

Confederate Major.—"General, I have been long enough a soldier to know that a grave mistake has been committed, but I also know that the fault is not on my side."

Fed. Gen.—"You are right—I ask your pardon. But why did you inquire for General Pleasanton, and what in the world induced you to suppose that he was in command here? I do not myself know where General Pleasanton is—at this moment he may be on your side of the Potomac."

Confed. Major.—"Where General Pleasanton is to-day I am certainly not able to tell; but as I had the pleasure of seeing him with my own eyes last night returning with considerable haste to this side of the river, I had the right to suppose that he was here."

Fed. Gen. (laughing).—" I can have no objection to your conjecture. When do you think to join General Stuart again?"

Confed. Major.—"Should I ride all night, I may hope to reach him some time to-morrow morning." (I was dancing at half-past ten o'clock that same night at "The Bower.")

Fed. Gen. (again laughing).—"You seem to enjoy riding at night."

Confed. Major.—"Very much, at this delightful season of the year."

The General now very courteously offered me some refreshments, which I declined, saving and excepting a single glass of brandy-and-water. I then delivered my despatches, pocketed my receipt for them, and took leave of a man whom I could not help admiring for his amenity of manners and high soldierly bearing. General Fitzjohn Porter proved to be too much of the gentleman for the Northern Government. He was very soon afterwards dismissed from the service for faults alleged to have been committed during Pope's campaigns, but I have pleasure in bearing my testimony (that of an enemy) to his qualities as a gallant soldier and an excellent fighter.

I availed myself of this opportunity of writing from the tent of the Adjutant-General a private note to Major Von R., a former brother officer of mine in the Prussian army, who was serving on M'Clellan's Staff, looking to an interview, possibly under similar circumstances as had now brought me into the Federal lines, which interview, however, never took place. Starting now upon my return, I could not help expressing to my escort how very much I regretted he should have incurred the displeasure of his general by conducting me to him. He had the amazing effrontery to deny that this was the case; but I knew better. Soon afterwards he offered me a cigar, which I thankfully accepted, and, finding it excellent, praised very highly; whereupon he said, that having a large supply of them, he should be only too happy if I would consent to take a few boxes as a present, adding that he believed we were entirely cut off from luxuries of this kind. I thanked him cordially, but declined his friendly proposal, assuring him that he was altogether mistaken as to this matter, inasmuch as the steamers that were constantly running the blockade kept us abundantly provided with havannas. This was not strictly true, and I made the little sacrifice to pride with an almost broken heart.

We had the same long roundabout ride on our return, and it was late in the evening when we arrived on the bank of the Potomac, through whose waters I was conducted half-way by my friendly foe, who, as we shook hands at parting, regretted that we were enemies to each other, and said that he hoped we should meet again, "when this cruel war was over," under happier circumstances. I thanked him for his kindly feeling, and begged him to take a lesson from me as a farewell offering. Showing him my pine-tree on the Maryland shore which had served me as landmark, I said to him—"My young friend, General Fitzjohn Porter's headquarters in a straight line are not three miles from that tree—he is in command of your right wing: to deceive me, you have conducted me all around the country, but I have always known where I was, and I have passed three divisions of your army; moreover, an important personage is every moment expected at General Porter's tent, and this personage is no other than President Lincoln." My courteous adversary laughed heartily at this, and said, "Well, I did not believe that in any other nation of the world there was a man who could fool a Yankee; you have shown me the contrary, and I accept the lesson." We then shook hands for the last time, and returned to our respective lines.[310]

CONFEDERATE GENERAL PATRICK R. CLEBURNE.

HE KNEW HE WAS AT THE TOP!

☛ The story is told that once, when in the city of Washington, [Southern] Bishop Galloway was accosted by a bootblack, with brush in hand, who said, "Senator——."

To which Galloway replied, "I am no Senator."
Quickly the bootblack retorted, "Judge."
And the bishop replied, "I am no judge."

"Well," said the boy, "what is ye, then?"

The bishop, smiling, answered, "I am a bishop of the Methodist Church, South."

Then answered the bootblack, "I knowed ye was at the top, whatever ye was!"[311]

GENERAL JACKSON'S NEW COAT

☛ From a long rest, after the dissipations of the past night, I was roused about noon by [C.S.] General Stuart, with orders to ride, upon some little matters of duty, to the camp of General Jackson. I was also honoured with the pleasing mission of presenting to old Stonewall, as a slight token of Stuart's high regard, a new and very "stunning" uniform coat, which had just arrived from the hands of a Richmond tailor. The garment, neatly wrapped up, was borne on the pommel of his saddle by one of our couriers who accompanied me; and starting at once I reached the simple tent of our great general just in time for dinner. I found him in his old weather-stained coat, from which all the buttons had been clipped long since by the fair hands of patriotic ladies, and which, from exposure to sun and rain and powder smoke, and by reason of many rents and patches, was in a very unseemly condition.

When I had despatched more important matters, I produced General Stuart's present, in all its magnificence of gilt buttons and sheeny facings and gold lace, and I was heartily amused at the modest confusion with which the hero of many battles regarded the fine uniform from many points of view, scarcely daring to touch it, and at the quiet way in which, at last, he folded it up carefully, and deposited it in his portmanteau, saying to me, "Give Stuart my best thanks, my dear Major the coat is much too handsome for me, but I shall take the best care of it, and shall prize it highly as a souvenir. And now let us have some dinner." But I protested energetically against this summary disposition of the matter of the coat, deeming my mission, indeed, but half executed, and remarked that Stuart would certainly ask me how the uniform fitted its owner, and that I should, therefore, take it as a personal favour if he would put it on. To this he readily assented with a smile, and, having donned the garment, he escorted me outside the tent to the table where dinner had been served in the open air.

The whole of the Staff were in a perfect ecstasy at their chief's brilliant appearance, and the old negro servant, who was bearing the roast-turkey from the fire to the board, stopped in mid-career with a most bewildered expression, and gazed in wonderment at his master as if he had been transfigured before him. Meanwhile, the rumour of the change ran like electricity through the neighbouring camps, and the soldiers came running by hundreds to the spot, desirous of seeing their beloved Stonewall in his new attire; and the first wearing of a fresh robe by Louis XIV, at whose morning toilet all the world was accustomed to assemble, never created half the sensation at Versailles, that was made in the woods of Virginia by the investment of Jackson in this new regulation uniform.[312]

GENERAL JACKSON GAVE HIM HEARTBURN

☛ The deep sleep which succeeded to the fatigues of the previous day had hardly fallen upon me, when I was aroused by the touch of Stuart's hand upon my shoulder. The General's wish was that I should bear him company, with several of our couriers and Dr. Eliason, who was well acquainted with all the roads in the neighbouring county, to the headquarters of General Jackson, who had encamped about twelve miles off, on the opposite side of the Shenandoah, near the village of Millwood. The command of our cavalry had been temporarily transferred to Colonel Rosser, who had instructions to hold his position as long as possible, and to keep General Stuart informed by frequent messengers of the progress of the impending fight.

A cold wind was blowing in our faces as we trotted through the village of Paris in the direction of the Shenandoah, and it was freezing hard when we reached the stream, about midnight, at a point where ordinarily it was easily fordable, but where we found it so much swollen by the recent rains in the mountains that we were compelled to cross it swimming. We reached the opposite bank in safety, but chilled through and with soaking garments. Such was the intensity of the frost, that in a very few minutes our cloaks and blankets were frozen quite stiff; and the water, as it dripped from the flanks of our horses, congealed into icicles, and the legs of the animals were rough with ice. But a sharp ride, as it promoted the circulation of the blood, kept us tolerably warm, and at two o'clock in the morning we arrived at Jackson's encampment. Stuart, being unwilling in his great tenderness for Old Stonewall to disturb his slumbers, proposed that we should seek rest for the remaining hours of the night; but in our frozen condition, it being first necessary that we should thaw out our garments before we could dry them, we preferred building a huge fire of logs, around whose cheerful blaze we sat and smoked our pipes, though, with teeth chattering like castanets, this was smoking under difficulties. Jackson, who, in accordance with his usual habit, awoke with the earliest glimmer of day, no sooner discovered us than he expressed his regret at our evident discomfort, but gave us the readiest consolation by ordering breakfast to be immediately prepared. Nothing was better calculated to restore our good spirits than the summons to the General's large breakfast-table, where the aroma rose in clouds of vapour from an immense coffee-pot, and where stood a magnificent haunch of venison, cold, a present from a neighbouring planter.

The good cheer had the happiest effect on Stuart, who enlivened our repast with abundant anecdote and the recital of many a joke at the expense of his companions-in-arms. It was his special delight to tease me on account of the little mistakes I [being a Prussian] still frequently committed in speaking the English language, which he always cleverly turned so as to excite the merriment of his auditors. During one of our many conversations concerning Old Stonewall, his personal traits and military character, while intending to say, "It warms my heart when he talks to me," I had employed the expression, "It makes my heart burn," etc. Stuart now took occasion to repeat my remark, and represented me most absurdly as having declared that "it gave me the heartburn to hear Jackson talk," which of course provoked the roaring laughter of our little company. Jackson himself alone did not participate in the boisterous mirth. Looking me straight in the face with his large expressive eyes, and pressing my hand warmly across the table as just the faintest smile broke over his features, he said, "Never care, Major, for Stuart's jokes; we understand each other, and I am proud of the friendship of so good a soldier and so daring a cavalier as you are." I was conscious of a blush reddening my cheeks under my beard at this, but I felt also a glow of pride, and I would not at that moment have exchanged the simple, earnest tribute of the great warrior for all the orders and crosses of honour of Europe. "Hurrah for Old Von! and now let us be off," said Stuart, and slapping me on the back to conceal his own slight embarrassment, he rose from the table, followed by his companions. In a few minutes we rode off at a gallop to fresh scenes of excitement and activity.[313]

HE COULDN'T HOLD HIS HORSE

☛ The battle of Baker's Creek, when Grant was investing Vicksburg, at which time our cause seemed very gloomy, numbers of our gallant officers and men having been killed in the day's fight, was an occasion which distinguished the Confederate soldier because all the highest elements of manhood were necessary to hold him in line. The enemy was pressing our rear guard very strongly with a large force, the shells and bullets were flying thick, tearing up the ground, topping trees, and doing mad work generally. Adams's Cavalry Brigade was resisting the advance as well as they could. Men and horses were being killed, and it required nerve and everything else to make a man stay at his post. There was a deathly silence on the part of the men. No one knew what the next moment would do for him. To increase the intensity, a fellow riding a good horse went dashing to the rear. He had lost his nerve. As he flew by, he holloed out: "I can't hold my horse." Munford Bacon, of Madison County, Miss., a friend of mine, who was a member of Adams's Brigade, saw the man and heard his explanation for leaving the line. Munford raised up in his stirrups and yelled out: "Boys, I will give one thousand dollars for one of them horses you can't hold." This created a laugh and a yell, which made the enemy halt long enough to allow our troops to get into better position, and what might have been a disaster was prevented by Munford's wit.[314]

A JOKER GETS JOKED

☞ After the Army of Northern Virginia had fallen back from the Peninsula to Richmond in the spring of 1862, and had camped on the south side of the Chickahominy, a few men from each company were allowed to go into the city for a day only. I was at that time a member of Company C of the 18th Mississippi Regiment. One of the comedians in the company was [Confederate soldier] Ben F. Muse, of Canton, Miss. Ben always had a joke on somebody, and was not happy unless he had the laugh on one of us. But we had the laugh on Ben once, as I will tell you. When his time came to go into town, he said to the boys: "You know I am a hornsnolger, and if you want anything from Richmond, come up with your canteens and your money." Several of the boys who had not tasted the ardent for many moons gave Ben their canteens and the needful, and off he went. I remember how he looked as he bade us goodbye. He was a fine specimen of manhood, handsome as could be, with magnificent development. He had never been accustomed to hardships, and until he went into the army never wanted for anything, but on this occasion his clothes consisted of a pair of old ragged pants, a greasy old flannel shirt and one "gallus" [set of suspenders]. But Ben's heart was as cheery as a mocking bird on a spring morning, as he capered off with seven or eight canteens around his neck. He had no thought of trouble, but spent the time thinking about the fun he would have when he reached town.

MISS GRACE RANKIN, SPONSOR FOURTH S.C.V. BRIGADE, CIRCA 1932.

Several of our men who had been wounded, and some who had been sick, but were well enough to sit around, had congregated at the Mississippi supply depot, where clothes and blankets were sent from home to be distributed among the Mississippi troops. Dr. W. W. Devine was in charge. Well, Ben Muse reached the Mississippi depot and found a number of friends, among them Uriah Eulah, David Rowland, Ed Hargon, and others. Ben had but a short time to tarry, and at once proceeded to tell the boys he wanted to fill the canteens the first thing he did. Eulah was a warm friend of Ben Muse, so were the others, but Eulah thought the opportunity was favorable to have some fun, and, consulting with others, said to Ben: "We can show you where you can get these filled." It will be remembered by the old soldiers that [C.S.] General Winder was the

Commandant of Richmond Post, and his office was a marble front building; and they will also remember that General Winder was a very stern and uncompromising man. Eulah said: "Now, Ben, you come with us and we will show you the place." Dave Rowland had lost a leg, so the four went down the street very slowly until they reached a point opposite General Winder's headquarters. "Now," said Eulah, "you go in that marble store, and you will see two or three soldiers sitting around in the front room. Tell them you want to see the General on private business, and they will let you pass into the next room, where you will find several men in citizens' clothes, writing. Tell them also that you want to see the General on an important matter, and they will pass you into a third room, where you will see an old man with bald head, wearing glasses, and he also has on citizens' clothes. Walk up to the old man, tap him on the shoulder, and point to your canteens. Tell him you want them filled, and don't forget to say you've got the spondulix. The old man will jump up and rear and swear at you, but when he does you just pat him on his bald head, and say: "Oh, yes; I knew you would do this, but I'm one of the boys. I don't talk; you can count on me."

Ben went over, while Eulah and Dave Rowland waited on the other side. In about three minutes, Ben rushed into the street, his canteens rattling, making a great noise as he ran down the street. The guards were after him, but Ben was too fleet, and he reached the "Rockets" ahead of all pursuers. General Winder rushed to the sidewalk and ordered the guards to shoot him.

When Ben patted the old man on the head, he knocked his glasses off, and this was the only thing that saved him. Ben reached camp about daylight, but he brought nothing back but the canteens and an empty stomach.[315]

MISS ALICE BAXTER, ATLANTA; PRESIDENT GEORGIA DIVISION UNITED DAUGHTERS OF THE CONFEDERACY.

CHAPTER TEN

THE POOR FLAG FLOPPERS
☛ The Confederate soldier, in spite of his rags and lack of rations, was always on the *qui-vive* for fun, and his sense of the humor was always appealed to when a column marched in sight of the men whom they called "flag floppers." It was hard for them to refrain such good-natured inquiries as, "Mister, is the flies a botherin' of you?" "Say, is mosquitoes plentiful around here?"[316]

A PEACE ACCORD THAT WORKED
☛ Turner Anderson Gill and Samuel Shortridge Oldham were both born in Western Missouri, Gill in Jackson and Oldham in Cass County. In 1862, they were mustered into Company A, 6th Missouri Volunteer Infantry, C.S.A. Both were wounded in the battle of Corinth, Miss.; but soon recovered from their wounds and returned to the Company.

. . . When [C.S. Gen.] Price had driven the enemy out of Independence, Mo., with [U.S. Gen.] Pleasanton pressing on his rear, and was moving on Kansas City, between him and the enemy was Shelby's Brigade. It chanced that about four miles from Independence, Sam Oldham had an aunt, a Mrs. Thompson.

"Say, Cap," he said, "let's hitch our horses here, and go in yonder. I have an aunt living there."

Gill agreed, and they went in, and [Father] Time, according to an ancient habit, one of which he has never broken, seeing the two young Confederates having a good time, whisked along with surprising celerity. When the visitors finally arose to go and reached the outside, there sat on their horses very complacently, five young Federal troopers, their carbines resting across the pommels of their saddles. Here was a dilemma. To submit to arrest meant disgrace and months of captivity; to resist was certain death. The two Confederates conferred a minute, then Gill, with no display of trepidation, but with his hand resting on the grip of his six-shooter, thus addressed the five troopers:

"Young men, I propose a parley. The facts are plain. You are five, we but two. For us to fight and probably kill each other would have no effect on the war. We are all young men. Why should we fight, and kill each other? I admit we would both be killed, but, being fairly good shots, would be sure to get two of you, possibly four or five. Our proposition is this: let me and my comrade mount our horses and ride away. We will not draw nor try to trick you. You have our word. What do you say?"

After a brief confab, one of the Federals said:

"All right, Johnnies. We recognize the right stripe in you and accept your proposal, so mount and away before our Colonel comes up and spoils it all."

"We rode away," Gill told me long afterward, "but keeping an anxious look behind. But not a shot was sent after us by that astonished bunch of Boys in Blue."[317]

A SCHOOLBOY'S LOGIC

☞ Father criticized the sermon, mother disliked the blunders of the organist, and the eldest daughter thought the choir's singing atrocious. The subject had to be dropped when the small boy of the family, with the schoolboy's love of fair play, chipped in with a remark: "Dad, I think it was a jolly good show for a penny."[318]

THINGS WE NEED TO GET RID OF

☞ [Conservative] Street orator: "We must get rid of radicalism, Socialism, Bolshevism, Communism, and Anarchism." Voice from the crowd: "And while we're about it, why not throw in rheumatism?"[319]

EVERY MOTHER IS AN ARTIST

☞ "Do you do any literary work?" asked a neighbor of a mother.

"Yes," she replied. "I am writing two books."

"What are their titles?"

"*John and Mary*," she answered. "My business is to write upon the minds and hearts of my children the lessons they will never forget."

Every mother is an artist and her material is not the perishable marble, but immortal souls.

> I took a piece of living clay
> And gently formed it day by day,
> And molded with my power and art,
> A young child's soft and yielding heart.
> I came again when years were gone;
> It was a man, I looked upon.
> He still that early impress bore,
> And naught could change it any more.

The greatest need of America today is Christian mothers who will bring up their children "in the nurture and admonition of the Lord."[320]

SAGE ADVICE FROM THE CONFEDERACY

☞ The father of Success is Work. The mother of Success is Ambition. The oldest son is Common Sense. Some of the other boys are Perseverance, Honesty, Thoroughness, Foresight, Enthusiasm, and Co-operation. The oldest daughter is Character. Some of her sisters are

Cheerfulness, Loyalty, Courtesy, Care, Economy, Sincerity, and Harmony. The baby is Opportunity. Get well acquainted with the "old man," and you will be able to get along pretty well with the rest of the family.[321]

A CONSERVATIVE COMPLAINT FROM 1932

☛ The breaking down of old-fashioned principles of morality and integrity in America is the fundamental cause of much of the general distress existing today, Judge Drain said in his charge to the County Grand Jury. He had no remedy to suggest, but it was the duty of courts, officers, and juries to do what they could to get the public mind back to the old-time reverence for law and right living. "Nothing else will bring this country back to where it should be," he said. "I am not a professional reformer, but I do believe that greater respect for our laws, and for the people who are chosen to enforce them, will have a vital bearing upon our welfare in the future."[322]

"MY ITHER LEG"

☛ "How are you today, Sandy?" asked the landlord of his Scotch tenant.
"Verra well, sir," replied Sandy, "if it wasna for the rheumatism in my right leg."
"Ah, you must not complain, Sandy. You are getting old, like the rest of us, and old age does not come alone."
"Auld age, sir?" exclaimed Sandy. "Auld age has nothing to do with it. Here's my ither leg just as auld an' it's sound."[323]

JEFFERSON DAVIS ON GENERAL LEE'S SENSE OF HUMOR

☛ He was not of the grave, formal nature that he seemed to some who only knew him when sad realities cast dark shadows upon him; but even then the humor natural to him would occasionally break out. For instance, General Lee called at my office for a ride to the defenses of Richmond, then under construction. He was mounted on a stallion which some kind friend had recently sent him. As I mounted my horse, his was restive and kicked at mine. We rode on quietly together, though Lee was watchful to keep his horse in order. Passing by an encampment, we saw near a tent two

CONFEDERATE MONUMENT, WILMINGTON, DELAWARE.

stallions tied at a safe distance from one another. "There," said he, "is a man worse off than I am." When asked to explain, he said: "Don't you see, he has two stallions? I have but one."[324]

THE TRUTH FROM A SOUTHERNER
☛ Wars are full of tragedies, with just a little of comedy once in a while. Take the experiences of any soldier of 1861-65, and there will be found tragedies at home as well as at the front. Wife and mother at home, with children, practically unprotected, except by the negroes whom John Brown, Lincoln, and others wanted to arm for insurrection against the whites. But how loyal those slaves were to their masters; they would work the fields, tend the stock, and gather the crops while "Ole Marster" was off to the war fighting for the perpetuation of slavery, according to Brown, Lincoln, Stevens, and others; but that was as untrue as that the war was a "rebellion."[325]

NAUGHTY LITTLE JIM
☛ Naughty little Jim was put into his room to stay there until he was good. After an hour his mother went and said: "Well, Jim, are you a good boy again now?"
Jim: "No, Mummy. I'll ring when I am!"[326]

HE WOULDN'T BE U.S. PRESIDENT
☛ Teacher—"Is there any boy in this class who would not want to be president of the United States?"
Boy—"I wouldn't, teacher."
Teacher—"Why not?"
Boy—"My father says it's best to have a steady job."[327]

WHO IS THE SINNER?
☛ "A gentleman called me handsome yesterday," said a rather elderly lady to her minister. "Do you think it is sinful of me to feel a little proud of the compliment?"
"Not at all, ma'am," replied the minister. "It's the gentleman who is the sinner, not you."[328]

BETTY & GRANDPA
☛ Grandpa, who is a little hard of hearing, used to tell Betty that if she prayed for anything she'd get it, which always was true for Betty, as grandpa usually supplied what she asked.
Betty wanted a new doll carriage and was praying loud and earnestly for it when her brother said: "Betty, you don't have to pray so loud. God isn't deaf."
"I know," responded Betty, "but grandpa is."[329]

"THANK GOD FOR THE DIFFERENCE"
☛ A Scotsman and an Englishman were arguing about their respective countries.
"Well, after all," said the Englishman, "there is very little difference between an Englishman and a Scotsman."

"Perhaps you are right, but thank God for the difference," replied the Scotsman.[330]

THE WITTY BARBER
☞ MacGregor: "Are you the mon who cut ma hair last time?"
Barber: "I don't think so, sir. I've only been here six months."[331]

OUR CLEVER CONFEDERATE WOMEN
☞ Many clever sayings have been handed down from these [Confederate] women of the [Eighteen] Sixties, full of humor and wit, that show their spirit and brilliancy. We know of a young "tar heel" girl, a brilliant talker, while her home was being pillaged by [U.S. Gen.] Sherman's "bummers," made a speech narrating the cause of the war, its beginning in the days of nullification and secession, quoting [Southern fire-eater] John C. Calhoun's speech in Congress down on through, until Sherman's men reached her own home. The soldiers closed about her listening, their hands unconsciously dropping the articles they had stolen. As she ceased, they said to her, "We never knew the South had so much to fight for; if we had, we would never have drawn gun or sword."

The courage displayed even by the young girls in the Confederacy was wonderful, and often their bright answers, even in the face of personal danger, showed a spirit that couldn't be put down, showing that woman's wit is greater than man's wisdom.

When Federal officers had their headquarters in the grove of "Sharon," the [Raleigh, NC] home of Gov. Jonathan Worth (then State Treasurer), they asked his charming young daughter, Miss Mary, to play while they sang the Northern song, "Tramp, Tramp, Tramp, the Boys are Marching," whereupon she replied that she would do so, but she would transpose the verses into those with Southern words.

On another occasion, when the Yankees were occupying the refugee country home of Miss Nellie Worth, of Wilmington, she was compelled by them to play the piano. She vowed to herself she would play nothing but Southern songs, so surrounded by her "deadly enemies" (to quote her), "I cooly sang the Bonnie Blue Flag and Dixie with all my might, breathing intense fire and hate in my soul [for the Yanks] in those two songs."

An old lady of Fayetteville was seated at a dinner party with the Federal officers who were occupying her home. "General," she said, to quote her own words, "Ain't you going to ask a blessing?" "Well, Grandma," he replied, "I don't know how; won't you do it for me?" So I asked a blessing and prayed a short prayer. I asked the Lord to turn their hearts away from their wickedness and make them go back to their homes and stop fighting us; and everything I was afraid to tell them, I told the Lord, and they couldn't say a word.[332]

KNOWN FOR HIS BORING SERMONS
☛ A minister was caught in a thunder shower on the way to church and got dripping wet. He sat in an unheated anteroom, trying to dry off a little before he appeared before his congregation. An old deacon found him there.

"I'm hardly a fit object to stand up before the people, am I, Brother Brown?" he said.

"O, I'd go ahead in," said Deacon Brown. "You'll be dry enough when you get in the pulpit."[333]

A NOT-SO TRICKY QUESTION
☛ A candidate in a recent election campaign made the following remark in the course of his address: "There is no question in the world which I cannot answer with just 'Yes' or 'No.'"

"Well, then, mister," said an old farm hand, "what's the time?"[334]

THE SODA FOUNTAIN WORKER
☛ "Are you a doctor?" she asked the young man at the soda fountain.

"No, madam," he replied, "I'm just a fizzician."[335]

THE FIDDLE HE PLAYED AT HOME
☛ "And is there any instrument you can play?" asked the hostess, who was pressing her guests to provide entertainment.

"Not away from home," Jenkins replied.

"That's queer! What do you play at home?"

"Second fiddle."[336]

THE HORSE WHO WOULDN'T HOLD HIS HEAD UP
☛ "The horse you sold me last week is a fine animal, but I can't get him to hold his head up."

"O, it's because of his pride. He'll hold it up as soon as he is paid for."[337]

THE "AVALANCHE" THAT FOOLED THE YANKS
☛ Our mountain campaigns were very hard and rough, but as yet we had not met with defeat or disaster, but in September, 1863, while holding the gateways through the Cumberlands and protecting transportation between the eastern and western armies, [U.S.] General Burnsides, commanding the 9th Army Corps, advanced from the north and threatened our position. The Confederates concentrated their scattered detachments at Cumberland Gap and resisted the approach of the army. The Federals gathered around the mountain thick and fast with an overwhelming force, which rendered further resistance impracticable. We had concentrated upon the lofty summit of Cumberland Gap mountain; this position was thought to be impregnable, but without supplies and munitions of war, no position can be impregnable. We had

previously obtained our supplies from the surrounding country, and such things cut off, we could not hold out long. Our troops consisted of the 55th Georgia, an Alabama regiment, a North Carolina regiment, infantry, and the Laton artillery of Atlanta, all under the command of [C.S.] Brigadier General Frazier [John W. Frazer]. On the 9th day of September, 1863, [U.S. Gen.] General Burnsides demanded our surrender. When the terms of the surrender were agreed upon and officially announced, the thickest gloom veiled the summit of that lofty mountain. Our faithful soldiers, who had endured extreme hardships and marched together through the dreadful consequences of war with a royal devotion to duty, were now victimized. Confusion, dismay, and disgust characterized the action and expression of every soldier, while the enemy, fifteen hundred feet in the valley below, were flushed with victory.

Notwithstanding the terms of our surrender had been agreed upon and orders to cease firing had been issued to each command, [C.S.] Lieutenant McIntire, commanding one section of the Laton artillery, continued to load and fire over the brink of a precipice down at the enemy, and when he was ordered the second time to cease firing, he threw his cannon, caisson and all, over the precipice, and they went down crashing with such force as to remove thousands of huge rocks from their places on the slope of the mountain, gathering in number and velocity, crushing everything down the mountain with irresistible force. The first relief of the enemy's picket line had been posted for the night along the foot of the mountain, and the reserve picket were indulging in camp revelry, cooking and eating, and rejoicing over their bloodless victory, when they heard a noise as of a mighty volcanic eruption, followed by a great mass of earth, stones, and timbers [falling] down into their midst. They fled in confusion, regardless of their rations or picket duties. When this alarm was reported and investigated, the Federals tried to keep their stampede a profound secret, but it was too good a joke to keep; the next day one of the guardsmen told the joke and enjoyed the laugh that was coming to us. Lieutenant McIntire, who created this confusion on the Federal picket line, came to Texas after the war and became a prominent citizen of Dallas, and, with the same indomitable will and push that dumped the cannon over the ill-fated brink, he accumulated an immense fortune and up to his death he enjoyed the full fruition of a life devoted to constructive progress.[338]

SOUTHERN WOMEN & "THE U.S. OATH OF ALLEGIANCE"
☛ In 1862, when Middle Tennessee was under Federal rule, and Fort Donelson had been surrendered, [U.S.] General Grant was in command at that post. Tennessee has always been the Volunteer State, and when called on for troops, Stewart County responded with her bravest and best. Only a few men, comparatively, were left at home, the majority of whom called themselves Union men. Of these, Grant had no fears; they

didn't count. It was the women he dreaded, for what these hot-headed Southern women can't think of was not in man to conceive. "They shall take the oath!" So the order was issued forthwith that every woman in the county must appear before him and take the oath of allegiance to the Federal government and Abraham Lincoln. A great military triumph, worthy of a great military leader! But "safety first" was not a bad slogan, even in General Grant's day.

A FRATERNAL GATHERING OF FAMOUS CONFEDERATES AND YANKS AT SULPHUR SPRINGS, WEST VIRGINIA, IN 1869. BACK ROW STANDING, L-R: GEN. JAMES CONNER, C.S.A.; GEN. JOHN W. GEARY, U.S.A.; GEN. JOHN B. MAGRUDER, C.S.A.; GEN. ROBERT D. LILLEY, U.S.A.; GEN. P. G. T. BEAUREGARD, C.S.A.; GEN. LEW WALLACE, U.S.A.; GEN. HENRY A. WISE, C.S.A.; GEN. JOSEPH L. BRENT, U.S.A.; SITTING L-R: BLACQUE BEY; GEN. ROBERT E. LEE, C.S.A.; GEORGE PEABODY; W. W. CORCORAN; JAMES LYONS.

A few days after the edict went forth, the "grand review" began its march and continued for days, "Pore white trash," as the negroes called them, in the majority. Some on foot, some horseback, muleback, a few in buggies, and hundreds in wagons—an immense army of intimidated women going to headquarters, where they would swarm like flies around the grand potentate who had summoned them and, with uplifted hand, swear allegiance to the enemy who had invaded their land and at that moment was trampling their rights in the dust.

There were eight women, all told, at our house, which would have swelled the ranks considerably. We often fed Yankee soldiers; they had a way of dropping in at meal time and were always invited to a seat at the table; Southern hospitality demanded that of us. But take that oath, when our men were in the Confederate army? Mother said: "No! never! Not if they put us in a dungeon." That slowly moving, motley crowd, marching day after day like a funeral procession, was nothing less than tragedy, but at the same time it was a picture for the funniest of the funny papers, an event of that stormy period in which we were then living I shall never forget.[339]

"HERE'S YOUR MULE!"
☞ Every soldier remembers the many popular calls, phrases, or sayings that were in vogue during the War between the States, and among them all, none was more widespread and generally used among the Confederates than "Here's Your Mule!" or "Mister, Here's Your Mule." There have been a number of attempts to explain its origin, no one account like the other, and none correct. This paper is written to give a correct account of how "Here's Your Mule!" started, and the correctness of what is here written will be attested by the few still left of those West Tennessee soldiers who were in the Camp of Instruction at Jackson, Tenn.

While the many companies were in said camp before and after the organization into regiments, all sorts of salable commodities were brought into camp in all sorts of conveyances. One of those camp hucksters, who was especially active in peddling pies and other edibles, brought them in a small and ancient looking wagon, drawn by a small, black, shaggy mule. This old fellow was quite an oddity in a way, and became quite well known in camp. The boys tried their usual pranks of speech on him and many of them came off "second best" in the encounter of rough wit. So one day a few of those who had failed to get ahead of the old countryman in the contest with tongues, determined to play a practical joke on him. Most of the soldiers were sheltered then by the old fashioned "A" tents which go in a straight line from the ridge pole down to the pegs that held the cover edge fast to the ground. During the temporary absence of the old huckster, these fellows slipped out the main parts of the harness from this mule, and, taking the animal to another part of the camp, placed him under one of the little "A" tents and fastened the flags down tight to the pegs, then loafed around the wagon until the owner appeared. He naturally was surprised to find that his mule was gone and at once began actively to look for him, the boys who had carried the mule away, amusing themselves at the owner's expense with various suggestions as to the cause of the animal's disappearance. The owner of the mule was too seriously concerned over his loss to give back in his usual style, and the mischievous jokers had a lot of fun at his expense. Soon those men (who had jointly hidden the mule in a place known to but few) spread the news around the camp that old "Pies" had lost his mule. Then one of them went to a distant point in the encampment and shouted at the top of his voice, "Mister, here's your mule!" At once the owner of the mule struck a lively gait in the direction of the voice, but found no mule and no one that could give information of him. Then he said to the men standing around: "Gentlemen, have any of you seen anything of a little black, shaggy mule around here?" In a few minutes the cry, "Mister, here's your mule!" came from another part of the camp, causing the man to go there on a run with the same result, followed by the same inquiry on his part. So he was kept going for a long time from one part of the camp to another by the same call, without finding the mule. As might be expected, quite a crowd followed him about, and as others, who knew nothing of the hiding of the mule, took up the call "Here's your mule!" from different points, the huckster knew he was being played with by the boys. His last summons had brought him to the vicinity of the tent where the mule had been hidden, and from there he did not go in response to other calls of "Here's your mule!" from distant points. All the while a large crowd stood around and gave him "the laugh." Finally, after standing this a while he raised his hands above his head in a beseeching gesture, which brought silence, and in a loud wail of distress, he said: "Gentlemen, for the love of God, has anybody seen anything of that 'ar mule?" Probably the mule recognized his owner's voice, and he lifted up his own voice in a loud bray. Then there arose such a general yell of "Here's your mule!" and led by the fellows who new in which tent to find him, the crowd overthrew the tent and brought forth the "little black, shaggy mule" to his distressed owner. It was a long time before the frolic ended and the countryman got away from the teasing boys, but he had sold all his load and found his lost mule, and he took the joking good naturedly.

From that afternoon, the cry, "Here's Your Mule!" gave rise to merriment in that camp, and as the different commands left the Camp of Instruction, they took with them the cry, "Here's Your Mule!" which spread rapidly through the army until it was in general use by soldiers who had no idea of how it originated, but understood that there was a joke behind it or connected with it some way. It was carried rapidly through all parts of the armies of the West and found its way to the Virginia army. Very few who used it, or heard it, knew how or where it originated, and the writer gives for publication this true history of "Here's Your Mule!" for the first time, as far as he knows. Parodies were gotten up on "Here's Your Mule" and sung around the camp fire. . . .[340]

CONFEDERATE VETERANS & THE BOY SCOUTS

☞ The week of February 14, [1929,] will be observed as Boy Scout Anniversary week, the 19th anniversary of the organizing of the Boy Scouts of America falling on the 8th. Approximately 800,000 active Scouts and Leaders will participate in this nation-wide celebration. Nearly four million American boys have been Scouts since 1910.

The Boy Scout movement stands as the greatest united effort on behalf of and by boys of which world history holds record. The organization seeks to build character in boys and to train them for the duties of citizenship. It is recognized as probably the greatest deterrent of youthful crime. It seeks to help boys to help themselves to gain good health, a strong physique, and mental and moral training. How wonderfully Boy Scouts have met their objectives is a matter of widespread public information.

Those of us who have seen the work of the Boy Scouts in connection with our Confederate reunions have been made to realize what wonderful training they have received in courtesy and helpfulness wherever it is needed. In fact, they add so much to the enjoyment of our reunions that we could not do without them. Hurrah for the Boy Scouts of America! May they grow in numbers until every boy of the country is enrolled![341]

LITTLE EMMA
☞ Little Emma was crossing the desert with her parents in their car. She became unusually silent for a while and then surprised them by saying: "Mother, I never saw so much nothing in all my life."[342]

FED UP WITH POLITICS
☞ Young Wife: "O, politics! politics! I'm fed up on the subject!" Hubby: "Well, my love, that's one thing you can be fed up on without taking on weight."[343]

HIRE YOURSELF OUT—TO YOURSELF!
☞ Some day when you feel gay, and you think you deserve a raise for your valuable services, this is what you should do: Put the shoe on the other foot and hire out to yourself. Just for a day or two, put yourself in your employer's place, and keep tab on the work you do. Let's see—you were late this morning. Only ten minutes? That's true, but whose time was it? You took pay for it, therefore you sold it. You can't sell eight hours of time and keep part of it—not unless you give short measure. How about that work you had to do over? You're not paid to be careless, you're paid to do work well. Not twice over, but once, that's enough! Then do it right! That's what you would say, if you worked for yourself. Hire out, then, to a man named "You," and imagine it's up to you to meet the payroll. Then see what difference it makes in the point of view. Try it once, for a day or two.[344]

PASTE THIS IN YOUR BIBLE (FROM 1929)
☞ An omer was six points.
A gerah was one cent.
A farthing was three cents.
A sheckel of gold was $8.
A talent of silver was $583.30.
A talent of gold was $13,809.
A cubit was nearly twenty-two inches.
A sheckel of silver was about fifty cents.
A hin was a gallon and two pints.
A mite was less than a quarter cent.

A piece of silver, or a penny thirteen cents.
A day's journey was about three and one-fifth miles.
A Sabbath day's journey was an English mile.[345]

PROPER CARE OF HUSBANDS
☞ "So you let your husband carry a latchkey?"

"O, just to humor him. He likes to show it to his friends to let them see how independent he is—but it don't fit the door!"[346]

HE NEEDS A HOLIDAY
☞ "My word, I'm badly overworked."
"What are you doing?"
"Oh, this and that."
"When?"
"Now and then."
"Where?"
"Here or there."
"Well, you must need a holiday."[347]

A HEART-RENDING SERMON
☞ A minister discovered a trouser button in the collection plate one. Sunday morning. In the evening, when he entered the pulpit, he announced: "I wish to remind you that there is a collection at the close of the service. The text I have chosen for the evening sermon is: 'Rend your heart and not your garments.'"[348]

A CURIOUS ELEPHANT INDEED
☞ Muriel had been to the Zoo for the first time and was giving her grandmother a long account of what she had seen. "And which animal did you like best, dear?" asked her grandmother when Muriel had finished. "O, the elephant!" was the reply. "It was wonderful to see him pick up buns with his vacuum cleaner!"[349]

THE "CONTRARY" SEX
☞ "An' yo' say dat little twin baby am a gal?" inquired Parson Jones of one of his colored flock.

"Yessah."

"An' de other one. Am dat of the contrary sex?"

"Yessah. She am a gal, too."[350]

THE STOLEN SAW
☞ A man stole a saw, and on his trial he told the judge that he only took it for a joke.

"How far did you carry it?" inquired the judge.

"Two miles," answered the prisoner.

"Ah, that's carrying a joke too far," said the judge; and the prisoner was sentenced to jail for three months.[351]

HUMOROUS STORIES FROM JEFF DAVIS' GRANDNIECE

☛ [By Miss Nannie Davis Smith:] That the South made history and the North wrote it (untruthfully) is realized by a generation too busy for research work, so octogenarians, reminded of the duty they owe posterity, are doing their endeavor.

Closely associated at Beauvoir with my beloved granduncle, Jefferson Davis, I regret not recording then and there incidents he related—humorous frontier experiences and personal adventures of which there is possibly no written evidence. An amusing anecdote had Mexico for its setting. [U.S.] General [Zachary] Taylor's favorite war horse having vanished mysteriously from securely locked stables, "Old Rough and Ready" was making the air blue with imprecations and dire threats, when Colonel Davis undertook to recover the missing steed in twenty-four hours, if given a free hand. That native Mexicans are expert thieves is an established fact. Aware also that a father confessor's influence was unbounded, Colonel Davis told the shepherd of this flock that, by way of reprisal, his horse might be taken unless General Taylor's was returned at once. Secrets of the confessional are never betrayed, but next morning the borrowed steed was in his stall.

UNVEILING THE STATUE OF JEFFERSON DAVIS IN STATUARY HALL, U.S. CAPITOL BUILDING, WASHINGTON, D.C., JUNE 2, 1931.

A very remarkable story was about a woman who, disguised as a man, fought under the [C.S.A.'s] Stars and Bars. Seeking an interview with President Davis, she told him that her husband and a brother being her only ties, she had enlisted and fought with them till both were killed, and fearing, if wounded, her sex would be discovered, she asked an honorable discharge and the privilege of serving as nurse in a hospital. That heroic woman was from Louisiana, my native State.

After our boys answered the call to arms in 1861, I visited relatives on their plantation in Mississippi, where several girl friends assembled and enjoyed long horseback rides. Returning from one of these excursions, we raced a steamboat, when, to our surprise, cheers went up from gray-clad men on deck, to which waving handkerchiefs responded; later newspaper clippings informed us we had welcomed the "Jeff Davis

Guard." Those gallant Kentucky volunteers never came our way again, and of the carefree group they cheered, I alone survive.

Safely lodged in a hilly region, watered by springs and bayous, I shall never forget my first experience of levee protection when the Mississippi River went on a rampage. As ladies in those primitive times didn't travel without an escort, my father intended coming for me, but, in that anxious period, New Orleans fell, and Uncle Joe Davis, whom I was visiting, moved to Vicksburg. When a steamboat hurrying up stream stopped at Hurricane, waves dashed over the levee, submerging a plank on which we walked aboard.

I gave a wide berth to New Orleans during [U.S. Gen. Benjamin] "Beast" Butler's reign, whose infamous [anti-woman] proclamation and penchant for silver spoons won undesirable notoriety. Another outward sign of loyalty was his attack on the Church, imprisoning ministers who refused to pray for Lincoln and the invaders of our soil. Straightway, Father Mullen, the beloved war priest, bade his flock, kneeling in silent prayer when he did, to pray for Jefferson Davis and the Confederacy.

A funny thing happened when Father Mullen was arraigned before Butler charged with having refused to bury a Federal officer. "A mistake, sir, I'd cheerfully bury the whole Yankee army," the fearless priest replied. After the war, rumor said that Ben Butler contemplated revisiting New Orleans. The "Beast" didn't return, however, neither did he return those historic spoons, prized presumably as souvenirs. In the wake of progress, old landmarks have been removed, some of them destroyed, but St. Patrick's Church, Father Mullen's stronghold, is still in evidence.

Brierfield, President Davis's home, and his brother's adjoining plantation were plundered in approved Yankee fashion, valuable books, furniture, even marble mantels carried off, and ornamental oaks, the growth of years, were wantonly destroyed. A beautiful marble bust of little Samuel Davis was saved by his old [black] nurse, Betsy, who buried it before the vandals arrived. This same Betsy had been Mrs. Davis's much-indulged waiting maid. At a hotel where they boarded, Mr. Davis told his wife: "My dear, I am mortified. If you need wine, order it by the bottle sent to your room." "What do you mean? I don't need wine," she replied. On an itemized bill appeared glasses of choice beverages, whereof the maid had evidently partaken *ad libitum*. Angrily her master exclaimed, "Woman, this is too much. Never come near me again! I set you free—go!" "I ain't gwine nowhar," Betsy calmly assured him. "You's my marster an' you's got ter spote me." So much for "the white man's burden," imposed on our Southland by Great Britain and New England.

The following is another instance of freedom rejected under very different circumstances. A slave who risked his own life in saving one of my ancestors from drowning, declined an offer of liberty and transportation to Africa. According to Daddy Fortune's story, he was chief of a warlike tribe, had been captured [by fellow Africans] long years ago, and brought here by slave traders; there would be no one to welcome his return, he said, and he elected to remain with his white friends. I remember Daddy Fortune in helpless old age being tenderly cared for by my maternal grandmother. Madame Guibert, who told me many interesting truths, none more thrilling than Grandfather Guibert's escape from San Domingo—but that's another story.[352]

DRINKING "THICK" WATER

☛ I had not had a drink of water since early in the day and was very thirsty, "dry as a sponge," so as soon as we got down into the valley, and before I had found my horse, I began to look for water—a well, riverlet, run, or creek. All canteens were empty. Starting out on a hunt through a low-hanging mist that rose from the damp ground after a warm day's thawing, and a gloom that was almost impenetrable, I stumbled into what appeared to be a dry run. No water there, but the promise of a pool lower down. I decided to follow its course down until I came to water, if any was to be found. After stumbling along the dry course for nearly a hundred yards, as a near guess, my foot struck a very soft spot, very damp. Edging along cautiously, feeling along, I caught a gleam of water. Putting my hand down, I assured myself that it was a very shallow pool of yellow water, and thicker than the water we had waded through that morning when we forded the river. What matter of that? It was water anyhow, even if a bit muddy. Laying my rifle on the bank, I stooped down and, making a scoop of my two hands, scooped up a double handful of the "thicker than water" liquid and took in a big swallow. One swallow was enough. Ugh! I can taste it yet after sixty-four years. The mud in it was not much worse than the "Big Muddy's" (Missouri); but the taste? Ah! that was something else. But I kept it down. I had a stout stomach in those days.[353]

MISS ELLA KING TRADER, THE "FLORENCE NIGHTINGALE OF THE SOUTH."

SOUTHERN TOADYISM

☛ There is no desire on the part of the most extreme Southerner to deprive Lincoln of any glory that is rightfully his, but the effort to make the South glorify him should have no recognition by a self-respecting people. Lincoln has enough adulation from the North and East and West, and we have enough to do in seeing that our own great men are not forgotten—and they have been sadly neglected. It is, therefore, rather irritating, to say the least of it, to note the effort, as reported by the daily press, that is made by some Southerners to especially observe the 13th of February and to laud the man who brought war on the South. The action of the Virginia legislature especially seems without excuse. This is what the Associated Press gave out:

> "Richmond, Va., February 13: In response to a resolution of Representative R. Lindsay Gordon, Louisa County delegate, with the statement that 'every Southern gentleman now agrees with Abraham Lincoln on the question of slavery,' the Virginia general assembly to-day for the first time officially honored the civil war President by adjournment of the lower house out of respect to his memory."

Those hard-working legislators evidently needed a holiday, and any pretext served; but why should this Virginia legislator speak for "every Southern gentleman." Lincoln certainly [dis]honored Virginia by refusing to allow the State Assembly to meet just after the surrender. This legislator has forgotten his birthright. There must be a lot of people in Virginia who are not "Southern gentlemen," for there are many in that State who would not agree that slavery was the cause of the war, as this gentleman assumes; even Lincoln would not agree to that. He needs to get better informed on Southern history. This action of the lower House of the Virginia Assembly has occasioned wide comment and indignant protest, and the Louisa delegate may be better informed thereby. The Senate took no action on that day.

And this is reported of one who claims she is proud of her Southern birth: "London, February 13: Viscountess Astor, extolling Abraham Lincoln at a birthday luncheon honoring the American civil war President to-day, discussed Anglo-American relations and assailed the '100-per cent citizen' as a menace to international amity." She regarded Lincoln not as the typical American, but as the embodiment of the best qualities of the citizens of all countries.

Why not of the worst qualities, since he approved of the atrocities of his [U.S.] generals in the South, by which they tried to make it a desert waste? For such as this Germany was condemned by the world.

And this from the seat of government—but it needn't have been inflicted by a Southern representative:

> "Washington, February 13: The tribute of the land of Dixie to Abraham Lincoln was given in the Senate to-day by Senator Robinson of Arkansas, the Democratic [by then Liberal] party leader: 'As a representative in this body of what has come to be known as the New South, I bow my head to-day in reverence,' he said. 'I cut a wild rose blooming in the garden of Dixie and lay it on the tomb of the great, humble, awkward, immortal Lincoln, whose courage and charity excel that which has been exemplified by the leadership of armed forces nowhere, at no time, in the annals of human history.'"

And Washington himself "should laugh."[354]

HE MET EMMA SANSOM
☛ In the year of 1892-93, Mr. Johnson, Emma Sansom's husband, employed me to do some machinery work for him, and the first day of my work he introduced me to his wife. At the dinner table, Mr. Johnson asked me if I was in the war, and "What command." I replied: "The 8ᵗʰ Tennessee Cavalry, under General Forrest." I was with Joseph E. Johnston, the best general in the South!" exclaimed Mr. Johnson. "O, no, Mr. Johnson," I said, "if Forrest could have had the men in number with Johnston, he would have gone into Washington and took Abe Lincoln by the ears and 'blowed' him up like a bat." Well, this caused a great laugh. After a little while, Mrs. Johnson said: "I agree with Mr. West. I think Forrest one of the greatest men of the South!" She then asked me if I was with Forrest in the pursuit and capture of Colonel Streight. I told her no, that our regiment was sent to Florence and Bainbridge. "Well, do you remember anything about a girl getting up behind General Forrest on horseback and showing him an old ford on Black Creek so he could cross in pursuit of the Yankees?" I said I remembered the circumstance, but I could not remember the name. "Well," she said, "I am Emma Sansom." She also told me about two girls who captured the Yankees at that time.

. . . As best I can remember, [Emma] . . . died in the year of 1902, and was laid to rest in Little Mound Cemetery, about twelve miles west of Gillmore, Tex., near the home she loved so well. I lived in the neighborhood of the Johnson family for twenty-five years, and I know whereof I write. I am now eighty-two years old [signed, Uncle Johnny West].[355]

JUDICIOUS COUNSEL FROM THE U.D.C. PRESIDENT
☛ The new President of the Louisiana Division [of the United Daughters of the Confederacy], Mrs. F. P. Jones, of Leesville, has sent out her first circular letter, setting forth her desires concerning the Division and the general organization. If each member would do as she asks, the Division would soon cover every phase of the U.D.C. activity. It would be fine if all would do as she concludes her letter: "Think deeply, speak gently, love much, laugh often, work hard, give freely, pay promptly, pray earnestly, and be kind. That's enough." After this, if there's one request of hers to be added, it is: "Answer letters."[356]

ANNOUNCING HIS FATHERHOOD
☛ "I'm a father!" cried young Jones as he burst into the office. "So's your old man," replied the boss. "Get to work."[357]

THE IRISH OF IT
☛ Two Irishmen were walking down the road on their way to work. One was a little, short fellow, and was having trouble keeping up with his taller companion.

"I say, Pat, you walk fast, don't you?"
"I walk faster than this when I'm by meself," returned Pat.
"Faith, an' I'd hate to be walkin' with ye when ye was by yerself."[358]

BEFORE WOMEN WERE ACCEPTED IN "MEN'S" PROFESSIONS
☛ A tramp rang a doctor's doorbell and asked the young woman who answered if she would be so kind as to ask the doctor if he had a pair of old trousers he would give away. "I am the doctor," said the young woman, and the tramp fell down the steps.[359]

THE IRISHMAN WHO GOT A JOB
☛ "Yis, sor, work is scarce; but Oi got a job last Sunday that brought me a quid."
"What, Pat; you broke the Sabbath?"
"Well, sor, it wuz me or the Sabbath. Wan of us had to be broke."[360]

AN UNUSUAL CHICKEN SOUP
☛ He had ordered some chicken soup in the lunchroom and, having tasted, he said to the waitress: "What is this you have brought me?"
"'Deed, sah, dat's chicken soup," was the reply.
"Well, there is no chicken in it."
"No, sah; dere ain't no dog in dog biscuits, either!"[361]

CHICKEN FOUR TIMES A WEEK
☛ There were callers at the house, and little Charles felt that he should contribute something to the conversation. "We've had chicken four times this week," he said, politely. "Four times? What extravagance!" exclaimed one of the visitors. "Oh, but it was the same chicken," hastened Charles.[362]

THE DISAPPROVING GRANDMOTHER
☛ Granddaughter (being lectured)—"I seem to have heard that the girls of your period 'set their caps' at men."
Disapproving Grandmother.—"But not their kneecaps."[363]

THE OLD DUFFER & THE CUTE LITTLE TRICK
☛ In a night club an old duffer was seen peeling off several golden notes from a hefty wad and passing them to one of those cute little tricks with a curl and a lisp. "And a little child shall bleed them," sighed the hostess.[364]

THE DUMBEST GIRL
☛ A Broadwayite [New York City] writes he has found the dumbest girl. She was fired from a five-and ten-cent store because she could not remember the prices.[365]

CIGARETTES & THE PORRIDGE PAN
☞ He: "I've seen the specialist, and he tells me I must give up smoking cigarettes at once!"

She: "Can't you go on a little longer? We only want twenty-two more coupons to get a porridge pan!"[366]

THE CIRCULAR ARGUMENT
☞ Agnes: "Sally told me that you told her that secret I told you not to tell her."

Marie: "She's a mean thing! I told her not to tell you I told her."

Agnes: "Well, I told her I wouldn't tell you she told me, so don't tell her I did."[367]

CONFEDERATE VETERAN LIEUTENANT COMMANDER DABNEY MINOR SCALES OF HOLLY SPRINGS, MISSISSIPPI. WHY DID LT. SCALES SIDE WITH THE CONFEDERACY? HE BELIEVED, "AS OUR FOREFATHERS DID AND AS THE TRUTH TAUGHT US, THAT THE UNITED STATES WAS CREATED AS AN ASSOCIATION OF SOVEREIGN STATES AND THAT THE FIRST DUTY OF EVERY CITIZEN WAS TO THE SOVEREIGN STATE IN WHICH HE WAS BORN."

CHAPTER ELEVEN

THE NEXT BEST THING
☛ "The best thing for you to do," said the doctor, "is to give up smoking, drinking anything but water at your meals, late hours . . ."
"Wait," entreated the patient; "what's the next best thing?"[368]

THE JOLLY CONFEDERATE SOLDIER
☛ The private Confederate soldier was the jolliest, gayest, happiest man I ever met. If there was a grouch in the Confederate army, I did not meet him.

Here is a good one you have heard at many a reunion. I do not tell new stories. Nobody understands them. No one wants to hear them.

Near the close of the war a squad of soldiers were gathered around a camp fire near Richmond. A Mississippi man belonging to the Stonewall Brigade had been on a furlough to Richmond, and the boys were questioning him.

"Been in Richmond?"

"Yep; spent three days and [a] bunch of money."

"Stay at a hotel?"

"One night; they did not have any room, but they gave me a cot and let me put it down in the end of the hall. They charged me twenty dollars in good Confederate money for that cot. I slipped out early in the morning with that cot. *It was my cot.* Found a lady way out in the suburbs who had a vacant room; let me have it and gave me three good meals for two days for five dollars and the cot."

CONFEDERATE GENERAL ALEXANDER P. STEWART.

"Did she feed you well?"

"Did she? Spoon bread, hot biscuits, lye hominy, and 'Rye' coffee, and, O boy! *Sorghum.*"

"Stop it," yelled the crowd.

"Did you go to the theater?"

"Yes sir, saw Ben De Bar and his company in a war play. Five Confederates captured twenty Yankees, then the conscript officer came in and captured both armies and stopped the show."

"See 'em making money?"

"Yes; by the ton."

"Suppose you saw George Washington?"

"I did, way up on top of a monument of marble; he was marble too, and so was the horse."

"What did the horse look like?"

"Traveler [Lee's horse]; he sure was some horse."

"Go out to the hospital?"

"Yes; saw a lot of our boys. Sent their love to you and said they never did want to get well."

"Did you see the nurses' home?"

"Say, you asking too many questions. *I saw one of the nurses home, but that is none of your business.*"

The Confederate private would laugh and joke marching twenty-five miles a day and winning two battles; he would joke in the hospital, joke dying on the battle field, joke when he was ragged, nearly barefooted, and nearly starved to death.

The stone soup story has been told around many a camp fire and at many a reunion. It is good enough to be true:

Down the Valley, below Staunton a piece, a long, lank, lean, hungry-looking C.S.A. private stopped in front of a home and said:

"I am one of Jackson's private cavalry. I got left. I am trying to catch up with 'em, and I am hungry. Can you give me a breakfast?" "No," said the lady, "I am sorry, but breakfast is over, but if you can wait until twelve o'clock, I will try to give you a good dinner."

"Thank you, ma'am. I am mighty sorry I can't wait; but if you will let me have that pot and give me some wood and that nice smooth stone, I will make some stone soup."

"Why, yes. You can take the pot and some wood, and I will bring you out some coal, and of course you can have the stone; but I never heard of anybody making soup out of a stone."

He filled the pot with water, put it over the fire, picked up the stone, washed it off at the pump, and put it carefully in the water, which now began to boil merrily.

"Have you a little salt and pepper?"

"Yes; wait a minute and I will bring it." She came back with the salt and a piece of fat meat, and said: "That will help."

"Indeed it will," and into the pot they went.

"Now," said the soldier, "you haven't got a couple of potatoes, have you?"

"Indeed I have," and she brought them out. He dropped them in the pot with a couple of hard tack, and said: "Now get two plates, deep ones. Come out, and we will have some soup together."

The lady said: "That is nice soup, but why use the stone?"

"Well," said the soldier, full and happy, "it was a good foundation."[369]

THE YANKS TARGET A POT OF CONFEDERATE VEGETABLES

☛ The ladies of the city were always trying to help us [Confederate soldiers] out. In April, 1864, they sent us a cargo of vegetables, knowing that every one longs for a taste of green in the spring and that we could not get out to appropriate vegetables for ourselves. We had no way of cooking, so we ate all we could raw, then began to search for some way to cook the remainder. We had an immense kettle to boil our clothes in; so after much washing and scouring, we decided to use this kettle. We put in all our vegetables, all our meat, and all our hard-tack and boiled it together. It smelled so good, and every man was standing ready to dip his cup in the kettle when a shell from the enemy's gun came over, singing "Tu- wicker, Tu- wicker," and fell in that pot of vegetables! Instead of getting that soup inside of us, it was all scattered on the outside. We can laugh over it now, but it was a tragic moment then.[370]

WITH GENERAL FORREST AT CHICKAMAUGA

☛ When General Forrest appeared on our line, encouraging us to hold on, our friends in the brush opened up on the cavalcade with all they had, big guns and little, and yet not a man went down. I never could account for it to my own satisfaction fully. I have often read of the General's fearlessness and contempt of danger. In this instance, he showed not even the least excitement. I could see no trace of any emotion whatsoever about him, and he passed within two feet of me. By my side stood a stripling of my own age who had just rammed home a cartridge in his "Minie" and was fumbling for a cap as the General came up to him, and, stooping down, patted the boy on the shoulder in a fatherly way and said to him: "Go it, my little man!" "Bob" looked up, surprised, and, seeing who was addressing

THE CONFEDERATE SCULPTURE AT STONE MOUNTAIN, GEORGIA.

him so familiarly, started for a big pine tree a few paces in front of the line, laid his "Minie" against the side of the tree, and blazed away at the brush. Perhaps the General never laughed—I have never heard of his doing so—but I certainly thought I detected a grin on his face. The whole incident was comical to those near by, and we had a hearty laugh over it then and afterwards. But "Bob" remained as sober as ever. What added to our hilarity was the fact that the night previous Bob's horse happened to step on the rifle barrel and his weight caused it to bend, so that a charge could with difficulty be rammed home, and the bullet would hit fifteen degrees to the left of the object aimed at, and he would take no other gun.[371]

THE STOLEN TURKEY
☞ His master asked an old Negro servant to get him a good Christmas turkey. "Mind you, Sam," he said, "I don't want a wild turkey."
"I'll get you a tame one, boss," said Sam.
The turkey arrived. When the father of the family began to carve it his knife struck something hard. It proved to be a pocket of shot. He sent for Sam.
"I told you not to bring me a wild turkey," he said.
"Dat was tame turkey, boss."
"But I found the shot in him."
"Don't you worry, boss. Dat shot were intended for dis niggah."[372]

A GROUP OF WHITE AND BLACK CONFEDERATE VETERANS (WEARING THEIR MILITARY MEDALS) AT HUNTSVILLE, ALABAMA, CIRCA 1928.

THE PLAY ON WORDS DIDN'T SAVE HIM
☞ "I saw him," said the witness, "steal a hammer from a hardware store and bolt for the door, upon which I had noticed he rivetted his attention from the first."
"Yes," said the judge, kindly.
"Well, I tried to hold him, but he gave me a wrench and got a weigh, and then I called a policeman, who nailed him."
"You employed great tack," said the Judge, gravely. "Tin months."[373]

THEIR FORTUNES WERE MADE
☞ Two young Irishmen in a Canadian regiment were going into the

trenches [of World War I] for the first time, and their captain promised them five shillings each for every German they killed.

Pat lay down to rest, while Mick performed the duty of watching. Pat had not lain long when he was awakened by Mick shouting:

"They're comin'! They're cornin'!"

"Who's comin'?" asks Pat.

"The Germans," replies Mick.

"How many are there?"

"About fifty thousand."

"Begorra," shouts Pat, jumping up and grabbing his rifle, "our fortune's made!"[374]

REGISTERING IN MISSOURI

☛ An old negro went to the office of the Commissioner of Registration in a Missouri town and applied for registration papers.

"What is your name?" asked the official.

"George Washington," was the reply.

"Well, George, are you the man who cut down the cherry tree?"

"No, sah; I ain't de man. I ain't done no work for nigh onto a year."[375]

GREECE OR GREASE?

☛ As a ship was entering the harbor of Athens a well-dressed young woman passenger approached the captain and, pointing to the distant hills, inquired:

"What is that white on the hills, captain?"

"That is snow, madam," replied the captain.

"Well," remarked the woman, "I thought so myself, but a gentleman just told me it was Greece."[376]

MEASURING BY SMELL

☛ Little May's grandmother had an old-fashioned way of measuring a yard by holding one end of the goods to her nose and then stretching the piece at arm's length.

One day May found a piece of ribbon. Carrying it to her grandmother, she requested gravely: "Grandma, smell this and see how long it is."[377]

A GEORGIA GIRL IN NEW YORK CITY

☛ A little story on that famous "fireman," [U.S. Gen.] Sherman, was brought out in a conversation on the statues in New York City, and especially that of Sherman at the Fifth Avenue entrance to Central Park, which has a female figure in front—evidently a guiding angel. A bride from Georgia was in New York on her wedding trip and asked who was the man who had a girl to lead his horse. When she was told, she groaned out: "Now, isn't that just like Sherman—to let the woman walk?"[378]

THE BEACH "TAN"
☞ "Molly has just returned from the seaside." "Did she get brown?" "No. I think his name was Thompson."[379]

AN APPEAL FOR PANTS
☞ A speaker at a ministers' meeting in Boston told the story of a negro clergyman who so pestered his bishop with appeals for help that it became necessary to tell him that he must not send any more appeals. His next communication was as follows: "This is not an appeal, it is a report. I have no pants."[380]

MARRIED OUTSIDE THE JAILHOUSE
☞ "Did Liza Jane git a good man when she ma'ied down in Memphis?" "Sho' did! Ma'ied right outen de jail house. He didn't have no time t' git in no trouble."[381]

HOW SCHOOLBOYS SEE THE WORLD
☞ The following are from some schoolboy examination papers:
"Things which are equal to the same thing are equal to anything else."
"A grass widow is the wife of a dead vegetarian."
"Oceania is that continent which contains no land."
"In India a man out of a cask may not marry another woman out of another cask."
"Parallel lines are the same distance all the way and do not meet unless you bend them."
"Gravitation is that which if there were none we should all fly away."
"Louis XVI was gelatined during the French Revolution."
"Horse power is the distance one horse can carry a pound of water in an hour."
"Paulsy is a kind of new writer's dance."
"Letters in sloping print [italics] are hysterics."[382]

THE CHANGING TIMES
☞ Blink: "Times have changed."
Jinks: "I'll say. It used to be when a man was run down he took a tonic, now he takes an ambulance."[383]

THE PRISONER'S SISTER
☞ "Have you ever been married?" asked the judge.
"Ye-es," stammered the prisoner.
"To whom?"
"A woman."
"Of course it was a woman," snapped the judge; "did you ever hear of anyone marrying a man?"
"Yes, sir," said the prisoner, brightly, "my sister did."[384]

JACKSON'S GRIM HUMOR

☛ "[During Lincoln's War,] I was sitting on a fence, with a chum, on the old Warrenton road just before the Second Manassas battle, when Stonewall and his staff rode up from the east, while [C.S.] General Stuart approached from the west, stopping directly in front of us. General Stuart had just made a raid around [U.S. Gen.] Pope's army, capturing his headquarters. General Stuart had little of the West Point etiquette, and, as he approached General Jackson, he called out: 'Hello, Jackson! I've got Pope's coat; if you don't believe it, there's his name,' holding up a magnificent new major general's coat, which made General Jackson's old gray look like second-hand clothing. Stuart's staff evidently expected a loud laugh, but General Jackson, with his hand at salute, said: 'General Stuart, I would much rather you had brought General Pope instead of his coat.'"[385]

MISS MARGARET GRACE VALENTINE, MAID OF HONOR FOR THE SOUTH.

FROM X TO O

☛ A negro woman came into the office of the estate for which she worked to received her monthly wages. As she could not write, she always made her mark on the receipt—the usual cross. But on this occasion she made a circle.

" What's the matter, Linda?" the man in charge asked, "Why don't you make a cross as usual?"

"Why," Linda explained earnestly, "Ah done got married yesterday an' changed mah name."[386]

FAMILY TREE FUN

☛ At a recent meeting of the Classical Association at Lexington, Ky., a group of teachers during the lunch hour were discussing the tracing of genealogies. "I never wanted to trace mine very far back," said one, jokingly. "I'm afraid I might find some one hanging on my family tree." "By the neck or tail?" asked another.[387]

SHE'S DONE HER BEST

☛ "Is your wife one of those women who look at their husbands and say: 'I made a man of him!'" asked the impertinent friend. "No," answered Mr. Meekton. "My Henrietta is very unassuming. She merely says she has done her best."[388]

THINGS TO REMEMBER
☛ The value of time.
The success of perseverance.
The pleasure of working.
The dignity of simplicity.
The worth of character.
The power of kindness.
The influence of example.
The obligation of duty.
The wisdom of economy.
The virtue of patience.
The importance of talent.
The joy of originating.[389]

EVAPORATIN' TIDAL FLATS
☛ "Flats is gettin' so small," said Uncle Eben, "dat purty soon dar won't be much left of 'home, sweet home' 'ceptin' de tune."[390]

THE LIFE INSURANCE POLICY
☛ Old Uncle Eben Jones went into a life insurance office and requested a policy. "Why, uncle," said the president, "you are too old for us to take the risk. How old are you?" "Ninety-seven come next August," said the old man, and added testily, "If you folks will take the trouble to look up your statistics, you'll find that mighty few men die after they're ninety-seven."[391]

A SPINSTER'S REGRET
☛ The middle-aged spinster was in a retrospective mood. "Sometimes," she sighed, "I wish I had married before I was old enough to have sense enough not to do it."[392]

MARRYING FOR MONEY
☛ Madge: "Then you believe in marrying for money?"
Marie: "I wouldn't say that exactly, but when you marry a man it's just as well to know there's something about him you will always like."[393]

WHAT IS A "NIXIE"?
☛ It is a piece of mail so incorrectly or incompletely addressed, or so improperly prepared, that it cannot be delivered or returned without special treatment, and it goes to the post office hospital for a postal operation. It differs from a dead letter in that a dead letter, parcel, or circular can neither be delivered nor returned and goes to the post office morgue for burial.[394]

CONVERSATION AT A NEGRO FESTIVAL
☛ During the course of a negro festival in a Southern town, Miss Mandy

Johnson, a guest from a rival community nearby, to whom such a function was a novelty, was approached by a Mr. Spencer, who inquired with great suavity: "Miss Johnson, am yo' program full?" "Lordy, no, Mr. Spencer," said the lady, "it takes mo' dan a san' wich an' two olives to fill mah program!"[395]

SHE PREFERS YOUNGER MEN
☞ The American heiress had just come back from her first trip to Europe. At dinner her neighbor inquired: "Did you see many picturesque old ruins during your trip?" "Yes," she replied. "And six of them proposed to me."[396]

HALF DOLLARS ARE SAFER
☞ Small nephew: "That dime you gave me slipped through a hole in my pocket." Uncle: "Well, here's another. Don't let it do the same." Nephew: "Perhaps half a dollar would be safer, wouldn't it, uncle?"[397]

A "GENTLE" HINT
☞ He: "I am a thought reader, and I can read your thoughts now." She: "Well, why don't you go, then?"[398]

RAISING FUNDS AT THE AFRICAN BAPTIST CHURCH
☞ They were making a drive to raise funds for an addition to the African Baptist Church. Two colored sisters called on old Uncle Berry, an aged negro, who lived on the outskirts of the village, and explained the purpose of their visit and asked the aged darky to give something toward the cause.

"Lawsy, sisters, I sho' would like to help you-all along," he said, "but I just ain't got it. Why, I has the hardest time to keep paying a little something on what I already owes around here." "But," said one of the collectors, "you know you owe the Lord something, too." "Yes, dat's right, sister," said the old man, "but he ain't pushing me like my other creditors is."[399]

U.S. MONEY ORDERS THROUGH AN IRISHMAN'S EYES
☞ "This is a great country, Pat!"
"An' how's that, Mike?"
"Sure, an' th' paper says yez kin buy a foive-dollar money order for three cents."[400]

THE VICAR & THE BAZAAR
☞ In his announcement on a Sunday morning the vicar regretted that money was not coming in fast enough—but he was no pessimist. "We have tried," he said, "to raise the necessary money in the usual manner. We have tried honestly. Now we are going to see what a bazaar can do."[401]

A QUESTION THAT MIGHT EARN YOU AN "E" IN SCHOOL!
☛ Professor: "I will use my hat to represent the planet Mars. Are there any questions before I go on?" Student: "Yes. Is Mars inhabited?"[402]

ROMANCE OR FOOD?
☛ "But I don't love you," the lady objected. "Then why," demanded the indignant youth, hastily referring to divers memoranda in his pocket diary, "did you eat fifty-two pounds of sweetmeats I bought for you during the past year?" "Because," said the lady, "I love them."[403]

SO MUCH FOR THE "EDUCATED" NORTH
☛ Another illustration of the shallowness and uselessness of much of the education of this country was given by no less an outfit than the undergraduates of the University of Maine. A questionnaire was sent out as to who was Henry James. Quite a number of the students had never heard of any James but the two-gun bandit who shot up so much of Missouri. Other questions were answered to the effect that Martin Luther was the son of Moses, the author of "Vanity Fair" was Shakespeare, Disraeli was a poet, and Moses was a Roman ruler.[404]

THE BRITISH MUSIC LESSON
☛ A schoolmaster, giving a music lesson, inquired whether the pupils had any favorite anthem they would like to sing. "'God Save the King,' sir," responded one of the lads. "A very patriotic suggestion, Tommy," said the master. "Now tell me what made you think of the national anthem." "Because," replied the boy, glancing toward the clock, "it's time to go home."[405]

THE "LAW" OF GRAVITY
☛ The teacher was giving a class a lecture on "gravity." "Now, children," she said, "it is the law of gravity that keeps us on this earth." "But, please, teacher," inquired one small child, "how did we stick on before the law was passed?"[406]

ROBINSON CRUSOE'S NEIGHBORS
☛ "Do you suppose there ever was a human being who didn't talk about his neighbors?" asked the cynical man. "Yes," said his companion. "Name him." "Robinson Crusoe."[407]

THE UNSCHOOLED ALABAMA WOMAN WHO HATED YANKEES
☛ A crowd of wounded [Confederate] boys were sitting around the stove in the Bragg Hospital, when heavy jokes and left-handed compliments were passed on different Southern States. The manners, customs and languages were freely discussed and freely criticised. Some sharp and telling things were said by an Alabamian about East Tennessee. A Tennesseean took up the defense, and said: "Well, boys, I admit that

there is too much ignorance in East Tennessee, but some of her neighbors have not much to boast of. I got my first bad wound in 1862, and as my home was in the Yankees' hands, I was furloughed to go where I pleased, and I went to Alabama. I took up my abode with an old lady, who was a fire-eating hater of Yankees, and had as much toleration for a Blue Coat as for the Queen's English. One day, when the conversation turned, rather gloomily, upon the prospect of the final success of the Yankees, she flew into a great passion, and cried out: "Never, never; they may captivate all the men, they may arrogate all the women, they may fisticate all the land, but they can never conjugate the South. Never! never!!!"[408]

A MODERN DAY INCIDENT & YOUR EDITOR

☛ In the Fall of 2015 Sea Raven Press was set up at a "Civil War" trade show in Nashville, Tennessee, selling Lochlainn Seabrook's books. He was signing individual volumes for the fans and customers that were excitedly swarming around him, when an unhappy looking man in the crowd aggressively approached our table.

Pushing his way through, he leaned forward, and, glaring furiously at Lochlainn, he demanded: "Have you written any books about how the Confederates were *racist traitors who tried to preserve slavery?*"

Lochlainn replied drily: "No sir, I only write nonfiction books." (Snickers from the crowd.)

Not ready to surrender, the angry man launched a second volley: "The South lost! Why aren't you writing Civil War books from the North's perspective?"

Lochlainn: "That angle's been well covered by communist historians and the university presses, sir." (Loud laughter from the crowd.)

Realizing that he wasn't going to win this particular skirmish, the uneducated South-hater quickly turned and fled back into the throng.[409]

The End

IN MEMORIAM—C.S.A.: "THE HEART OF AMERICA."

NOTES

1. Woods, p. 47.

2. On Lincoln's socialistic, Marxist, and communist thoughts, ideas, and tendencies, see my books: 1) *Lincoln's War: The Real Cause, The Real Winner, the Real Loser*; 2) *Abraham Lincoln Was a Liberal, Jefferson Davis Was a Conservative: The Missing Key to Understanding the American Civil War*; 3) *Abraham Lincoln: The Southern View*. Also see McCarty, passim; Browder, passim; Benson and Kennedy, passim.

3. See J. W. Jones, TDMV, pp. 144, 200-201, 273.

4. See Seabrook, TAHSR, passim. See also, Pollard, LC, p. 178; J. H. Franklin, pp. 101, 111, 130, 149; Nicolay and Hay, ALCW, Vol. 1, p. 627.

5. Seabrook, ASHCSA (J. Davis), p. 59.

6. Seabrook, ASHCSA (J. Davis), pp. 55-56.

7. For more on the nihilistic, atheistic, anti-life, anti-tradition, anti-American, anti-Constitution, anti-capitalism, anti-South agenda of the Victorian Republican Party (then the Liberal Party) and the modern Democrat Party (now the Liberal Party), otherwise known as "The Communist/Socialist Rules for Revolution," see Hasselberg, pp. 2350-2351; Lenin, passim; Marx and Engels, passim; B. Dodd, passim.

8. *Confederate Veteran*, July 1901, Vol. 9, No. 7, p. 318.

9. See, e.g., *Confederate Veteran*, September 1896, Vol. 4, No. 9, p. 301.

10. Dinkins, pp. 70-71.

11. von Borcke, p. 280.

12. *Confederate Veteran*, February 1906, Vol. 14, No. 2, p. 73.

13. *Confederate Veteran*, May 1932, Vol. 40, No. 5, p. 168.

14. *Confederate Veteran*, September 1923, Vol. 31, No. 9, pp. 329-330. (My title, L.S.)

15. *Confederate Veteran*, January 1924, Vol. 32, No. 1, p. 38.

16. La Bree, p. 204.

17. *Confederate Veteran*, January 1893, Vol. 1, No. 1, p. 132. (My title, L.S.)

18. *Confederate Veteran*, March 1924, Vol. 32, No. 3, p. 117.

19. *Confederate Veteran*, June 1924, Vol. 32, No. 6, p. 245. (My title, L.S.)

20. *Confederate Veteran*, October 1893, Vol. 1, No. 10, p. 307. (My title, L.S.)

21. *Confederate Veteran*, July 1924, Vol. 32, No. 7, p. 287. (My title, L.S.)

22. *Confederate Veteran*, July 1924, Vol. 32, No. 7, p. 287. (My title, L.S.)

23. *Confederate Veteran*, October 1893, Vol. 1, No. 10, pp. 307-308. (My title, L.S.)

24. *Confederate Veteran*, October 1893, Vol. 1, No. 10, p. 308.

25. *Confederate Veteran*, July 1924, Vol. 32, No. 7, p. 287. (My title, L.S.)

26. *Confederate Veteran*, August 1924, Vol. 32, No. 7, p. 327. (My title, L.S.)

27. *Confederate Veteran*, October 1893, Vol. 1, No. 10, p. 308.

28. *Confederate Veteran*, October 1893, Vol. 1, No. 10, p. 308. (My title, L.S.)

29. *Confederate Veteran*, October 1893, Vol. 1, No. 10, p. 308. (My title, L.S.)

30. *Confederate Veteran*, August 1924, Vol. 32, No. 7, p. 327. (My title, L.S.)

31. *Confederate Veteran*, September 1924, Vol. 32, No. 9, p. 367. (My title, L.S.)

32. *Confederate Veteran*, October 1893, Vol. 1, No. 10, pp. 308-309.

33. *Confederate Veteran*, October 1893, Vol. 1, No. 10, p. 309.

34. *Confederate Veteran*, September 1924, Vol. 32, No. 9, p. 367. (My title, L.S.)

35. *Confederate Veteran*, October 1893, Vol. 1, No. 10, p. 309.

36. *Confederate Veteran*, October 1893, Vol. 1, No. 10, p. 309. (My title, L.S.)

37. *Confederate Veteran*, September 1924, Vol. 32, No. 9, p. 367. (My title, L.S.)

38. *Confederate Veteran*, September 1924, Vol. 32, No. 9, p. 367. (My title, L.S.)

39. *Confederate Veteran*, October 1893, Vol. 1, No. 10, pp. 309-310.

40. *Confederate Veteran*, September 1924, Vol. 32, No. 9, p. 367. (My title, L.S.)

41. *Confederate Veteran*, October 1893, Vol. 1, No. 10, p. 310. (My title, L.S.)

42. *Confederate Veteran*, October 1893, Vol. 1, No. 10, p. 310.

43. *Confederate Veteran*, September 1893, Vol. 1, No. 9, p. 267.

44. *Confederate Veteran*, October 1924, Vol. 32, No. 10, p. 407. (My title, L.S.)
45. *Confederate Veteran*, December 1924, Vol. 32, No. 12, p. 487.
46. Morgan, pp. 134-135. (My title, L.S.)
47. *Confederate Veteran*, June 1893, Vol. 1, No. 6, p. 165. (My title, L.S.)
48. *Confederate Veteran*, July 1893, Vol. 1, No. 7, p. 216.
49. *Confederate Veteran*, July 1893, Vol. 1, No. 7, p. 216.
50. *Confederate Veteran*, July 1893, Vol. 1, No. 7, p. 216. (My title, L.S.)
51. *Confederate Veteran*, July 1893, Vol. 1, No. 7, p. 216.
52. *Confederate Veteran*, February 1923, Vol. 31, No. 2, p. 79. (My title, L.S.)
53. *Confederate Veteran*, July 1893, Vol. 1, No. 7, p. 216.
54. *Confederate Veteran*, July 1893, Vol. 1, No. 7, p. 216.
55. *Confederate Veteran*, July 1893, Vol. 1, No. 7, p. 216.
56. *Confederate Veteran*, August 1893, Vol. 1, No. 8, p. 234. (My title, L.S.)
57. *Confederate Veteran*, August 1893, Vol. 1, No. 8, p. 237. (My title, L.S.)
58. *Confederate Veteran*, August 1893, Vol. 1, No. 8, p. 237. (My title, L.S.)
59. *Confederate Veteran*, August 1893, Vol. 1, No. 8, p. 239.
60. *Confederate Veteran*, February 1923, Vol. 31, No. 2, p. 79. (My title, L.S.)
61. *Confederate Veteran*, September 1893, Vol. 1, No. 9, p. 264.
62. *Confederate Veteran*, October 1893, Vol. 1, No. 10, p. 301.
63. *Confederate Veteran*, March 1893, Vol. 1, No. 3, p. 74. (My title, L.S.)
64. *Confederate Veteran*, October 1893, Vol. 1, No. 10, p. 312. (My title, L.S.)
65. *Confederate Veteran*, January 1894, Vol. 2, No. 1, p. 21. (My title, L.S.)
66. *Confederate Veteran*, May 1894, Vol. 2, No. 5, p. 151. (My title, L.S.)
67. *Confederate Veteran*, August 1894, Vol. 2, No. 8, p. 244. (My title, L.S.)
68. *Confederate Veteran*, September 1894, Vol. 2, No. 9, p. 279.
69. *Confederate Veteran*, March 1894, Vol. 2, No. 3, p. 89.
70. *Confederate Veteran*, March 1923, Vol. 31, No. 3, p. 119. (My title, L.S.)
71. *Confederate Veteran*, March 1923, Vol. 31, No. 3, p. 119.
72. *Confederate Veteran*, April 1923, Vol. 31, No. 4, p. 159.
73. *Confederate Veteran*, September 1894, Vol. 2, No. 9, pp. 334-335.
74. *Confederate Veteran*, April 1923, Vol. 31, No. 4, p. 159.
75. *Confederate Veteran*, April 1923, Vol. 31, No. 4, p. 159. (My title, L.S.)
76. *Confederate Veteran*, April 1923, Vol. 31, No. 4, p. 159.
77. *Confederate Veteran*, January 1894, Vol. 2, No. 1, p. 6.
78. *Confederate Veteran*, June 1894, Vol. 2, No. 6, p. 182.
79. *Confederate Veteran*, September 1894, Vol. 2, No. 9, p. 311.
80. *Confederate Veteran*, April 1923, Vol. 31, No. 4, p. 159.
81. *Confederate Veteran*, January 1895, Vol. 3, No. 1, p. 20. (My title, L.S.)
82. *Confederate Veteran*, April 1895, Vol. 3, No. 4, p. 98. (My title, L.S.)
83. *Confederate Veteran*, May 1895, Vol. 3, No. 5, p. 129. (My title, L.S.)
84. *Confederate Veteran*, September 1895, Vol. 3, No. 9, p. 271. (My title, L.S.)
85. *Confederate Veteran*, May 1923, Vol. 31, No. 5, p. 202.
86. *Confederate Veteran*, October 1895, Vol. 3, No. 10, p. 301. (My title, L.S.)
87. *Confederate Veteran*, January 1895, Vol. 3, No. 1, p. 14. (My title, L.S.)
88. *Confederate Veteran*, April 1895, Vol. 3, No. 4, p. 106. (My title, L.S.)
89. *Confederate Veteran*, May 1895, Vol. 3, No. 5, p. 144. (My title, L.S.)
90. *Confederate Veteran*, May 1895, Vol. 3, No. 5, p. 143. (My title, L.S.)
91. *Confederate Veteran*, May 1923, Vol. 31, No. 5, p. 199. (My title, L.S.)
92. *Confederate Veteran*, May 1923, Vol. 31, No. 5, p. 199. (My title, L.S.)
93. *Confederate Veteran*, May 1923, Vol. 31, No. 5, p. 199. (My title, L.S.)
94. *Confederate Veteran*, March 1895, Vol. 3, No. 3, pp. 77-78. (My title, L.S.)
95. La Bree, p. 29. (My title, L.S.)
96. *Confederate Veteran*, January 1895, Vol. 3, No. 1, p. 21.
97. *Confederate Veteran*, June 1923, Vol. 31, No. 6, p. 242. (My title, L.S.)

98. *Confederate Veteran*, June 1923, Vol. 31, No. 6, p. 242. (My title, L.S.)

99. *Confederate Veteran*, June 1923, Vol. 31, No. 6, p. 239. (My title, L.S.)

100. *Confederate Veteran*, June 1923, Vol. 31, No. 6, p. 239. (My title, L.S.)

101. *Confederate Veteran*, May 1895, Vol. 3, No. 5, p. 134. (My title, L.S.)

102. Seabrook, *A Rebel Born* (the book), 2015 ed., pp. 503-504. (My title, L.S.)

103. *Confederate Veteran*, August 1895, Vol. 3, No. 8, p. 238. (My title, L.S.)

104. *Confederate Veteran*, April 1896, Vol. 4, No. 4, pp. 118-119. (My title, L.S.)

105. *Confederate Veteran*, July 1923, Vol. 31, No. 7, p. 279. (My title, L.S.)

106. *Confederate Veteran*, July 1923, Vol. 31, No. 7, p. 279. (My title, L.S.)

107. *Confederate Veteran*, July 1923, Vol. 31, No. 7, p. 279. (My title, L.S.)

108. *Confederate Veteran*, August 1896, Vol. 4, No. 8, p. 261. (My title, L.S.)

109. *Confederate Veteran*, September 1896, Vol. 4, No. 9, pp. 301-303. (second half my title, L.S.)

110. La Bree, p. 212. (My title, L.S.)

111. *Confederate Veteran*, August 1923, Vol. 31, No. 8, p. 319. (My title, L.S.)

112. *Confederate Veteran*, August 1923, Vol. 31, No. 8, p. 319.

113. *Confederate Veteran*, August 1923, Vol. 31, No. 8, p. 319. (My title, L.S.)

114. *Confederate Veteran*, August 1923, Vol. 31, No. 8, p. 319. (My title, L.S.)

115. *Confederate Veteran*, August 1923, Vol. 31, No. 8, p. 319. (My title, L.S.)

116. *Confederate Veteran*, September 1896, Vol. 4, No. 9, pp. 305-306. (First word of title mine, L.S.)

117. *Confederate Veteran*, September 1896, Vol. 4, No. 9, pp. 306-307. (My title, L.S.)

118. *Confederate Veteran*, September 1923, Vol. 31, No. 9, p. 359. (My title, L.S.)

119. *Confederate Veteran*, September 1923, Vol. 31, No. 9, p. 359. (My title, L.S.)

120. *Confederate Veteran*, September 1923, Vol. 31, No. 9, p. 359. (My title, L.S.)

121. *Confederate Veteran*, November 1896, Vol. 4, No. 11, p. 377. (My title, L.S.)

122. *Confederate Veteran*, November 1896, Vol. 4, No. 11, p. 377. (My title, L.S.)

123. *Confederate Veteran*, October 1923, Vol. 31, No. 10, p. 399.

124. *Confederate Veteran*, October 1923, Vol. 31, No. 10, p. 399. (My title, L.S.)

125. *Confederate Veteran*, October 1923, Vol. 31, No. 10, p. 399. (My title, L.S.)

126. *Confederate Veteran*, October 1923, Vol. 31, No. 10, p. 399. (My title, L.S.)

127. *Confederate Veteran*, November 1896, Vol. 4, No. 11, pp. 377-378. (My title, L.S.)

128. *Confederate Veteran*, October 1923, Vol. 31, No. 10, p. 399. (My title, L.S.)

129. *Confederate Veteran*, November 1896, Vol. 4, No. 11, p. 378. (My title, L.S.)

130. *Confederate Veteran*, November 1896, Vol. 4, No. 11, pp. 378-379. (My title, L.S.)

131. *Confederate Veteran*, October 1923, Vol. 31, No. 10, p. 399. (My title, L.S.)

132. *Confederate Veteran*, October 1923, Vol. 31, No. 10, p. 399.

133. *Confederate Veteran*, November 1896, Vol. 4, No. 11, p. 379. (My title, L.S.)

134. *Confederate Veteran*, October 1922, Vol. 30, No. 10, p. 412. (My title, L.S.)

135. *Confederate Veteran*, November 1922, Vol. 30, No. 11, p. 438. (My title, L.S.)

136. *Confederate Veteran*, November 1922, Vol. 30, No. 11, p. 438. (My title, L.S.)

137. *Confederate Veteran*, November 1922, Vol. 30, No. 11, p. 438. (My title, L.S.) Note: the official national anthem of the C.S.A. is "God Save the South." "Dixie," however, remains the unofficial national anthem.

138. *Confederate Veteran*, January 1921, Vol. 29, No. 1, p. 39. (My title, L.S.)

139. *Confederate Veteran*, October 1896, Vol. 4, No. 10, p. 345. (My title, L.S.)

140. La Bree, p. 29.

141. *Confederate Veteran*, October 1896, Vol. 4, No. 10, p. 345. (My title, L.S.)

142. *Confederate Veteran*, October 1896, Vol. 4, No. 10, p. 345. (My title, L.S.)

143. *Confederate Veteran*, October 1896, Vol. 4, No. 10, pp. 345-346. (My title, L.S.)

144. *Confederate Veteran*, July 1921, Vol. 29, No. 7, p. 279. (My title, L.S.)

145. *Confederate Veteran*, August 1921, Vol. 29, No. 8, p. 319.

146. *Confederate Veteran*, October 1896, Vol. 4, No. 10, p. 346. (My title, L.S.)

147. *Confederate Veteran*, October 1896, Vol. 4, No. 10, p. 346. (My title, L.S.)

148. *Confederate Veteran*, July 1921, Vol. 29, No. 7, p. 279. (My title, L.S.)

149. *Confederate Veteran*, February 1896, Vol. 4, No. 2, p. 45. (My title, L.S.)

150. *Confederate Veteran*, February 1896, Vol. 4, No. 2, p. 45. (My title, L.S.)

151. *Confederate Veteran*, July 1921, Vol. 29, No. 7, p. 279. (My title, L.S.)
152. *Confederate Veteran*, February 1896, Vol. 4, No. 2, p. 56. (My title, L.S.)
153. *Confederate Veteran*, February 1896, Vol. 4, No. 2, p. 56. (My title, L.S.)
154. *Confederate Veteran*, October 1896, Vol. 4, No. 10, pp. 337-338. (My title, L.S.)
155. *Confederate Veteran*, January 1896, Vol. 4, No. 1, p. 8. (My title, L.S.)
156. *Confederate Veteran*, January 1896, Vol. 4, No. 1, p. 23.
157. *Confederate Veteran*, March 1896, Vol. 4, No. 3, pp. 90-91. (My title, L.S.)
158. *Confederate Veteran*, March 1896, Vol. 4, No. 3, p. 91. (My title, L.S.)
159. *Confederate Veteran*, July 1896, Vol. 4, No. 7, pp. 218-219. (My title, L.S.)
160. *Confederate Veteran*, October 1921, Vol. 29, No. 10, p. 399. (My title, L.S.)
161. *Confederate Veteran*, September 1897, Vol. 5, No. 9, p. 486. (My title, L.S.)
162. *Confederate Veteran*, June 1897, Vol. 5, No. 6, p. 291. (My title, L.S.)
163. *Confederate Veteran*, January 1897, Vol. 5, No. 1, p. 11. (My title, L.S.)
164. *Confederate Veteran*, October 1921, Vol. 29, No. 10, p. 399. (My title, L.S.)
165. *Confederate Veteran*, January 1897, Vol. 5, No. 1, p. 12. (My title, L.S.)
166. *Confederate Veteran*, February 1897, Vol. 5, No. 2, pp. 55-56. (My title, L.S.)
167. *Confederate Veteran*, October 1897, Vol. 5, No. 10, p. 510. (My title, L.S.)
168. *Confederate Veteran*, December 1897, Vol. 5, No. 12, p. 624. (My title, L.S.)
169. *Confederate Veteran*, February 1897, Vol. 5, No. 2, p. 81. (My title, L.S.)
170. *Confederate Veteran*, March 1897, Vol. 5, No. 3, p. 106. (My title, L.S.)
171. *Confederate Veteran*, March 1897, Vol. 5, No. 3, p. 104. (My title, L.S.)
172. *Confederate Veteran*, March 1897, Vol. 5, No. 3, p. 104. (My title, L.S.)
173. *Confederate Veteran*, April 1897, Vol. 5, No. 4, p. 172. (My title, L.S.)
174. *Confederate Veteran*, October 1921, Vol. 29, No. 10, p. 399. (My title, L.S.)
175. *Confederate Veteran*, June 1897, Vol. 5, No. 6, pp. 277-281. (My title, L.S.)
176. *Confederate Veteran*, August 1897, Vol. 5, No. 8, p. 426. (My title, L.S.)
177. *Confederate Veteran*, November 1920, Vol. 28, No. 11, pp. 419-420. (My title, L.S.)
178. *Confederate Veteran*, January 1920, Vol. 28, No. 1, p. 42.
179. *Confederate Veteran*, October 1897, Vol. 5, No. 10, p. 527. (My title, L.S.)
180. *Confederate Veteran*, November 1897, Vol. 5, No. 11, p. 551. (My title, L.S.)
181. *Confederate Veteran*, November 1898, Vol. 6, No. 11, p. 521. (My title, L.S.)
182. *Confederate Veteran*, November 1898, Vol. 6, No. 11, p. 521.
183. *Confederate Veteran*, November 1898, Vol. 6, No. 11, p. 521. (My title, L.S.)
184. *Confederate Veteran*, November 1898, Vol. 6, No. 11, p. 521. (My title, L.S.)
185. *Confederate Veteran*, November 1898, Vol. 6, No. 11, pp. 521-522. (My title, L.S.)
186. *Confederate Veteran*, November 1898, Vol. 6, No. 11, p. 522. (My title, L.S.)
187. *Confederate Veteran*, January 1898, Vol. 6, No. 1, p. 37. (My title, L.S.)
188. *Confederate Veteran*, February 1898, Vol. 6, No. 2, p. 52. (My title, L.S.)
189. *Confederate Veteran*, March 1898, Vol. 6, No. 3, p. 135. (My title, L.S.)
190. *Confederate Veteran*, May 1920, Vol. 28, No. 5, p. 202.
191. *Confederate Veteran*, April 1898, Vol. 6, No. 4, pp. 150-151. (My title, L.S.)
192. *Confederate Veteran*, April 1898, Vol. 6, No. 4, p. 151. (My title, L.S.)
193. *Confederate Veteran*, May 1920, Vol. 28, No. 5, p. 202. (My title, L.S.)
194. *Confederate Veteran*, April 1898, Vol. 6, No. 4, pp. 152-153. (My title, L.S.)
195. *Confederate Veteran*, August 1898, Vol. 6, No. 8, p. 320. (My title, L.S.)
196. *Confederate Veteran*, April 1898, Vol. 6, No. 4, p. 379. (My title, L.S.)
197. *Confederate Veteran*, April 1898, Vol. 6, No. 4, p. 154. (My title, L.S.)
198. *Confederate Veteran*, April 1898, Vol. 6, No. 4, p. 160.
199. *Confederate Veteran*, December 1898, Vol. 6, No. 12, p. 568. (My title, L.S.)
200. *Confederate Veteran*, January 1898, Vol. 6, No. 1, p. 18. (My title, L.S.)
201. *Confederate Veteran*, October 1920, Vol. 28, No. 10, p. 399. (My title, L.S.)
202. *Confederate Veteran*, January 1898, Vol. 6, No. 1, pp. 18-19. (My title, L.S.)
203. *Confederate Veteran*, January 1898, Vol. 6, No. 1, p. 19. (My title, L.S.)
204. *Confederate Veteran*, July 1898, Vol. 6, No. 7, p. 297. (My title, L.S.)

205. *Confederate Veteran*, July 1898, Vol. 6, No. 7, p. 309. (My title, L.S.)
206. La Bree, p. 26.
207. La Bree, pp. 30-31.
208. La Bree, p. 31.
209. La Bree, p. 35.
210. La Bree, pp. 35-36.
211. La Bree, pp. 234-235.
212. La Bree, pp. 236-237.
213. La Bree, pp. 247-249.
214. *Confederate Veteran*, December 1920, Vol. 28, No. 12, p. 479. (My title, L.S.)
215. *Confederate Veteran*, December 1920, Vol. 28, No. 12, p. 479. (My title, L.S.)
216. La Bree, pp. 249-250.
217. La Bree, pp. 251-252.
218. La Bree, pp. 262-263.
219. La Bree, p. 263.
220. La Bree, p. 272.
221. La Bree, pp. 273-274.
222. La Bree, p. 274. (My title, L.S.)
223. La Bree, p. 287.
224. La Bree, pp. 287-288.
225. La Bree, pp. 302-304.
226. La Bree, pp. 306-307.
227. La Bree, p. 310.
228. La Bree, pp. 310-311.
229. La Bree, pp. 311-313. (My title, L.S.)
230. La Bree, p. 315.
231. La Bree, p. 315.
232. La Bree, p. 316. (My title, L.S.)
233. La Bree, p. 316.
234. La Bree, p. 317. (My title, L.S.)
235. La Bree, p. 317. (My title, L.S.)
236. La Bree, p. 318. (My title, L.S.)
237. La Bree, pp. 318-319. (My title, L.S.)
238. La Bree, p. 319. (My title, L.S.)
239. La Bree, p. 319. (My title, L.S.)
240. La Bree, p. 319. (My title, L.S.)
241. La Bree, p. 320. (My title, L.S.)
242. La Bree, p. 320. (My title, L.S.)
243. La Bree, p. 320. (My title, L.S.)
244. La Bree, pp. 320-321.
245. La Bree, pp. 321-322.
246. La Bree, p. 322. (My title, L.S.)
247. La Bree, p. 322. (My title, L.S.)
248. La Bree, pp. 322-323. (My title, L.S.)
249. La Bree, pp. 324-325. (My title, L.S.)
250. La Bree, pp. 327-328.
251. La Bree, pp. 348-349.
252. La Bree, p. 400. (My title, L.S.)
253. La Bree, p. 401. (My title, L.S.)
254. La Bree, p. 402.
255. La Bree, p. 404.
256. La Bree, pp. 404-405. (My title, L.S.)
257. La Bree, p. 405. (My title, L.S.)
258. La Bree, pp. 406-407. (My title, L.S.)

259. La Bree, p. 409. (My title, L.S.)

260. La Bree, pp. 409-410. (My title, L.S.)

261. Seabrook, *A Rebel Born* (the book), 2015 ed., p. 475. (My title, L.S.)

262. La Bree, pp. 410-411. (My title, L.S.)

263. La Bree, pp. 415-416. (My title, L.S.)

264. La Bree, pp. 498-499. (My title, L.S.)

265. La Bree, p. 499. (My title, L.S.)

266. La Bree, p. 499. (My title, L.S.)

267. La Bree, pp. 500-501. (My title, L.S.)

268. La Bree, pp. 503-504. (My title, L.S.)

269. La Bree, pp. 504-505. (My title, L.S.)

270. La Bree, p. 505. (My title, L.S.)

271. Seabrook, *A Rebel Born* (the book), 2015 ed., p. 477. (My title, L.S.)

272. La Bree, p. 508. (My title, L.S.)

273. La Bree, pp. 509-510. (My title, L.S.)

274. La Bree, p. 510. (My title, L.S.)

275. La Bree, pp. 510-511. (My title, L.S.)

276. La Bree, pp. 514-515. (My title, L.S.)

277. La Bree, p. 515. (My title, L.S.)

278. La Bree, p. 516. (My title, L.S.)

279. Morgan, pp. 136-137. (My title, L.S.)

280. Seabrook, *A Rebel Born* (the book), 2015 ed., p. 472. (My title, L.S.)

281. Morgan, pp. 158-164. (My title, L.S.)

282. Dinkins, p. 193. (My title, L.S.)

283. Dinkins, pp. 70-74. (My title, L.S.)

284. *Confederate Veteran*, July 1930, Vol. 38, No. 7, p. 250. (My title, L.S.)

285. Dinkins, pp. 128-132. (My title, L.S.)

286. *Confederate Veteran*, August 1930, Vol. 38, No. 8, p. 290.

287. Dinkins, pp. 161-164. (My title, L.S.)

288. *Confederate Veteran*, September 1931, Vol. 39, No. 9, p. 359. (My title, L.S.)

289. Dinkins, pp. 264-267. (My title, L.S.)

290. Kirkland, pp. 242-243. (My title, L.S.)

291. Dinkins, pp. 267-269. (My title, L.S.)

292. Robinson, pp. 41-42. (My title, L.S.)

293. Moore, p. 517. (My title, L.S.)

294. Moore, p. 317. (My title, L.S.)

295. von Borcke, pp. 277-280. (My title, L.S.)

296. von Borcke, pp. 232-233. (My title, L.S.)

297. *Confederate Veteran*, November 1930, Vol. 38, No. 11, p. 447. (My title, L.S.)

298. von Borcke, pp. 38-40. (My title, L.S.)

299. von Borcke, p. 40. (My title, L.S.)

300. von Borcke, pp. 47-48. (My title, L.S.)

301. *Confederate Veteran*, August 1926, Vol. 34, No. 2, p. 79. (My title, L.S.)

302. *Confederate Veteran*, May 1926, Vol. 34, No. 5, p. 199. (My title, L.S.)

303. von Borcke, pp. 50-54. (My title, L.S.)

304. *Confederate Veteran*, February 1931, Vol. 39, No. 2, p. 79. (My title, L.S.)

305. von Borcke, pp. 63-65. (My title, L.S.)

306. von Borcke, pp. 66-67. (My title, L.S.)

307. von Borcke, pp. 97-98. (My title, L.S.)

308. von Borcke, pp. 99-100. (My title, L.S.)

309. *Confederate Veteran*, February 1932, Vol. 40, No. 2, p. 82.

310. von Borcke, pp. 191-197. (My title, L.S.)

311. *Confederate Veteran*, April 1931, Vol. 39, No. 4, p. 159. (My title, L.S.)

312. von Borcke, pp. 203-204. (My title, L.S.)

313. von Borcke, pp. 245-247. (My title, L.S.)
314. *Confederate Veteran*, May 1932, Vol. 40, No. 5, p. 169. (My title, L.S.)
315. *Confederate Veteran*, May 1932, Vol. 40, No. 5, pp. 169, 198. (My title, L.S.)
316. *Confederate Veteran*, August 1932, Vol. 40, No. 8, p. 303. (My title, L.S.)
317. *Confederate Veteran*, November 1932, Vol. 40, No. 11, p. 387. (My title, L.S.)
318. *Confederate Veteran*, August 1932, Vol. 40, No. 8, p. 319. (My title, L.S.)
319. *Confederate Veteran*, August 1932, Vol. 40, No. 8, p. 319. (My title, L.S.)
320. *Confederate Veteran*, May 1932, Vol. 40, No. 5, p. 202. (My title, L.S.)
321. *Confederate Veteran*, April 1932, Vol. 40, No. 4, p. 162. (My title, L.S.)
322. *Confederate Veteran*, February 1932, Vol. 40, No. 2, p. 82. (My title, L.S.)
323. *Confederate Veteran*, February 1932, Vol. 40, No. 2, p. 39. (My title, L.S.)
324. *Confederate Veteran*, January 1931, Vol. 39, No. 1, p. 39. (My title, L.S.)
325. *Confederate Veteran*, May 1931, Vol. 39, No. 5, p. 189. (My title, L.S.)
326. *Confederate Veteran*, February 1931, Vol. 39, No. 2, p. 119. (My title, L.S.)
327. *Confederate Veteran*, February 1931, Vol. 39, No. 2, p. 79. (My title, L.S.)
328. *Confederate Veteran*, January 1931, Vol. 39, No. 1, p. 39. (My title, L.S.)
329. *Confederate Veteran*, January 1931, Vol. 39, No. 1, p. 39. (My title, L.S.)
330. *Confederate Veteran*, October 1931, Vol. 39, No. 10, p. 399. (My title, L.S.)
331. *Confederate Veteran*, July 1930, Vol. 38, No. 7, p. 250. (My title, L.S.)
332. *Confederate Veteran*, October 1930, Vol. 38, No. 10, pp. 374-375. (My title, L.S.)
333. *Confederate Veteran*, October 1930, Vol. 38, No. 10, p. 407. (My title, L.S.)
334. *Confederate Veteran*, October 1930, Vol. 38, No. 10, p. 407. (My title, L.S.)
335. *Confederate Veteran*, August 1930, Vol. 38, No. 8, p. 290. (My title, L.S.)
336. *Confederate Veteran*, November 1930, Vol. 38, No. 11, p. 447. (My title, L.S.)
337. *Confederate Veteran*, November 1930, Vol. 38, No. 11, p. 447. (My title, L.S.)
338. *Confederate Veteran*, June 1930, Vol. 38, No. 6, pp. 231-232. (My title, L.S.)
339. *Confederate Veteran*, April 1929, Vol. 37, No. 4, p. 127. (My title, L.S.)
340. *Confederate Veteran*, October 1929, Vol. 37, No. 10, pp. 373-374.
341. *Confederate Veteran*, February 1929, Vol. 37, No. 2, p. 44. (My title, L.S.)
342. *Confederate Veteran*, February 1929, Vol. 37, No. 2, p. 79. (My title, L.S.)
343. *Confederate Veteran*, July 1929, Vol. 37, No. 7, p. 279. (My title, L.S.)
344. *Confederate Veteran*, September 1929, Vol. 37, No. 9, p. 359. (My title, L.S.)
345. *Confederate Veteran*, September 1929, Vol. 37, No. 9, p. 359.
346. *Confederate Veteran*, March 1928, Vol. 36, No. 3, p. 119.
347. *Confederate Veteran*, March 1928, Vol. 36, No. 3, p. 119. (My title, L.S.)
348. *Confederate Veteran*, March 1928, Vol. 36, No. 3, p. 119. (My title, L.S.)
349. *Confederate Veteran*, March 1928, Vol. 36, No. 3, p. 119. (My title, L.S.)
350. *Confederate Veteran*, March 1928, Vol. 36, No. 3, p. 119. (My title, L.S.)
351. *Confederate Veteran*, March 1928, Vol. 36, No. 3, p. 119. (My title, L.S.)
352. *Confederate Veteran*, August 1928, Vol. 36, No. 8, p. 289. (My title, L.S.)
353. *Confederate Veteran*, January 1928, Vol. 36, No. 1, p. 19. (My title, L.S.)
354. *Confederate Veteran*, March 1928, Vol. 36, No. 3, p. 84.
355. *Confederate Veteran*, April 1928, Vol. 36, No. 4, p. 157. (My title, L.S.)
356. *Confederate Veteran*, September 1928, Vol. 36, No. 9, p. 351. (My title, L.S.)
357. *Confederate Veteran*, January 1928, Vol. 36, No. 1, p. 39. (My title, L.S.)
358. *Confederate Veteran*, January 1928, Vol. 36, No. 1, p. 39.
359. *Confederate Veteran*, February 1928, Vol. 36, No. 2, p. 79. (My title, L.S.)
360. *Confederate Veteran*, February 1928, Vol. 36, No. 2, p. 79. (My title, L.S.)
361. *Confederate Veteran*, February 1928, Vol. 36, No. 2, p. 79. (My title, L.S.)
362. *Confederate Veteran*, June 1928, Vol. 36, No. 6, p. 239. (My title, L.S.)
363. *Confederate Veteran*, July 1928, Vol. 36, No. 7, p. 279. (My title, L.S.)
364. *Confederate Veteran*, August 1928, Vol. 36, No. 8, p. 319. (My title, L.S.)
365. *Confederate Veteran*, August 1928, Vol. 36, No. 8, p. 319. (My title, L.S.)
366. *Confederate Veteran*, August 1928, Vol. 36, No. 8, p. 319. (My title, L.S.)

367. *Confederate Veteran*, August 1928, Vol. 36, No. 8, p. 319. (My title, L.S.)
368. *Confederate Veteran*, October 1928, Vol. 36, No. 10, p. 399. (My title, L.S.)
369. *Confederate Veteran*, April 1927, Vol. 35, No. 4, p. 147. (My title, L.S.)
370. *Confederate Veteran*, September 1927, Vol. 35, No. 9, p. 358. (My title, L.S.)
371. *Confederate Veteran*, October 1927, Vol. 35, No. 10, p. 382. (My title, L.S.)
372. *Confederate Veteran*, February 1927, Vol. 35, No. 2, p. 79. (My title, L.S.)
373. *Confederate Veteran*, February 1927, Vol. 35, No. 2, p. 79. (My title, L.S.)
374. *Confederate Veteran*, August 1927, Vol. 35, No. 8, p. 319. (My title, L.S.)
375. *Confederate Veteran*, August 1927, Vol. 35, No. 8, p. 319. (My title, L.S.)
376. *Confederate Veteran*, August 1927, Vol. 35, No. 8, p. 319. (My title, L.S.)
377. *Confederate Veteran*, August 1926, Vol. 34, No. 2, p. 79. (My title, L.S.)
378. *Confederate Veteran*, May 1926, Vol. 34, No. 5, p. 197. (My title, L.S.)
379. *Confederate Veteran*, June 1926, Vol. 34, No. 6, p. 239. (My title, L.S.)
380. *Confederate Veteran*, July 1926, Vol. 34, No. 7, p. 279. (My title, L.S.)
381. *Confederate Veteran*, July 1926, Vol. 34, No. 7, p. 279. (My title, L.S.)
382. *Confederate Veteran*, August 1926, Vol. 34, No. 8, p. 319. (My title, L.S.)
383. *Confederate Veteran*, September 1926, Vol. 34, No. 9, p. 359. (My title, L.S.)
384. *Confederate Veteran*, October 1926, Vol. 34, No. 10, p. 399. (My title, L.S.)
385. *Confederate Veteran*, June 1926, Vol. 34, No. 6, p. 221.
386. *Confederate Veteran*, February 1925, Vol. 33, No. 2, p. 79. (My title, L.S.)
387. *Confederate Veteran*, February 1925, Vol. 33, No. 2, p. 79. (My title, L.S.)
388. *Confederate Veteran*, February 1925, Vol. 33, No. 2, p. 79. (My title, L.S.)
389. *Confederate Veteran*, February 1925, Vol. 33, No. 2, p. 79.
390. *Confederate Veteran*, June 1925, Vol. 33, No. 6, p. 239. (My title, L.S.)
391. *Confederate Veteran*, June 1925, Vol. 33, No. 6, p. 239. (My title, L.S.)
392. *Confederate Veteran*, June 1925, Vol. 33, No. 6, p. 239. (My title, L.S.)
393. *Confederate Veteran*, July 1925, Vol. 33, No. 7, p. 279.
394. *Confederate Veteran*, July 1925, Vol. 33, No. 7, p. 279.
395. *Confederate Veteran*, July 1925, Vol. 33, No. 7, p. 279. (My title, L.S.)
396. *Confederate Veteran*, July 1925, Vol. 33, No. 7, p. 279. (My title, L.S.)
397. *Confederate Veteran*, August 1925, Vol. 33, No. 8, p. 319. (My title, L.S.)
398. *Confederate Veteran*, August 1925, Vol. 33, No. 8, p. 319. (My title, L.S.)
399. *Confederate Veteran*, August 1925, Vol. 33, No. 8, p. 319. (My title, L.S.)
400. *Confederate Veteran*, September 1925, Vol. 33, No. 9, p. 359. (My title, L.S.)
401. *Confederate Veteran*, October 1925, Vol. 33, No. 10, p. 399. (My title, L.S.)
402. *Confederate Veteran*, October 1925, Vol. 33, No. 10, p. 399. (My title, L.S.)
403. *Confederate Veteran*, November 1925, Vol. 33, No. 11, p. 439. (My title, L.S.)
404. *Confederate Veteran*, January 1924, Vol. 32, No. 1, p. 22.
405. *Confederate Veteran*, November 1925, Vol. 33, No. 11, p. 439. (My title, L.S.)
406. *Confederate Veteran*, November 1925, Vol. 33, No. 11, p. 439. (My title, L.S.)
407. *Confederate Veteran*, December 1925, Vol. 33, No. 12, p. 479. (My title, L.S.)
408. La Bree, p. 214.
409. Lochlainn Seabrook.

BIBLIOGRAPHY
And Suggested Reading

Alexander, Edward Porter. *Military Memoirs of a Confederate*. New York: Charles Scribner's Sons, 1907

Anderson, Mabel Washbourne. *Life of General Stand Watie: The Only Indian Brigadier General of the Confederate Army and the Last General to Surrender*. Pryor, OK: self-published, 1915.

Armstrong, J. M. *The Biographical Encyclopedia of Kentucky of the Dead and Living Men of the Nineteenth Century*. Cincinnati, OH: J. M. Armstrong and Co., 1878.

Ashe, Samuel A'Court. *History of North Carolina*. 2 vols. Greensboro, NC: Charles L. Van Noppen, 1908.

Benson, Al, Jr., and Walter Donald Kennedy. *Lincoln's Marxists*. Gretna, LA: Pelican, 2011.

Boyd, James P. *Parties, Problems, and Leaders of 1896: An Impartial Presentation of Living National Questions*. Chicago, IL: Publishers' Union, 1896.

Brock, Robert Alonzo (ed.). *Southern Historical Society Papers*. 52 vols. Richmond, VA: Southern Historical Society, 1876-1943.

Browder, Earl. *Lincoln and the Communists*. New York, NY: Workers Library Publishers, Inc., 1936.

Bryan, William Jennings. *The First Battle: A Story of the Campaign of 1896*. Chicago, IL: W. B. Conkey Co., 1896.

Burns, James MacGregor. *The Vineyard of Liberty*. New York, NY: Alfred A. Knopf, 1982.

Carpenter, Stephen D. *Logic of History - Five Hundred Political Texts: Being Concentrated Extracts of Abolitionism; Also Results of Slavery Agitation and Emancipation; Together With Sundry Chapters on Despotism, Usurpations and Frauds*. Madison, WI: self-published, 1864.

Christian, George Llewellyn. *Abraham Lincoln: An Address Delivered Before R. E. Lee Camp, No. 1 Confederate Veterans at Richmond, VA, October 29, 1909*. Richmond, VA: L. H. Jenkins, 1909.

——. *A Capitol Disaster: A Chapter of Reconstruction in Virginia*. Richmond, VA: self-published, 1915.

——. *Confederate Memories and Experiences*. Richmond, VA: self-published, 1915.

Confederate Veteran (Sumner Archibald Cunningham, ed.). 40 vols. Nashville, TN: Confederate Veteran, 1893-1932.

Davis, Jefferson. *The Rise and Fall of the Confederate Government*. 2 vols. New York, NY: D. Appleton and Co., 1881.

Dean, Henry Clay. *Crimes of the Civil War, and Curse of the Funding System*. Baltimore, MD: self-published, 1869.

Dinkins, James. *1861-1865, by an Old Johnnie: Personal Recollections and Experiences in the Confederate Army*. Cincinnati, OH: The Robert Clarke Co., 1897.

Dodd, Bella. *School of Darkness*. New York, NY: P. J. Kennedy and Sons, 1954.

Early, Jubal Anderson. *A Memoir of the Last Year of the War for Independence, in the Confederate States of America*. Lynchburg, VA: Charles W. Button, 1867.

Edmonds, George. *Facts and Falsehoods Concerning the War on the South, 1861-1865*. Memphis, TN: self-published, 1904.

Evans, Clement Anselm (ed.). *Confederate Military History*. 12 vols. Atlanta, GA: Confederate Publishing Co., 1899.

Franklin, John Hope. *Reconstruction After the Civil War*. Chicago, IL: University of Chicago Press, 1961.

Gardiner, C. *Acts of the Republican Party as Seen by History*. Washington, D.C.: self-published, 1906.

Hasselberg, P. D. (ed.). *Parliamentary Debates: First Session, Fortieth Parliament, 1982, House of Representatives* (Vol. 445). Wellington, New Zealand: Government Printer, 1982.

Johnson, Robert Underwood, and Clarence Clough Buel (eds.). *Battles and Leaders of the Civil War*. 4 vols. New York, NY: The Century Co., 1884-1888.

Johnstone, Huger William. *Truth of War Conspiracy, 1861*. Idylwild, GA: H. W. Johnstone, 1921.

Jones, John Beauchamp. *A Rebel War Clerk's Diary at the Confederate States Capital*. Philadelphia, PA: J. B. Lippincott and Co., 1866.

Jones, John William. *The Davis Memorial Volume; Or Our Dead President, Jefferson Davis and the World's Tribute to His Memory*. Richmond, VA: B. F. Johnson, 1889.

Kirkland, Frazar. *The Pictorial Book of Anecdotes of the Rebellion, or the Funny and Pathetic Side of the War, Embracing the Most Brilliant and Remarkable Anecdotal Events of the Great Conflict in the United States*. Omaha, NE: F. H. Rogers and Co., 1891.

La Bree, Ben (ed.). *Camp Fires of the Confederacy: Confederate Poems and Selected Songs*. Louisville, KY: self-published, 1898.

Lenin, Vladimir. *"Left Wing" Communism: An Infantile Disorder*. Detroit, MI: The Marxian Educational Society, 1921.

Livermore, Thomas L. *Numbers and Losses in the Civil War in America, 1861-65*. 1900. Carlisle, PA: John Kallmann, 1996 ed.

Magliocca, Gerard N. *The Tragedy of William Jennings Bryan: Constitutional Law and the Politics of Backlash*. New Haven, CT: Yale University Press, 2011.

Marx, Karl, and Frederick Engels. *Manifesto of the Communist Party*. Chicago, IL: Charles H. Kerr and Co., 1906.

McCarty, Burke (ed.). *Little Sermons in Socialism by Abraham Lincoln*. Chicago, IL: The Chicago Daily Socialist, 1910.

McPherson, James M. *Abraham Lincoln and the Second American Revolution*. New York, NY: Oxford University Press, 1991.

Meriwether, Elizabeth Avery (pseudonym, "George Edmonds"). *Facts and Falsehoods Concerning the War on the South, 1861-1865*. Memphis, TN: A. R. Taylor and Co., 1904.

Miller, Francis Trevelyan, and Robert S. Lanier (eds.). *The Photographic History of the Civil War*. 10 vols. New York, NY: The Review of Reviews Co., 1911.

Minutes of the Eighth Annual Meeting and Reunion of the United Confederate Veterans, Atlanta, GA, July 20-23, 1898. New Orleans, LA: United Confederate Veterans, 1907.

Minutes of the Ninth Annual Meeting and Reunion of the United Confederate Veterans, Charleston, SC, May 10-13, 1899. New Orleans, LA: United Confederate Veterans, 1907.

Minutes of the Twelfth Annual Meeting and Reunion of the United Confederate Veterans, Dallas, TX, April 22-25, 1902. New Orleans, LA: United Confederate Veterans, 1907.

Moore, Frank. *Anecdotes, Poetry and Incidents of the War: North and South, 1860-1865*. New York: Arundel, 1882.

Moore, John Trotwood. *Songs and Stories From Tennessee*. Philadelphia, PA: Henry T. Coates, 1903.

Morgan, Mrs. Julia Irby. *How It Was: Four Years Among the Rebels*. Nashville, TN: self-published, 1892.

Muzzey, David Saville. *The United States of America: Vol. 1, To the Civil War*. Boston, MA: Ginn and Co., 1922.

——. *The American Adventure: Vol. 2, From the Civil War*. 1924. New York, NY: Harper and Brothers, 1927 ed.

Nicolay, John G., and John Hay (eds.). *Abraham Lincoln: A History*. 10 vols. New York, NY: The Century Co., 1890.

——. *Complete Works of Abraham Lincoln*. 12 vols. 1894. New York, NY: Francis D. Tandy Co., 1905 ed.

——. *Abraham Lincoln: Complete Works*. 12 vols. 1894. New York, NY: The Century Co., 1907 ed.

ORA (full title: *The War of the Rebellion: A Compilation of the Official Records of the Union and Confederate Armies*). 70 vols. Washington, DC: Government Printing Office, 1880.

ORN (full title: *Official Records of the Union and Confederate Navies in the War of the Rebellion*). 30 vols. Washington, DC: Government Printing Office, 1894.
Pollard, Edward Alfred. *The Lost Cause*. New York, NY: E. B. Treat and Co., 1867.
Richardson, John Anderson. *Richardson's Defense of the South*. Atlanta, GA: A. B. Caldwell, 1914.
Robinson, Nina Hill. *Aunt Dice: The Story of a Faithful Slave*. Nashville, TN: M. E. Church, 1897.
Rogers, William P. *The Three Secession Movements in the United States: Samuel J. Tilden, the Democratic Candidate for Presidency; the Advisor, Aider and Abettor of the Great Secession Movement of 1860; and One of the Authors of the Infamous Resolution of 1864; His Claims as a Statesman and Reformer Considered*. Boston, MA: John Wilson and Son, 1876.
Rove, Karl. *The Triumph of William McKinley: Why the Election of 1896 Still Matters*. New York, NY: Simon and Schuster, 2015.
Rutherford, Mildred Lewis. *Truths of History: A Fair, Unbiased, Impartial, Unprejudiced and Conscientious Study of History*. Athens, GA: n.p., 1920.
Seabrook, Lochlainn. *Carnton Plantation Ghost Stories: True Tales of the Unexplained from Tennessee's Most Haunted Civil War House!* 2005. Franklin, TN, 2016 ed.
——. *Nathan Bedford Forrest: Southern Hero, American Patriot*. 2007. Franklin, TN, 2010 ed.
——. *Abraham Lincoln: The Southern View*. 2007. Franklin, TN: Sea Raven Press, 2013 ed.
——. *The McGavocks of Carnton Plantation: A Southern History - Celebrating One of Dixie's Most Noble Confederate Families and Their Tennessee Home*. 2008. Franklin, TN, 2011 ed.
——. *A Rebel Born: A Defense of Nathan Bedford Forrest*. 2010. Franklin, TN: Sea Raven Press, 2011 ed.
——. *A Rebel Born: The Screenplay* (for the film). 2011. Franklin, TN: Sea Raven Press.
——. *Everything You Were Taught About the Civil War is Wrong, Ask a Southerner!* 2010. Franklin, TN: Sea Raven Press, revised 2019 ed.
——. *The Quotable Jefferson Davis: Selections From the Writings and Speeches of the Confederacy's First President*. Franklin, TN: Sea Raven Press, 2011.
——. *The Quotable Robert E. Lee: Selections From the Writings and Speeches of the South's Most Beloved Civil War General*. Franklin, TN: Sea Raven Press, 2011 Sesquicentennial Civil War Edition.
——. *Lincolnology: The Real Abraham Lincoln Revealed In His Own Words*. Franklin, TN: Sea Raven Press, 2011.
——. *The Unquotable Abraham Lincoln: The President's Quotes They Don't Want You To Know!* Franklin, TN: Sea Raven Press, 2011.
——. *Honest Jeff and Dishonest Abe: A Southern Children's Guide to the Civil War*. Franklin, TN: Sea Raven Press, 2012.
——. *Encyclopedia of the Battle of Franklin - A Comprehensive Guide to the Conflict that Changed the Civil War*. Franklin, TN: Sea Raven Press, 2012.
——. *The Quotable Nathan Bedford Forrest: Selections From the Writings and Speeches of the Confederacy's Most Brilliant Cavalryman*. Spring Hill, TN: Sea Raven Press, 2012.
——. *Forrest! 99 Reasons to Love Nathan Bedford Forrest*. Spring Hill, TN: Sea Raven Press, 2012.
——. *Give 'Em Hell Boys! The Complete Military Correspondence of Nathan Bedford Forrest*. Spring Hill, TN: Sea Raven Press, 2012.
——. *The Constitution of the Confederate States of America Explained: A Clause-by-Clause Study of the South's Magna Carta*. Spring Hill, TN: Sea Raven Press, 2012 Sesquicentennial Civil War Edition.
——. *The Great Impersonator: 99 Reasons to Dislike Abraham Lincoln*. Spring Hill, TN: Sea Raven Press, 2012.
——. *The Old Rebel: Robert E. Lee As He Was Seen By His Contemporaries*. Spring Hill, TN: Sea Raven Press, 2012 Sesquicentennial Civil War Edition.
——. *The Quotable Stonewall Jackson: Selections From the Writings and Speeches of the South's Most Famous General*. Spring Hill, TN: Sea Raven Press, 2012 Sesquicentennial Civil War Edition.
——. *Saddle, Sword, and Gun: A Biography of Nathan Bedford Forrest for Teens*. Spring Hill, TN: Sea Raven Press, 2013.

——. *The Alexander H. Stephens Reader: Excerpts From the Works of a Confederate Founding Father.* Spring Hill, TN: Sea Raven Press, 2013.

——. *The Quotable Alexander H. Stephens: Selections From the Writings and Speeches of the Confederacy's First Vice President.* Spring Hill, TN: Sea Raven Press, 2013 Sesquicentennial Civil War Edition.

——. *Give This Book to a Yankee! A Southern Guide to the Civil War for Northerners.* Spring Hill, TN: Sea Raven Press, 2014.

——. *The Articles of Confederation Explained: A Clause-by-Clause Study of America's First Constitution.* Spring Hill, TN: Sea Raven Press, 2014.

——. *Confederate Blood and Treasure: An Interview With Lochlainn Seabrook.* Spring Hill, TN: Sea Raven Press, 2015.

——. *Nathan Bedford Forrest and the Battle of Fort Pillow: Yankee Myth, Confederate Fact.* Spring Hill, TN: Sea Raven Press, 2015.

——. *Everything You Were Taught About American Slavery War is Wrong, Ask a Southerner!* Spring Hill, TN: Sea Raven Press, 2015.

——. *Confederacy 101: Amazing Facts You Never Knew About America's Oldest Political Tradition.* Spring Hill, TN: Sea Raven Press, 2015.

——. *The Great Yankee Coverup: What the North Doesn't Want You to Know About Lincoln's War!* Spring Hill, TN: Sea Raven Press, 2015.

——. *Slavery 101: Amazing Facts You Never Knew About America's "Peculiar Institution."* Spring Hill, TN: Sea Raven Press, 2015.

——. *Confederate Flag Facts: What Every American Should Know About Dixie's Southern Cross.* Spring Hill, TN: Sea Raven Press, 2016.

——. *Nathan Bedford Forrest and the Ku Klux Klan: Yankee Myth, Confederate Fact.* Spring Hill, TN: Sea Raven Press, 2016.

——. *Seabrook's Bible Dictionary of Traditional and Mystical Christian Doctrines.* Spring Hill, TN: Sea Raven Press, 2016.

——. *Everything You Were Taught About African-Americans and the Civil War is Wrong, Ask a Southerner!* Spring Hill, TN: Sea Raven Press, 2016.

——. *Nathan Bedford Forrest and African-Americans: Yankee Myth, Confederate Fact.* Spring Hill, TN: Sea Raven Press, 2016.

——. *Women in Gray: A Tribute to the Ladies Who Supported the Southern Confederacy.* Spring Hill, TN: Sea Raven Press, 2016.

——. *Lincoln's War: The Real Cause, the Real Winner, the Real Loser.* Spring Hill, TN: Sea Raven Press, 2016.

——. *The Unholy Crusade: Lincoln's Legacy of Destruction in the American South.* Spring Hill, TN: Sea Raven Press, 2017.""

——. *Abraham Lincoln Was a Liberal, Jefferson Davis Was a Conservative: The Missing Key to Understanding the American Civil War.* Spring Hill, TN: Sea Raven Press, 2017.

——. *All We Ask is to be Let Alone: The Southern Secession Fact Book.* Spring Hill, TN: Sea Raven Press, 2017.

——. *The Ultimate Civil War Quiz Book: How Much Do You Really Know About America's Most Misunderstood Conflict?* Spring Hill, TN: Sea Raven Press, 2017.

——. *Rise Up and Call Them Blessed: Victorian Tributes to the Confederate Soldier, 1861-1901.* Spring Hill, TN: Sea Raven Press, 2017.

——. *Victorian Confederate Poetry: The Southern Cause in Verse, 1861-1901.* Spring Hill, TN: Sea Raven Press, 2018.

——. *Confederate Monuments: Why Every American Should Honor Confederate Soldiers and Their Memorials.* Spring Hill, TN: Sea Raven Press, 2018.

——. *The God of War: Nathan Bedford Forrest as He Was Seen by His Contemporaries.* Spring Hill, TN: Sea Raven Press, 2018.

——. *The Battle of Spring Hill: Recollections of Confederate and Union Soldiers.* Spring Hill, TN: Sea Raven Press, 2018.

——. *I Rode With Forrest! Confederate Soldiers Who Served With the World's Greatest Cavalry Leader.* Spring Hill, TN: Sea Raven Press, 2018.

——. *The Battle of Nashville: Recollections of Confederate and Union Soldiers.* Spring Hill, TN: Sea Raven Press, 2018.

——. *The Battle of Franklin: Recollections of Confederate and Union Soldiers*. Spring Hill, TN: Sea Raven Press, 2018.

——. (ed.) *A Short History of the Confederate States of America* (Jefferson Davis, Belford Company, NY, 1890). A Sea Raven Press Reprint. Spring Hill, TN: Sea Raven Press, 2020.

——. (ed.) *Prison Life of Jefferson Davis: Embracing Details and Incidents in his Captivity, With Conversations on Topics of Public Interest* (John J. Craven, Sampson, Low, Son, and Marston, London, UK, 1866). A Sea Raven Press Reprint. Spring Hill, TN: Sea Raven Press, 2020.

——. *What the Confederate Flag Means to Me: Americans Speak Out in Defense of Southern Honor, Heritage, and History*. Spring Hill, TN: Sea Raven Press, 2021.

——. *Heroes of the Southern Confederacy: The Illustrated Book of Confederate Officials, Soldiers, and Civilians*. Spring Hill, TN: Sea Raven Press, 2021.

——. *America's Three Constitutions: Complete Texts of the Articles of Confederation, Constitution of the United States of America, and Constitution of the Confederate States of America*. Spring Hill, TN: Sea Raven Press, 2021.

Steel, Samuel Augustus. *The South Was Right*. Columbia, SC: R. L. Bryan Co., 1914.

Stephens, Alexander Hamilton. *Speech of Mr. Stephens, of Georgia, on the War and Taxation*. Washington, D.C.: J & G. Gideon, 1848.

——. *A Constitutional View of the Late War Between the States; Its Causes, Character, Conduct and Results*. 2 vols. Philadelphia, PA: National Publishing, Co., 1870.

——. *Recollections of Alexander H. Stephens: His Diary Kept When a Prisoner at Fort Warren, Boston Harbour, 1865*. New York, NY: Doubleday, Page, and Co., 1910.

Thompson, Holland. *The New South: A Chronicle of Social and Industrial Evolution*. New Haven, CT: Yale University Press, 1920.

von Borcke, Heros. *Memoirs of the Confederate War for Independence*. Philadelphia, PA: J. B. Lippincott and Co., 1867.

Warner, Ezra J. *Generals in Gray: Lives of the Confederate Commanders*. 1959. Baton Rouge, LA: Louisiana State University Press, 1989 ed.

——. *Generals in Blue: Lives of the Union Commanders*. 1964. Baton Rouge, LA: Louisiana State University Press, 2006 ed.

Woods, Thomas E., Jr. *The Politically Incorrect Guide to American History*. Washington, D.C.: Regnery, 2004.

MEET THE AUTHOR

NEO-VICTORIAN SCHOLAR LOCHLAINN SEABROOK, a descendant of the families of Alexander Hamilton Stephens, John Singleton Mosby, Edmund Winchester Rucker, and William Giles Harding, is a 7th generation Kentuckian and the most prolific pro-South writer in the world today. Known by literary critics as the "new Shelby Foote" and by his fans as the "Voice of the Traditional South," he is a recipient of the prestigious Jefferson Davis Historical Gold Medal. As a lifelong writer he has authored and edited books ranging in topics from history, politics, science, and biography, to nature, religion, music, and the paranormal; books that his readers describe as "game changers," "transformative," and "life altering."

One of the world's most popular living historians, he is a 17th generation Southerner of Appalachian heritage who descends from dozens of patriotic Revolutionary War soldiers and Confederate soldiers from Kentucky, Tennessee, North Carolina, and Virginia. A proud member of the Sons of the Confederate Veterans, he is a true Renaissance Man. Besides being an accomplished and well respected author-historian and Bible authority, he is also a Kentucky Colonel, eagle scout, screenwriter, nature, wildlife, and landscape photographer, artist, graphic designer, songwriter (3,000 songs), film composer, multi-instrument musician, vocalist, session player, music producer, genealogist, former history museum docent, and a former ranch hand, zookeeper, and wrangler.

His over 70 adult and children's books contain some 60,000 well-researched pages that have earned him accolades from around the globe. His works, which have sold on every continent except Antarctica, have introduced hundreds of thousands to vital facts that have been left out of our mainstream books. He has been endorsed internationally by leading experts, museum curators, award-winning historians, bestselling authors, celebrities, filmmakers, noted scientists, well regarded educators, TV show hosts and producers, renowned military artists, esteemed heritage organizations, and distinguished academicians of all races, creeds, and colors. Colonel Seabrook holds the world record for writing the most books on Southern icon Nathan Bedford Forrest: 12.

Of northern, western, and central European ancestry, he is the 6th great-grandson of the Earl of Oxford and a descendant of European royalty. His modern day cousins include: Johnny Cash, Elvis Presley, Lisa Marie Presley, Billy Ray and Miley Cyrus, Patty Loveless, Tim McGraw, Lee Ann Womack, Dolly Parton, Pat Boone, Naomi, Wynonna, and Ashley Judd, Ricky Skaggs, the Sunshine Sisters, Martha Carson, Chet Atkins, Patrick J. Buchanan, Cindy Crawford, Bertram Thomas Combs (Kentucky's 50th governor), Edith Bolling (second wife of President Woodrow Wilson), Andy Griffith, Riley Keough, George C. Scott, Robert Duvall, Reese Witherspoon, Lee Marvin, Rebecca Gayheart, and Tom Cruise.

A constitutionalist and avid outdoorsman and gun advocate, Colonel Seabrook is the author of the international blockbuster, *Everything You Were Taught About the Civil War is Wrong, Ask a Southerner!* He lives with his wife and family in beautiful historic Middle Tennessee, the heart of the Confederacy.

For more information on author Mr. Seabrook visit

LOCHLAINNSEABROOK.COM

MORE CONFEDERATE HUMOR FROM
LOCHLAINN SEABROOK

The Bondurants of New Orleans

COPYRIGHT © LOCHLAINN SEABROOK 2021

Mother: "Charlotte, why don't you invite that new neighborhood girl over, the one from Massachusetts."
Daughter: "Oh, we don't get along at all mother."
Father: "Why ever not dear?"
Daughter: "I don't speak Yankee and she doesn't speak Confederate."

If you enjoyed this book you will be interested in Colonel Seabrook's popular related titles:

☞ ABRAHAM LINCOLN WAS A LIBERAL, JEFFERSON DAVIS WAS A CONSERVATIVE
☞ EVERYTHING YOU WERE TAUGHT ABOUT THE CIVIL WAR IS WRONG, ASK A SOUTHERNER!
☞ ALL WE ASK IS TO BE LET ALONE: THE SOUTHERN SECESSION FACT BOOK
☞ EVERYTHING YOU WERE TAUGHT ABOUT AMERICAN SLAVERY IS WRONG, ASK A SOUTHERNER!
☞ CONFEDERATE FLAG FACTS: WHAT EVERY AMERICAN SHOULD KNOW ABOUT DIXIE'S SOUTHERN CROSS
☞ LINCOLN'S WAR: THE REAL CAUSE, THE REAL WINNER, THE REAL LOSER

Available from Sea Raven Press and wherever fine books are sold

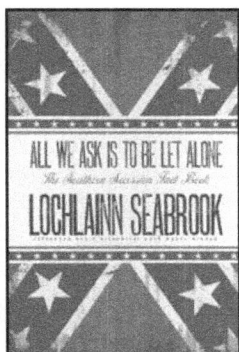

ALL OF OUR BOOK COVERS ARE AVAILABLE AS 11" X 17" COLOR POSTERS, SUITABLE FOR FRAMING

SeaRavenPress.com

www.ingramcontent.com/pod-product-compliance
Lightning Source LLC
Chambersburg PA
CBHW031939110426
42744CB00029B/189